READY-TO-USE MULTICULTURAL ACTIVITIES FOR THE AMERICAN HISTORY CLASSROOM

Four Centuries of Diversity from the 1600s to the Present

HALLIE ANN WANNAMAKER

THE CENTER FOR APPLIED RESEARCH IN EDUCATION
West Nyack, N.Y. 10995

THE CENTER FOR APPLIED
RESEARCH IN EDUCATION

West Nyack, New York

10 9 8 7 6 5 4 3 2 1

Library of Congress Cataloging-in-Publication Data

Wannamaker, Hallie Ann.
Ready-to-use multicultural activities for the American history classroom : four centuries of diversity from the 1600s to the present / Hallie Ann Wannamaker.
p. cm.
Includes bibliographical references
ISBN 0-87628-858-1
1. United States—History—Study and teaching—Activity programs.
2. Pluralism—Study and teaching—Activity programs—United States.
I. Center for Applied Research in Education. II. Title.
E175.8.W34 1996 95-33598
973'.07—dc20 CIP

ISBN 0-87628-858-1

Printed in the United States of America

DEDICATION

To the staff of Schomburg Satellite Academy High School—
a group of dedicated and creative educators.

ACKNOWLEDGMENTS

Thanks to the following people for their many contributions and inspirations: Oscar Forne, Vic Klein, Flory Perini, Pat Alfieri, Susan Schaffel, Gail Gordon, Noel Jardines, Vincent Brevetti, and the Academy for Advancement of Science and Technology.

PERMISSIONS

PHOTO CREDITS

1–8a The first Labor Walkout: "Jamestown Glassblowers" by Richard Frear (the National Park Service #266–580)

3–14 A Woman's Fate: "Woman Whipping Female Slave" (1834) (Library of Congress, #LC-US262-80825)

3–28 Close Quarters: "Ada McColl On the Prairie Near Lakim, Kansas Gathering Buffalo Chips" (1938) (The Kansas State Historical Society, Topeka, Kansas)

3–29b African American Pioneers: "Negro Refugees Waiting on Levee" (1897) (Library of Congress, #LC-US262-26365)

4–13 Internment Camps for Japanese Americans: "Children Awaiting Evacuation" (5/8/1942) by Dorothea Lange (National Archives #210-G-2C-155)

ILLUSTRATION CREDITS

Illustrations by Pat Alfieri

1–4 Matrilineal Society

1–5 Going to a Dance

1–10 Stepmothers and Stepfathers

1–13 Economic Class Tensions?

1–16 Grilled Cheese Sandwich

2–3 Stereotypes

2–11 Point of View

2–13 What Did They Say to One Another?

2–15 Follow the Army

2–20 The Iroquois Constitution

2–21 Which Side of the Road?

2–23 Benjamin Banneker

2–24 Everyday Life

3–4 Sacagawea

3–5 York

3–6 Spelling

3–12 Frederick Douglass

3–17 Do You Agree?

3–18 The Story of Tin Fook

3–25 African American Soldiers

3–27 Robert Brown Elliot

3–31 Cheyenne Native American Game

3–39 Queen Liliuokalani

4–3 Child Labor

4–12 Women and World War II

4–22 Hillary Rodham Clinton

4–25 Immigration by Sea

4–32 Bringing in the New Year

Illustrations by Katherine Wu

1–3 Generations

1–14 Tight Quarters

1–15 Indentured Servants

Illustration by Leah Obias

1–18 Guns

Illustrations by Alex Ramniceanu

1–2 How Much Do We Know? (1600s)

1–9 Enslaved!

2–2 How Much Do We Know? (1700s)

3–2 How Much Do We Know? (1800s)

4–2 How Much Do We Know? (1900s)

Illustrations by Philip Santiago

3–13 Frederick Douglass

About the Author

Hallie Ann Wannamaker was born and raised in St. Paul, Minnesota, and graduated from the City University of New York Graduate Center in 1989 with an M.A. in Liberal Studies/American Studies. She taught social studies from 1986 to 1992 at Schomburg Satellite Academy, an alternative NYC public high school located in the South Bronx. Besides teaching all periods of U.S. history, she has created thematic courses such as History of Women and the Great Depression. Her B.A. degree is in dance from Adelphi University. She taught creative movement, modern dance, and ballet to preschoolers, K–6, and adults in the Boston and New York City areas from 1976 to 1985.

Hallie Ann Wannamaker lives in Teaneck, New Jersey, with her husband, Vincent Brevetti, her stepson, John, and her daughter, Hallie Emma. She is currently the project coordinator of the Northeastern New Jersey Provisional Teacher Training Consortium—Teaneck Lead District.

About the Author

About This Resource

The approach used in this resource has enticed students away from the "History is boring" addage and sparked both their interest and thinking. After all, history is about us; human beings interacting with each other and our environments, constantly looking forward toward our future. And what American teenagers are not interested in themselves, their peers, and their future? We are all aware that history is much more than a dull regurgitation of facts and dates. To understand history, we must explore the fascinating stories, analyze the interesting data, relate the personal experiences of our lives to those of the past, and create history projects to express to others what we have discovered!

This multicultural social studies activity book of American history, from 1600 to the present day, endeavors to make American history come alive for today's teenagers. Its purpose is to:

1. Develop a base of factual information about American history our students can use and explore.
2. Develop a sensitivity to the many different viewpoints of historical events (male, female, African American, Native American, Asian American, European American, Hispanic American, Pacific Islander Americans, working class, young, and others).
3. Develop a sense of "what life was like" (eating, sleeping, clothing, traveling, housing) in time past.
4. Develop writing skills to express what has been learned.
5. Develop critical analysis skills to interpret why certain historical events occurred.

6. Develop ideas for creating history projects to teach others about the earlier generations of their families and communities.
7. Develop an appreciation for what has and has not been accomplished in America.
8. Develop skills such as map reading, creation of graphs, interpretation of charts, oral history, and original and secondary research.

An introductory section of *Ready-to-Use Multicultural Activities for the American History Classroom* presents the concept of multiculturalism to your students. Following the introduction you will find a section of activities for each century of our country's existence—activities that touch on events of that period. These activities will encourage your students to conceptualize, analyze, and remember these important historical people and events. The activities will also encourage them to empathize with past struggles, develop and test hypotheses, and create projects. Each section begins with a map exercise and a survey to peak your students' interest in the century, and ends with a "People to Remember" exercise.

Students will remember what they have learned and be able to apply it to their own lives if they can relate to it, make predictions about the future based on their knowledge of the past, and teach the information to others—peers, siblings, and parents. Do not hesitate to change the exercises to fit your particular needs.

Hallie Ann Wannamaker

Contents

About This Resource . . . . *xi*

INTRODUCTION ***1***

Teachers' Guide to Activities for the Introduction 3

Activities

A–1 What Is Multicultural History? 4

A–2 From All Over the World 6

A–3 What Is Your Heritage? 8

A–4 The "All American" Teenager 9

SECTION ONE: THE 1600s ***13***

Teachers' Guide to Activities for the 1600s 15

Activities

1–1 Draw! 19

1–2 How Much Do We Know? 21

1–3 Generations . . . 24
1–4 Matrilineal Society . . . 26
1–5 Going to a Dance? . . . 28
1–6 Important Dates! . . . 29
1–7 A Love Story . . . 30
1–8 Polish Americans Lead the First Labor Walkout . . . 31
1–9 Enslaved! . . . 34
1–10 Stepmothers and Stepfathers . . . 36
1–11 Children or No Children? . . . 38
1–12 Needs/Economic Interests . . . 40
1–13 Economic Class Tension? . . . 43
1–14 Tight Quarters . . . 45
1–15 Indentured Servants . . . 47
1–16 Grilled Cheese Sandwich . . . 50
1–17 European American Women's Position in Society . . . 53
1–18 Guns! . . . 54
1–19 English American Names . . . 56
1–20 People to Remember . . . 62

SECTION TWO: THE 1700s . . . 63

Teachers' Guide to Activities for the 1700s . . . 65

Activities

2–1 Draw! . . . 70
2–2 How Much Do We Know? . . . 71
2–3 Stereotypes . . . 74
2–4 The Environment . . . 76
2–5 Spanish Colonization . . . 77
2–6 French Colonization . . . 80
2–7 Hats and Lingo . . . 83
2–8 Three Cultures . . . 84
2–9 European American Medical Care . . . 86

2–10 Childbirth and Midwifery 88

2–11 Point of View 89

2–12 Whose Side Are You On? 91

2–13 What Did They Say to Each Other? 94

2–14 Should Women Be Soldiers? 97

2–15 Follow the Army 99

2–16 Home Alone (with All the Work!) 103

2–17 Inspiration 104

2–18 Abigail Adams Writes a Letter 105

2–19 Too Far or Not Far Enough? 107

2–20 The Iroquois Constitution 110

2–21 Which Side of the Road? 111

2–22 The Cajuns 113

2–23 Benjamin Banneker 115

2–24 Everyday Life 117

2–25 What If? 119

2–26 Sagoyewatha 120

2–27 Tragedy 121

2–28 The Du Sables 124

2–29 Benjamin Franklin's Parody 125

2–30 People to Remember 126

SECTION THREE: THE 1800s 127

Teachers' Guide to Activities for the 1800s 129

Activities

3–1 Draw! 136

3–2 How Much Do We Know? 138

3–3 Decisions and Choices 141

3–4 Sacagawea 143

3–5 York 145

3–6 Spelling 147

3–7 Rewrite History 148
3–8 Trail of Tears 149
3–9 Working Conditions 154
3–10 Men, Women, and Money 158
3–11 Fight, and if You Can't Fight, Kick 162
3–12 Frederick Douglass 164
3–13 Telling Her Story 166
3–14 A Woman's Fate 167
3–15 Abolitionists Working Together 171
3–16 Susan B. Anthony Goes to Jail 173
3–17 Do You Agree? 175
3–18 The Story of Tin Fook 177
3–19 I've Been Working on the Railroad 179
3–20 Lee Yick 181
3–21 The Mexican War 183
3–22 Juan Nepomuceno Cortina 186
3–23 Mexican Americans 187
3–24 The Civil War—For Whom Would You Fight? 188
3–25 African American Soldiers 192
3–26 Abraham Lincoln 194
3–27 Robert Brown Elliot 196
3–28 Close Quarters 197
3–29 African American Pioneers 199
3–30 Cowboy Quiz 201
3–31 Cheyenne Native American Game 202
3–32 What Do They Have in Common? 204
3–33 Immigration 205
3–34 Words We Use Every Day 208
3–35 German Americans 209
3–36 Jewish Americans 211
3–37 Little Bags of Irish Earth 213
3–38 The Growth of the Cities 215

3–39 Queen Liliuokalani 218
3–40 People to Remember 219

SECTION FOUR: THE 1900s *221*

Teachers' Guide to Activities for the 1900s 223

Activities

4–1 Draw! 230
4–2 How Much Do We Know? 231
4–3 Child Labor 234
4–4 Shovel and Pick 237
4–5 Ida B. Wells Fights Mob Violence 239
4–6 W. E. B. Du Bois and Booker T. Washington 241
4–7 First Woman in Congress 242
4–8 World War I 243
4–9 The Suffrage Movement 245
4–10 "Roaring Twenties" Bingo 248
4–11 The Great Depression 250
4–12 Women and World War II 254
4–13 Internment Camps for Japanese Americans 256
4–14 The Civil Rights Movement 259
4–15 Where Would You Stand? 263
4–16 The 1960s 266
4–17 Oral History Interview—the 1960s 270
4–18 Oral History Interview—The Vietnam War 273
4–19 The Vietnam War—Pro or Con? 276
4–20 Gender Stereotypes 279
4–21 Working Outside the Home 281
4–22 Eleanor Roosevelt and Hillary Rodham Clinton 284
4–23 Puerto Rico—Commonwealth, State, or Independence? 286
4–24 Trying to Fit In 288
4–25 Immigration by Sea 290

4–26 Sweatshops . . . 293
4–27 The Farmworkers and Nonviolence . . . 295
4–28 Separation or Assimilation? . . . 297
4–29 A Basketball Star . . . 298
4–30 Smiles a Lot . . . 300
4–31 Arab Americans . . . 302
4–32 Bringing in the New Year . . . 304
4–33 Typecasting . . . 306
4–34 American as Apple Pie? . . . 308
4–35 Names . . . 310
4–36 Majority-Minority . . . 312
4–37 Ancestries . . . 315
4–38 Asian and Pacific Islander Americans . . . 317
4–39 Hispanic Americans . . . 320
4–40 People to Remember . . . 322

REFERENCES . . . *323*

BIBLIOGRAPHY . . . *333*

TOPICAL INDEX . . . *341*

INTRODUCTION

Teachers' Guide to Activities for the Introduction

A–1 WHAT IS MULTICULTURAL HISTORY?

This exercise will help your students create their own definition of multiculturalism and explore its importance.

A–2 FROM ALL OVER THE WORLD

It is interesting and helpful to know the ethnic makeup of U.S. society. Making a visual representation of this (i.e., a colorful pie graph) is an entertaining and useful exercise.

A–3 WHAT IS YOUR HERITAGE?

This is a good homework exercise. Encourage your students to interview a parent, guardian, or other family member who has information about their family history. The results are fun to share in class the next day!

A–4 THE "ALL AMERICAN" TEENAGER

Students often do not realize how "multicultural" their everyday existence is. Doing this exercise will make them look at their everyday world very differently!

Name ______________________________ *Date* ____________

A–1
WHAT IS MULTICULTURAL HISTORY?

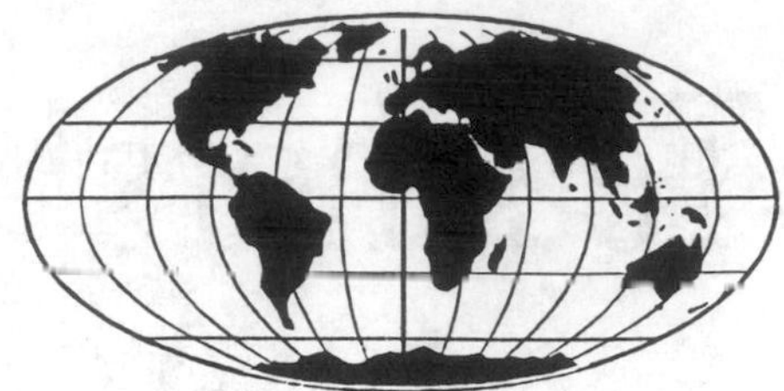

What words come to your mind when you hear the terms "multi," "culture," and "history"? Write these words around the terms encircled below.

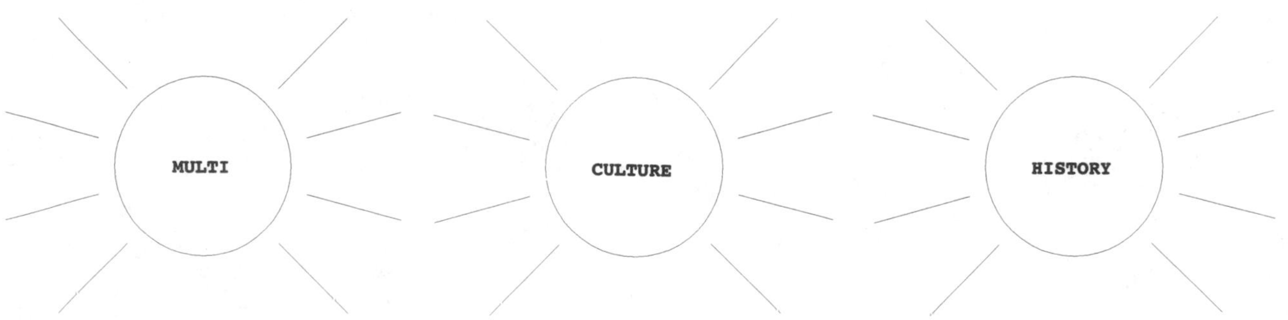

Look up the te rms "history," "culture," and "multiculture" in your dictionary. Write the definitions you find below.

HISTORY

CULTURE

MULTICULTURAL

When you are studying the history of the United States, you are studying an experiment in human history. With advances in technology (e.g., ship construction, navigation, mapmaking), people from around the world began to meet each other and people already living on the North American continent in the 1600s, and they still do so today. Make a list of the continents and islands from which Americans originated.

____

____

____

____

Some historians see the result of this great experiment to be very positive and use the analogy of a "melting pot"—the melting together of many cultures into one—to describe it. Other historians see the result of this great experiment to be very negative and use the analogy of a "tossed salad"—the inability of cultures to understand one another and communicate—to describe it. With which of these two camps of historians do you agree? Is the United States a country where people of different cultures understand one another? Or is there great division? Answer these questions in the space provided below:

Imagine you are a writer. You write U.S. history textbooks for today's American teenagers. You must write a 300-page book including information on four centuries of U.S. history (1600–2000) to be published this year. Which of the groups you mentioned on the previous page would you include? Would you emphasize one group (e.g., Asian Americans, European Americans, African Americans) more than others or would you give each group "equal time"? Is it important for teenagers to learn about different cultures or is it sufficient for them to know only about their own? Describe your book in the space provided below.

Name ______________________ *Date* ____________

A–2

FROM ALL OVER THE WORLD

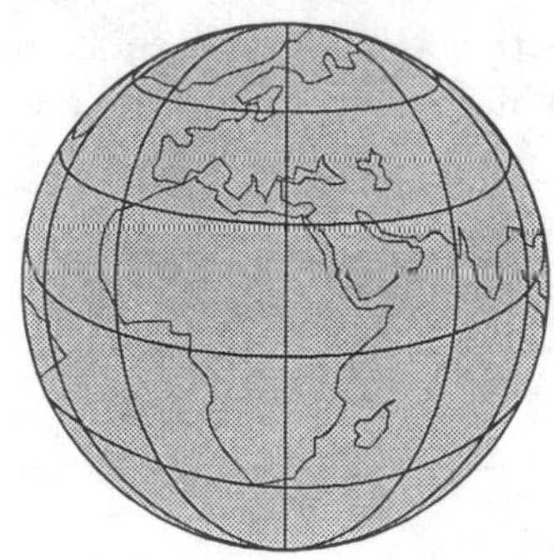

The cultural composition of the American population has constantly changed since the first census was taken in 1790. Read the statistics below, which tell the 1990 population statistics of Native Americans, African Americans, European Americans, Asian and Pacific Islander Americans, and Hispanic Americans.[(1)]

Origin	*Total*	*Percentage of U.S. Population*	*Color Code*
Native Americans	1,959,000	.8%	
African Americans	29,986,000		
European Americans	199,686,000		
Asian and Pacific Islander Americans	7,274,000		
Hispanic Americans	22,354,000		

What percent of the *total* U.S. population (248,710,000) is each of the above groups? Look at the example below, then compute the rest and complete the chart above.

Native Americans (1,959,000) are what percentage of the total U.S. population (248,710,000)?

STEP ONE: $1{,}959{,}000 = \frac{X}{100} \cdot 248{,}710{,}000$

STEP TWO: $X = \frac{1{,}959{,}000}{2{,}487{,}100}$

STEP THREE: X = .8% (rounded off to the nearest .1%)

For the next part of the exercise, you will need five differently colored markers, pencils, or crayons. Choose one color for each of the groups (blue for African Americans, green for European Americans, etc.) and fill in the "color code" box in the chart. Look at the pie chart on the next page, which visualizes the percentage each of these groups is of the total U.S. population. Figure out which part of the pie represents each of the five populations. Then color that part of the pie graph with the color you have chosen to represent that group. Be sure to label it also!

A-2 (continued)

THE CULTURAL COMPOSITION OF THE UNITED STATES

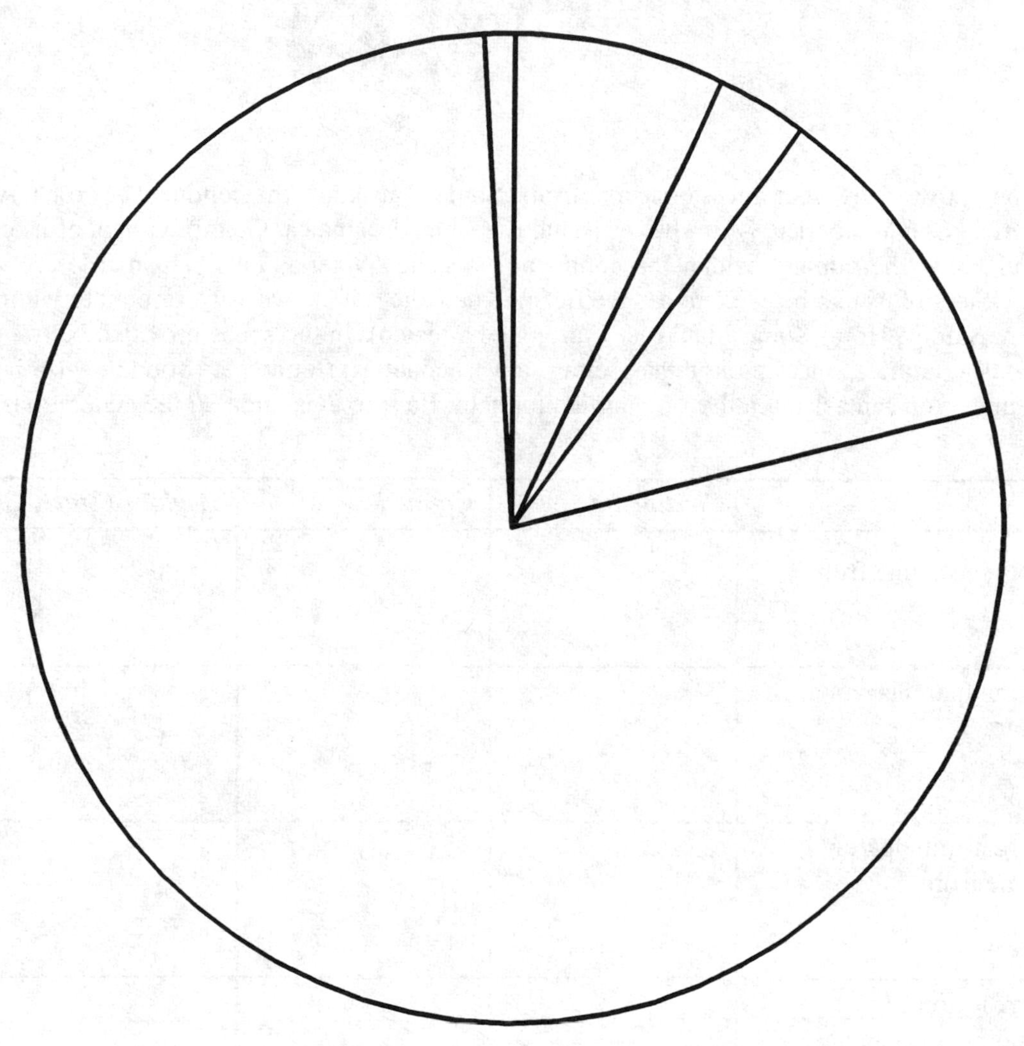

Name ______________________ Date ____________

A–3
WHAT IS YOUR HERITAGE?

Do you know where your ancestors came from? Some of us know the continent (Europe, Asia, Africa, North America, South America, Australia) or island (Greenland, Jamaica, Guam). Others of us can be more specific and know the country within the continent or island (Nigeria, Italy, Japan, Mexico, Dominican Republic). Others of us can be even more specific and know the state, town, city, or county within the country (London, Sidney, Hong Kong, Managua, Cairo, New Mexico). In the space provided below, write down the continents, countries, and regions (states, cities, towns, counties) from where you know (or believe) your ancestors came. You can ask a relative or guardian for help! Be sure to include *all* the generations you know!

	Continents	*Countries*	*Regions (State, City, etc.)*
My parents came from			
My grandparents came from			
My great-grandparents came from			
My great-great grandparents and other past generations came from			

Now compare your findings with those of your classmates. How many of them are from just one continent, country, and region? Some people—although they are getting fewer and fewer—can trace their heritage to a single place like Sicily, Italy, Europe. Others of us are combinations of many continents, countries, and regions. Write your findings below.

1. ____________ of my classmates are from just one continent, country, and region.
2. ____________ of my classmates are from many continents, countries, and regions.

Name ______________________________ Date ______________

A–4

THE "ALL AMERICAN" TEENAGER

Do you know in which part of the world the things you use in your everyday life originated? Our ever-day experience is actually very "multicultural"! Read the following story (which is perhaps not too far from your own life as an American teenager) to find out how multicultural our everyday lives are!

THE "ALL AMERICAN" TEENAGER

The "All American" teenager wakes up in the morning on a bed built on a pattern that originated in northern Africa. He or she climbs out of the sheets made of cotton, originally domesticated in Asia (India), and from under the blankets of wool, also originating in Asia. She or he slips on moccasins, invented by the Native Americans of North America, and goes to the bathroom to wash with soap invented by the Phoenicians of northern Africa. The "All American" teenager slips off pajamas, a garment invented in Asia (India); and puts on Levi jeans, which originated with a Jewish peddler from Europe (Germany) named Levi Strauss; a shirt of silk, the use of which was discovered in Asia (China); and sneakers with soles of rubber, which was discovered by the Native Americans of South America (Brazil).

As he or she goes downstairs, the teenager glances through the window of glass, invented by the Romans in southern Europe; and decides to bring an umbrella, invented in southeast Asia, to school because it is raining. She or he tries to decide whether to have an egg, from a bird (chicken) originally domesticated in East Asia, and bagel, a bread originated by Jewish Europeans (Germans); or a waffle, invented in northern Europe (Sweden), and maple syrup, invented by the Native Americans of North America. He or she finally decides to have just a glass of juice made from oranges, originally cultivated in Asia (China); and thin strips of the flesh of an animal (pig) domesticated in East Asia, which have been salted and smoked by a process developed in northern Europe.

Before walking to school he or she swallows a vitamin pill, invented by a man from Europe (Poland); grabs some extra paper, invented in Africa; puts a stamp on a letter of application to a university, first developed in Africa; and makes a quick call to a friend to make after-school plans for a hamburger, which originated in Europe (Germany); with ketchup, invented in Asia (China); mustard, invented in Europe (France); and pickle, invented in Europe (Holland); plus fries, made from potatoes which were originally cultivated by Native Americans; and a Coke, made from a plant first grown in South America (Peru).

In closing the outside door, she or he breathes a sigh of relief at being truly an "All American" teenager!

DIRECTIONS: Write all the underlined words around the world map on the next page. Then, draw a line from each word surrounding the map to the continent or country in which this item originated. EXTRA CREDIT! Continue the story above by looking up the origins of more things you use in your everyday life in the encyclopedia of your local school or library. Write these words around the map, drawing lines to their origins.

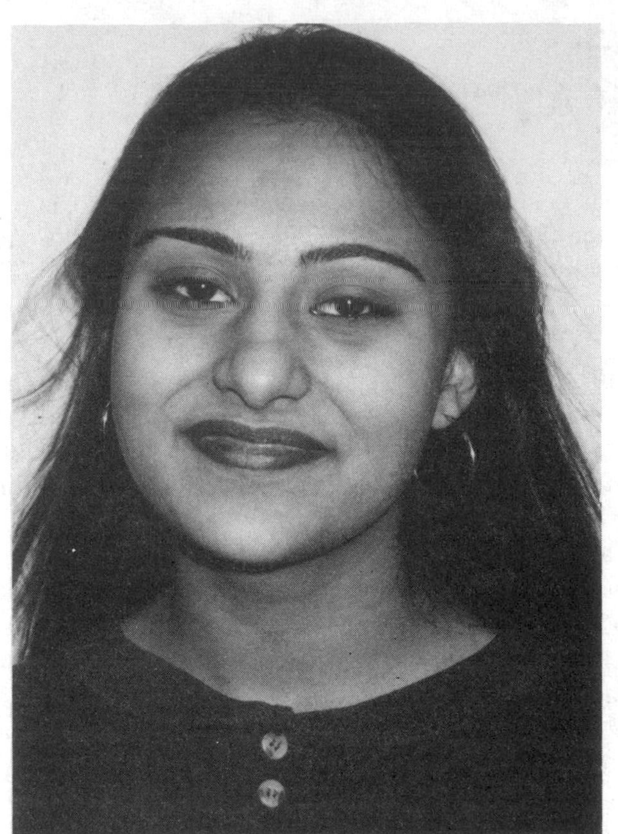

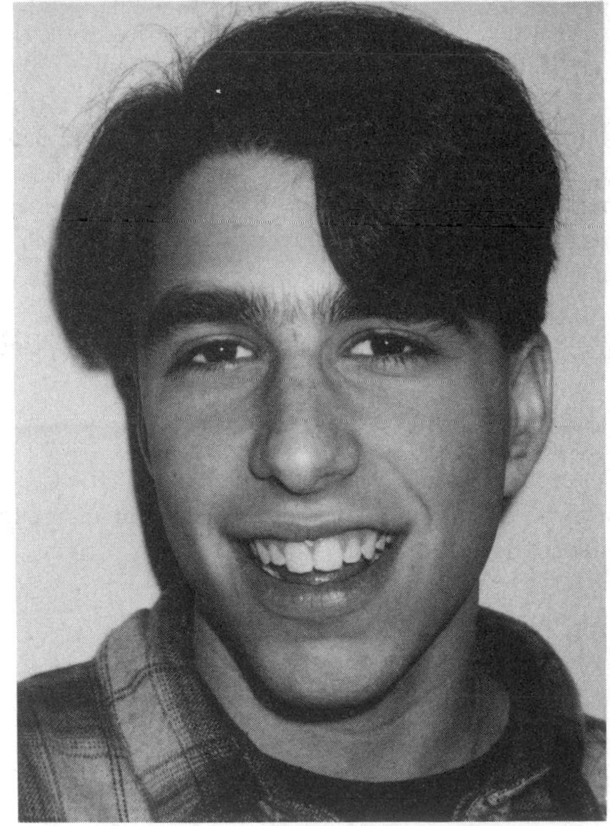

A-4 (continued)

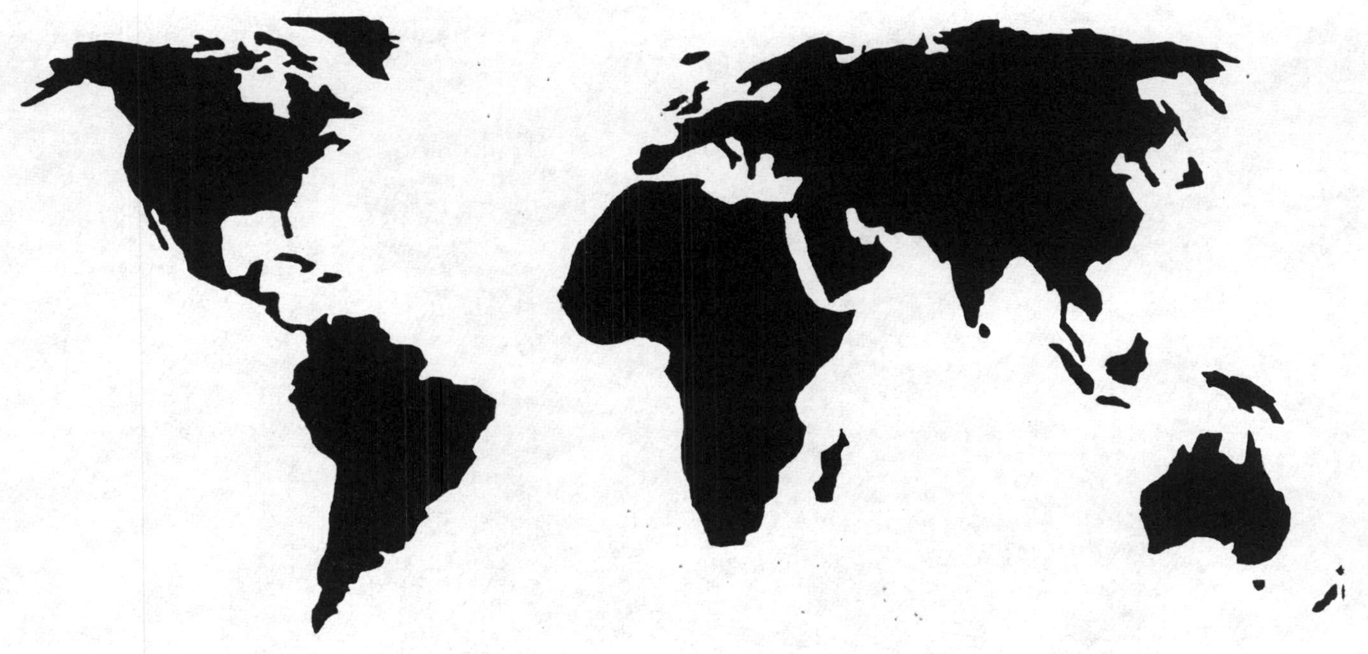

Section *One*

The 1600s

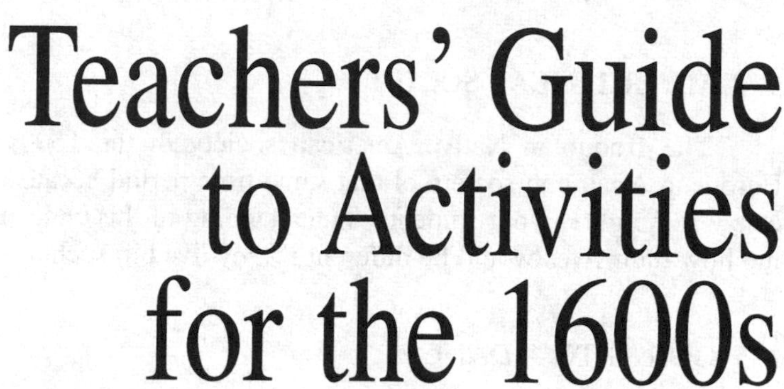

Teachers' Guide to Activities for the 1600s

1–1 DRAW!

It is critical that students learn geography and begin to appreciate how it can affect historical developments. Tracing a map or just filling in information on a ready-made map will not have the same learning value as actually creating it. By drawing the shape of the landforms, seas, and lakes themselves, your students will be far more engaged and will therefore learn more. Some of your students will not believe they can draw a map. Be sure to encourage them that they *can* do it. Some of their creations will not be exact, but that is not important; they will remember the geography if they must recreate it themselves! Also, it is important for students to understand that the Europeans and Africans did not just "fill up" an empty continent! They need to know the extent of the Native American civilizations that existed here before foreigners arrived.

1–2 HOW MUCH DO WE KNOW?

Before students launch into studying a subject area anew, it is important to review their *prior* knowledge. It is also important to see what biases and misconceptions they may bring to the subject area. This is a survey exercise that will help them to ponder what they do and do not know about the 1600s and hypothesize as to why many people may have these misconceptions. ANSWERS: (1) Italian (2) The Americas (3) Spain (4) said "hello Englishmen" (5) over 50% (6) sold as servants and wives (7) indentured servants (8) Iroquois Native Americans (9) all of the above (10) woman

1–3 GENERATIONS

Students often look at history as abstract information, people, and dates. They often cannot imagine that one of their relatives actually lived at every period of human history. This exercise will help students study their own family history. It will help them conceptualize history as the story of their ancestors.

1–4 MATRILINEAL SOCIETY

The Iroquoian Native American society in the 1600s was very different from the European American society of that same time period because it was *matrilineal*. This exercise will heighten your students' understanding of this concept and challenge them to imagine how their lives would be different if they lived in such a society today.

1–5 GOING TO A DANCE?

Socializing is something most teenagers enjoy. It is revealing to them to reflect on the idea that teenagers from many different cultural backgrounds and at many different time periods went through the same process they are going through—meeting new friends, especially of the opposite sex! These excerpts will give students new insights into Native American teenagers of the past and put smiles on their faces.

1–6 IMPORTANT DATES!

Significant dates are easy to forget—unless they are on the tip of your tongue. One way to keep them there is to put them into a poem or song. This is a delightful way to make facts "stick" to your tongue and your brain!

1–7 A LOVE STORY

What do Shakespeare and soap operas have in common? Most of us love a good love story—especially those of us between 13 and 19 years of age! Use these facts to encourage your students to write a "faction" (fact and fiction) story.

1–8 POLISH AMERICANS LEAD THE FIRST LABOR WALKOUT

This dramatic exercise will put your students in the shoes of the first Jamestown colonists and give them an appreciation for one of the ten largest ancestral groups in America—the Polish Americans.

1–9 ENSLAVED!

It is difficult for our students to fathom living under slavery. Reading the excerpts in this exercise will give them a better understanding of the horrors of this existence and challenge them to use their imaginations.

1–10 STEPMOTHERS AND STEPFATHERS

Stories are an important aspect of our lives. It is revealing to analyze the historical context of the many fairy tales with which we grew up. Mean stepmothers and stepfathers were not a figment of someone's imagination. They were an unfortunate reality for many children living in the 1600s. This exercise helps students understand why this was so and gives them a chance to explore the stereotype that has survived until today.

1–11 CHILDREN OR NO CHILDREN?

Hypothesizing about why certain historical phenomena occurred challenges teenagers to use their critical thinking skills. This exercise will also encourage them to "walk in someone else's shoes" and imagine what decisions *they* would have made if *they* had been in a similar situation.

1–12 NEEDS/ECONOMIC INTERESTS

Being able to critically analyze economic interest groups to understand what mutual and conflicting interests they may have is an important skill to attain. This exercise may take some guidance from you as a teacher.

1–13 ECONOMIC CLASS TENSION?

Too often early America is seen as a place where people could "pull themselves up by their bootstraps" if they just worked hard enough. It is important for students to understand that there were definite economic classes and tough barriers for working-class people to overcome. This cartoon and quote will deepen students understanding of the issue.

1–14 TIGHT QUARTERS

Feel what it was like to be on a crowded ship for a long period of time. Planning and carrying out this exercise will help your students internalize the conditions of most Europeans traveling to this country in the 1600s.

1–15 INDENTURED SERVANTS

The extent of the European immigrants who came to America as indentured servants is often unknown or misunderstood. This exercise will shed new light on this topic and challenge your students to use their contrast-and-compare skills.

1–16 GRILLED CHEESE SANDWICH

We often forget how different our everyday lives are compared with living four centuries ago. This exercise encourages your students to analyze their lives, labor, and food to better understand the difficulties of living in the 1600s.

1–17 EUROPEAN AMERICAN WOMEN'S POSITION IN SOCIETY

The role of women throughout our nation's development has all too often been trivialized or even excluded from U.S. history books. This exercise offers information your students may never have encountered and an opportunity to compare the 1600s with present-day conditions for women.

1–18 GUNS!

Some of the issues we face in the 1990s were also faced in the 1600s. It can be fascinating for students to imagine a historical figure living in the present-day world and voicing his or her opinion in ongoing debates. Encourage your students to make William Penn's opinions come alive today!

1–19 ENGLISH AMERICAN NAMES:

How much can we learn about our country's history and culture by just analyzing our last names? Your students will never look at the phone book in the same way after doing this exercise! ANSWERS: *topographical features* (Lake, Rivers, Hill, Dale, Shore, Brooks, Ford, Woods, Banks, Park, Glenn, Forest); *forenames* (Williams, Davies, Thomas, Charles, Allan, Phillips, Roberts, David, James, Martin); *descriptive adjectives* (Young, Black, Brown, Reid, Strong, Short, Long, Little, Armstrong, Elder); *occupations* (Taylor, Weaver, Smith, Farmer, Tanner, Miller); *rank* (Bishop, Priest, Rector, Chaplain, Deacon, Earl, Squire, Sheriff, Major, Sergeant, Prentice, Masters); *places in England* (York, Kent, English, Scott, Walsh).

1–20 PEOPLE TO REMEMBER

Women, men, Native Americans, African Americans, and European Americans are all on this list! Divide your class into small groups and have them use the library resources (encyclopedias and other references.) to see who can finish the list first! ANSWERS: (1) C (2) K (3) L (4) J (5) H (6) F (7) M (8) E (9) D (10) I (11) G (12) N (13) B (14) A (15) O

Name ______________________________ Date ______________

1–1
DRAW!

The map below shows where many of the Native American tribes and nations (Dakota, Cherokee, etc.) lived before European colonization. It also shows the seven Native American cultural regions (Eastern Woodlands, Great Plains, etc.). Using a larger piece of paper (legal size or larger construction paper), a pencil, and your eyes, redraw this map. Do not trace or use an overhead projector to enlarge the image! You can do it! Using colored pencils or markers, color each Native American cultural region differently. Then, with a black pencil or marker, write in the names of all the nations and tribes. This will give you an idea of the many different Native American cultures that existed before the Europeans arrived!

1-1 (continued)

STATES, CITIES, AND TOWNS: For this part of the exercise, you will need a good map of the United States, one that shows you the names of states, cities, and towns. You can find this map in your school or local library. Look at the map showing you where many of the Native American tribes and nations lived before Europeans arrived. In the space provided below, list states, cities, and towns that are named after the Native Amerians who originally lived in this area.

I found _____ states named after Native American tribes and nations. They are:

1.

2.

3.

4.

5.

6.

7.

I found _____ cities and towns named after Native American tribes and nations. They are:

1.

2.

3.

4.

5.

6.

7.

8.

9.

10.

(Write additional names on the back of this paper.)

Name ______________________ Date ____________

1–2

HOW MUCH DO WE KNOW?

How much do we Americans know about the early history of our country? Many times there are myths and misconceptions that people have learned. Put your name in the first box of this survey and answer the questions to the best of your knowledge. Then go over the correct answers with your teacher. Finally, choose five people (neighbors, relatives, friends, anyone!) and ask them the questions, recording their answers on the chart.

NAMES							
1. The land "America" was named after: a. an Italian b. an Englishman c. a Spaniard							# correct _____ # incorrect ____
2. Which had a larger population in the 1600s? a. The Americas b. Europe							# correct _____ # incorrect ____
3. The European country that first formed a permanent settlement on land now called the United States was: a. England b. Spain c. France							# correct _____ # incorrect ____

NAMES							
4. The first Native American who saw the Pilgrims: a. said "Hello Englishmen" b. attacked them c. fled in terror							# correct ____ # incorrect ____
5. The percentage of Europeans who came to America in the seventeenth and eighteenth centuries as indentured servants was: a. 10% b. 25% c. over 50%							# correct ____ # incorrect ____
6. The first women who sailed from England to Virginia were: a. sold as servants and wives b. the wives of other passengers c. owners of their own farms							# correct ____ # incorrect ____
7. The first Africans who landed in Jamestown were: a. slaves b. indentured servants c. free men and women							# correct ____ # incorrect ____
8. Which group first practiced democratic principles in eastern North America? a. English b. French c. Iroquois Native Americans							# correct ____ # incorrect ____

NAMES							
9. The following were accused of witchcraft and executed: a. women b. men c. dogs d. all of the above							# correct ____ # incorrect ____
10. The first poet to publish a book of English poetry in America was a: a. woman b. man							# correct ____ # incorrect ____

Use your math skills to answer the following questions:

1. How many responses did you receive? (Add up the total number of people who took the quiz and multiply by ten.) ____________________

2. How many responses were correct? What percentage of the total responses was this number?

   ____

3. How many responses were incorrect? What percentage of the total responses was this number?

   ____

4. Why do you think people do not know all the answers to these questions? Write two hypotheses below:

   Hypothesis 1 ____________________

   ____

   Hypothesis 2 ____________________

   ____

Name ________________________________ *Date* ____________

1–3

GENERATIONS

How many generations of a family are born every century? Let's do some research about *your* family to discover the answer to this question. First, complete the following sentence:

1. I, ______________________________, was born in the year 19 _____.

Now do some research about your family. Find out the following information by asking a family member (father, mother, grandmother, grandfather, aunt, uncle). If it is impossible to find out this information, work with a family member to make an educated guess.

2. My mother, ______________________________, was born in the year 19 _____.
3. My grandmother, ______________________________, was born in the year 19 _____.
4. My great-grandmother, ______________________________, was born in the year 19 _____.

Were you all born within the last 100 years (the 1900s or the twentieth century)?______________

Now, let's estimate about past generations of your family. Using 25 years as the average span of years between generations, complete sentences 5–16.

5. My great-great grandparents were born in the year 18 _____.
6. My great-great-great grandparents were born in the year 18 _____.
7. My great-great-great-great grandparents were born in the year 18 _____.
8. My great-great-great-great-great grandparents were born in the year 18 _____.
9. My great-great-great-great-great-great grandparents were born in the year 17 _____.
10. My great-great-great-great-great-great-great grandparents were born in the year 17 _____.
11. My great-great-great-great-great-great-great-great grandparents were born in the year 17 _____.
12. My great-great-great-great-great-great-great-great-great grandparents were born in the year 17 _____.
13. My great-great-great-great-great-great-great-great-great-great grandparents were born in the year 16 _____.
14. My great-great-great-great-great-great-great-great-great-great-great grandparents were born in the year 16 _____.
15. My great-great-great-great-great-great-great-great-great-great-great-great grandparents were born in the year 16 _____.
16. My great-great-great-great-great-great-great-great-great-great-great-great-great grandparents were born in the year 16 _____.

1-3 (continued)

WRITE A LETTER TO YOUR RELATIVE IN THE 1600s: Your great-great-great-great-great-great-great-great-great-great-great-great-great grandmother or grandfather may have lived in Africa, Europe, Asia, North America, South America, or Australia. Write a letter to him or her. Be sure to describe what life is like for a teenager of the 1990s. Remember, this relative has no knowledge of the United States or modern technology (e.g., car, TV, VCR, computer or refrigerator), so you have a lot to explain. At the end of your letter, think of five questions you would like to ask your relative about life in the 1600s.

Dear ______________________________,

____

____

____

____

____

____

____

____

Question 1 ____

____

Question 2 ____

____

Question 3 ____

____

Question 4 ____

____

Question 5 ____

____

(Continue on the back.)

Sincerely,

Name ______________________________ *Date* ______________

1–4

MATRILINEAL SOCIETY

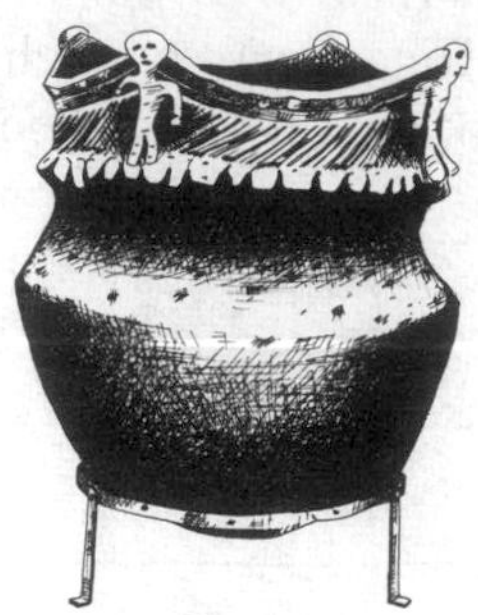

One group of Native Americans, the Iroquois, was a confederation of five nations—the Senecas (Great Hill People), the Mohawks (People of the Flint), the Oneidas (People of the Stone), the Onondagas (People of the Mountain), and the Cayugas (People of the Landings). They lived along the great lakes that border present-day New York and Pennsylvania. Many European Americans (missionaries, hunters, colonizers) remarked, when coming in contact with the Iroquoian civilization, that it differed greatly from their own civilization because it was *matrilineal*. Write around the circle below the words that come to your mind when you hear this term.

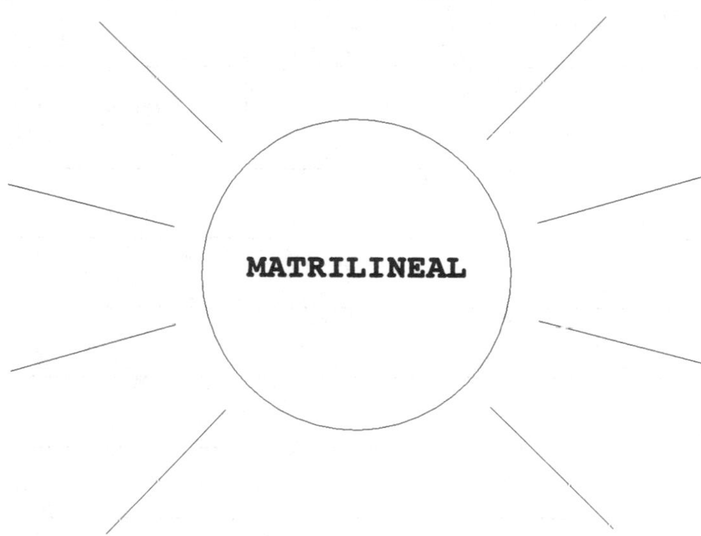

Look up the word "matrilineal" in the dictionary and write its definition in the space provided below:

MATRILINEAL

Read the facts about Iroquoian society in the seventeenth century; they will give you an idea of how this matrilineal society operated.

1. The mother was the head of Iroquoian families and family descent was traced through her.
2. When daughters reached puberty and married, they would bring their new husbands to live in the house of their mothers.

3. When sons reached puberty and married, they would go to live in the households of their new wives.
4. Many generations of a family lived together (sisters, aunts, uncles, cousins, grandparents) and became an "extended family."
5. Each extended family lived in a "long house" (a house made of wood and bark, in the shape of a long rectangle).
6. Each extended family was grouped together with other extended families to form a "clan."
7. A village was made up of a dozen or more clans.
8. The women of each clan elected a "matron" to represent them in village affairs.
9. Matrons organized agricultural labor and household management.
10. Each matron selected a man to represent the clan at village councils. The matron stood behind her selected man as he sat in a circle at village council meetings; she watched how the selected man spoke and voted and removed him from this position if he strayed too far from her wishes.
11. Matrons of the village got together to select the man from their village to represent them at tribal council meetings. (Each tribe consisted of many villages.)
12. Matrons had the power to impeach the men they had selected to represent them at the tribal council level, if they were not pleased with their performance.
13. Women tended the crops; land was owned and worked in common.
14. Men hunted and fished; catch was divided equally among the members of the village and was controlled by the women once it was brought back to the long house.
15. Women were in control of food, both agricultural and hunted, once it was within the long house.
16. When a woman wanted a divorce from her husband, she set her husband's things outside the door of the long house.
17. Women arranged their children's marriages and kept the children in the case of divorce.
18. Houses and land were considered common property. The idea of private property was foreign to the Iroquois. A French Jesuit priest who encountered them in the 1650s wrote "No poorhouses are needed among them, because they are neither mendicants nor paupers. . . . Their kindness, humanity and courtesy not only makes them liberal with what they have, but causes them to possess hardly anything except in common."

DIRECTIONS: Consider your own life. How would it be different if you lived in Iroquoian society of the seventeenth century? Where would you live? Who would be the members of your "extended family"? Whom would you marry? Where would you live after marriage? What kind of work would you perform? Would you be happy living in a society organized in this manner? Write a story describing your life with the Iroquois. Be sure to explain the advantages and disadvantages (from your point of view!) this life held.

____

____

____

____

(Continue on the back.)

Name ________________________ Date ____________

1–5

GOING TO A DANCE?

What was it like to be a teenage Native American living in seventeenth-century America? You probably already know that there were (and still are) many Native American nations and tribes. Each tribe or nation had different customs for teenage girls and boys to meet each other. Read this excerpt from *Daughters of the Earth: The Lives and Legends of American Indian Women*, by Carolyn Niethammer, which describes the customs of the Sioux Native Americans:

The Sioux also arranged a "formal ball" for their young people. The Night Dance took place on a summer evening in a large tipi set up near the center of the camp. . . . As is typical of young people's dances even now, the girls sat on one side of the lodge and the boys congregated on the other side. When the drumming began, each girl walked over to the boys' side and chose a partner by kicking the sole of his moccasin. The couples, holding each other by the belt, formed a line and danced in a two-step motion around the fire. The next dance it was the boys' turn to choose partners. Midway in the dancing a feast was served—usually boiled puppy.[1]

In the space below describe a dance you have attended. Be sure to explain where it was held, what kind of music was played, and who asked whom to dance. How is your dance similar to the description of the Sioux dance? How is it different from the description?

____

____

____

____

____

____

(Continue on the back.)

Name ____ *Date* _______________

1–6

IMPORTANT DATES!

How often have you been asked to memorize important dates in a history or social studies class? Sometimes this task is made easier by making up a rhyme for important historical events and their dates. For example, complete the following verse:

COLUMBUS SAILED THE OCEAN BLUE
IN FOURTEEN HUNDRED NINETY _________."

Read the following information about seventeenth century America and rhymes that were created from this information. Work with a friend and try to memorize the first three examples. Then work by yourself, or with a friend, to create rhymes for the last three examples:

1. Approximately 10 million Native Americans lived in seventeenth-century North America.

   Ten million natives were there, you see
   To live through the seventeenth century.

2. In 1619, the first 20 Africans landed on the east coast of America in the colony of Virginia.

   A frightening trip was surely seen
   By Africans landing sixteen nineteen.

3. About 105 British settlers established Jamestown colony in 1607.

   One-hundred-five arrived from England (not heaven)
   Remember the year, sixteen-zero-seven.

4. The first large group of European women (144) to land on the east coast of America were brought to Virginia in 1619 and sold as wives or servants.

   ____

   ____

5. The Pilgrims arrived at Plymouth Rock, Massachusetts, in 1620.

   ____

   ____

6. The Puritans arrived in Massachusetts Bay in 1630.

   ____

   ____

Memorize these simple jingles; your teacher may ask you to say them out loud in class!

Name ______________________________ *Date* ____________

1–7
A LOVE STORY

Do you have a favorite love story? Romeo and Juliet? West Side Story? Did you know that many authors write historical fiction? That is a combination of historical fact and context with imagination. Let's see if you can write a short piece of historical fiction based on facts regarding one of the first love stories experienced by African Americans in the "New World."

FACTS!

1. Antoney and Isabella, two African indentured servants who were brought to Jamestown in 1619, fell in love and got married.
2. Isabella gave birth to the first African American baby, named William, in 1623. He was baptized in the Church of England.
3. The first African settlers voted, owned land, testified in court, owned other African and European indentured servants and mingled with other free Europeans on a more or less equal basis.
4. According to the first detailed census, the 23 Africans who lived in Virginia constituted 2% of the population in 1624.
5. One of America's first African American communities was established in the 1650s on the banks of the Pungoteague River of Virginia.

Write a short love story (one to two pages) using some or all of the above information. Use your imagination to write descriptions, characters, and dialogue. Give your story a title.

TITLE ______________________________

____

____

____

____

____

____

(Continue on the back.)

Name ______________________________________ Date ______________

1–8

POLISH AMERICANS LEAD THE FIRST LABOR WALKOUT

What do you associate with the term "walkout"? Write whatever word(s) come to your mind when you hear this term around the circle below.

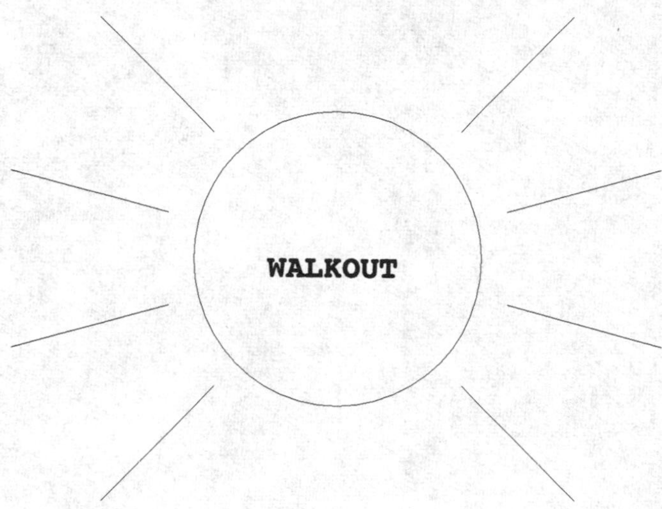

Polish Americans, who are the ninth largest ancestral group in the United States, have made many contributions to this country—including the invention of vitamins by Casimir Funk, the movement to establish playgrounds for children in cities by Dr. Marie Elizabeth Zakrzewska, and participation in the War of Independence. Their first contribution to this country, however, was their fight for civil rights and leadership in the first labor walkout. Read the facts from *The Poles in America*, by Joseph A. Wytrwal, to find out what this struggle was all about.

1. Several Poles were on board the ships of Englishmen that first landed in Jamestown, Virginia, in 1609. They were included in the expedition because of their expertise in the manufacture of glass, tar, and soap.
2. The Poles were hard workers. They dug wells, built shelters, cleared land, and cut down trees for the manufacture of wood products. They also constructed the first glass factory approximately one mile from the Jamestown settlement.
3. Within a few years, 50 Poles were living in Jamestown with the other English settlers.
4. At first, none of the settlers of Jamestown were allowed to create their own government. Instead, an administrator of the English king ran all the governmental affairs. After 1619, the London Company gave the English men the right to form their own government. The Polish men, however, were not granted this right.
5. On July 30, 1619, the first Virginia Assembly of English men *only* was held. The Polish settlers staged a demonstration at this assembly to protest the fact that they were not given the right to participate in the new fledgling democracy.
6. On that same day, the Polish factory workers staged a walkout from their workplace, refusing to work until they were granted the same voting privileges as those of the English settlers.

1-8 (continued)

THE FIRST LABOR WALKOUT:
"Jamestown Glassblowers" by Richard Frear
(The National Park Service #266-580).

7. The governor of Jamestown, Sir George Yeardley, gave the following account of the outcome of this protest and walkout: "Upon some dispute of the Polonians [Polish] resident in Virginia, it was now agreed (notwithstanding any former order to the contrary) that they shall be enfranchised and made free as any inhabitant there whatsoever. . . ."(1)

DIRECTIONS: Create a short play depicting the fist labor walkout in America. First, you must divide your classmates into two groups—the Poles and the English. Establish one area of the classroom as the site for the Virginia Assembly meeting of July 30, 1619, then designate another area of the classroom as the site for the glass factory. The English will begin in the area designated for the Virginia Assembly; the Poles will begin in the area for the factory. In the space provided below, write the dialogue among the English in the Virginia Assembly, *before* the Poles staged their protest and walkout. Then write the dialogue among the Poles in the factory *before* they staged their protest in front of the Virginia Assembly and the walkout.

DIALOGUE AMONG THE ENGLISH IN THE VIRGINIA ASSEMBLY

DIALOGUE AMONG THE POLES IN THE FACTORIES

Now, time for the protest and walkout! In the space provided below write the dialogue between the English and the Poles during the protest and walkout.

DIALOGUE BETWEEN THE ENGLISH AND THE POLES

(Continue on the back.)

Name ______________________ Date ______________

1–9

ENSLAVED!

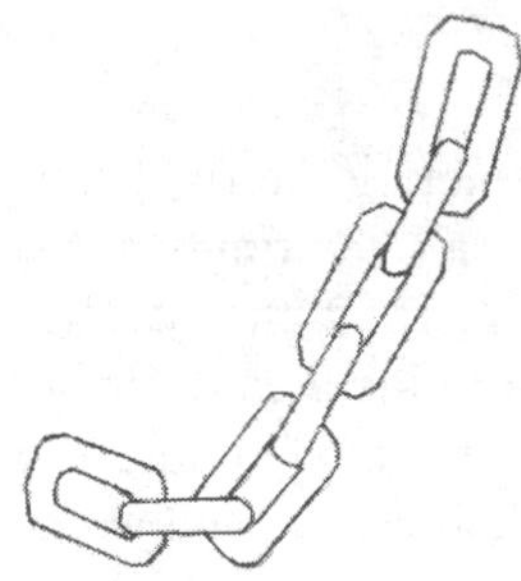

The European practice of enslaving Africans and bringing them to the Western hemisphere began shortly after Christopher Columbus journeyed to the Americas. By 1619, over 1 million Africans had been captured, transported, and forced to labor in the Caribbean and South America. During most of the 1600s, most African Americans were forcibly brought to America, but, as Lorenzo J. Greene states in his classic book entitled *The Negro in Colonial America*, "Until the end of the seventeenth century the records refer to Negroes as 'servants' and not 'slaves'." Indeed, many of the first generation of African Americans worked for European masters as indentured servants, eventually earning their freedom; however, by the end of the 1600s, that had changed. Great profits realized in the tobacco market and the slave trade encouraged an end to the era of African American indentured servants and ushered in the institutionalization of African American slavery in America. Read the excerpts that describe the experience of being captured in Africa, transported to America, sold in America, and forced to live and work in America.

CAPTURED IN AFRICA

". . . we were alarmed one morning, just at the break of day, by the horrible uproar caused by the mingled shouts of men. . . . The village was surrounded by enemies, who attacked us with clubs, long wooden spears, and bows and arrows. After fighting for more than an hour, those who were not fortunate enough to run away, were made prisoners. It was not the object of our enemies to kill; they wished to take us alive and sell us as slaves. I was knocked down by a heavy blow of a club, and when I recovered from the stupor that followed, I found myself tied fast. . . . We were immediately led away from this village. . . . We traveled three weeks in the woods . . . and arrived one day at a large river with a rapid current. . . . When our raft came near the ship, the white people . . . assisted to take us on deck. . . . The people who brought us down river received payment for us . . . in various articles, of which I remember that a keg of liquor, and some yards of blue and red cotton cloth were the principal."(1)

TRANSPORTED TO AMERICA

"The height, sometimes, between the decks [of slave ships], was only eighteen inches; so that the unfortunate human beings could not turn around, or even on their sides, the elevation being less than the breadth of their shoulders; and here they are usually chained to the decks by the neck and legs. In such a place the sense of misery and suffocation is so great, that the Negroes . . . are driven to a frenzy."

SOLD IN AMERICA

"Every first Tuesday slaves were brought in from Virginia and sold on the block. . . . They would stand the slaves up on the block and talk about what a fine-looking specimen of black manhood or womanhood they was, tell how healthy they was, look in their mouth and examine their teeth just like they was a horse, and talk about the kind of work they would be fit for and could do."[(2)]

LIVING IN AMERICA

"We lodged in log huts and on the bare ground. Wooden floors were an unknown luxury. In a single room were huddled, like cattle, ten or a dozen persons, men, women and children. All ideas of refinement and decency were, of course, out of the question. There were neither bedsteads, nor furniture of any description. Our beds were collections of straw and old rags, thrown down in the corners and boxed in with boards, a single blanket the only covering . . . . The wind whistled and the rain and snow blew in through the cracks, and the damp earth soaked in the moisture till the floor was miry as a pigsty. Such were our houses."[(3)]

WORKING IN AMERICA

"The work of the majority of slaves was physically demanding, dull and repetitive, offering blacks little challenge and only a slight possibility of better employment. Most slaves were kept to the routine tasks of raising tobacco and corn and tending livestock."[(4)]

What if this experience of enslavement had happened to you? Imagine that the world is invaded by aliens from another planet who have vastly superior military technology to that of the United States today. You are taken prisoner and taken to another planet to be enslaved. Write a short story describing your experience. Be sure to include a description of your capture, your journey to the other planet, how you were sold, your living conditions, and the kind of work you were forced to perform. Begin your story in the space provided below.

(Continue on the back.)

Name ______________________________ Date ______________

1–10

STEPMOTHERS AND STEPFATHERS

Do you remember reading about all of those mean stepmothers and stepfathers in stories like "Hansel and Gretel" or "Cinderella"? Those stories were created at a time when death of a parent was, unfortunately, a common occurrence for many children. In fact, one-third of all American children living in the southern colonies during the 1600s lost both parents before they reached adulthood. Having to deal with the death of one parent and remarriage of the other parent was also a fact of life for most seventeenth-century American children living in the South.

Consider the following true story about a 1600 European American colonial family.

Imagine you were the child, Walter, of the parents Mary and George Keeble. You and your three siblings (Mary, George, and Margaret) were left fatherless when your father died in 1666. Then your mother, Mary, married Robert Beverly and had five more children (Peter, Robert, Harry, John, and Mary). Then your mother, Mary, died (1678) and your new stepfather, Robert Beverly, married a woman named Katherine who had a son, Theophilus, Jr. Then your stepfather, Robert, died (1680) and your new stepmother married a man named Christopher Robinson, who had four children from a previous marriage (Anne, Christopher, Clara, John). Christopher and Katherine had four more children (Elizabeth, another Clara, another Theophilus, and Benjamin). Katherine died in 1692 and Christopher died in 1693.

Answer the following questions.

1. How many total stepsiblings and siblings did Walter have by 1693 and what were their names?

2. How many parents and stepparents had Walter had by the year 1693 and what were their names?

3. The average life expectancy of European American women in Virginia was 39 years and of European American men was 48 years during the 1600s. Why did Americans die at an earlier age in the 1600s? List your hypotheses.

Hypothesis 1 ______________________________

____

Hypothesis 2 ______________________________

____

Create a family tree of this European American colonial family by writing all the mothers, fathers, stepmothers, stepfathers, and children in the boxes provided below.

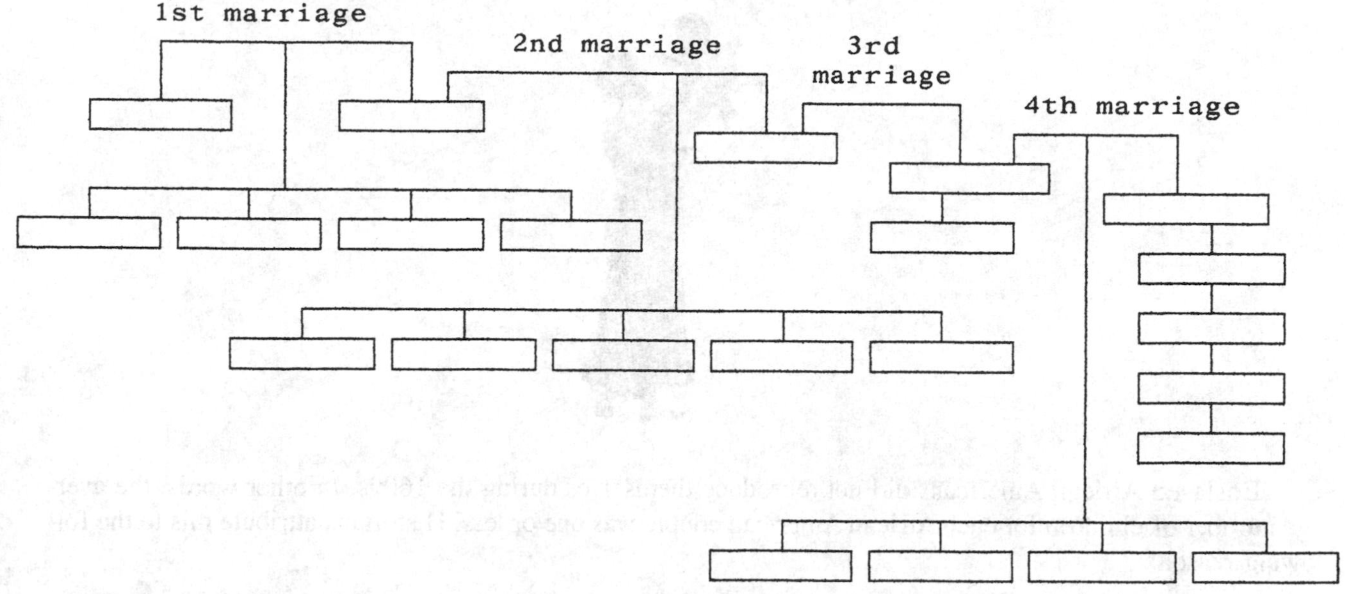

EXTRA CREDIT! Use your imagination and write a piece of fiction using this true historical information as a basis. This can take the form of a short story or a folk tale such as "Hansel and Gretel," "Snow White," "Br'er Rabbit," or "Cinderella." Be sure to describe the characters, the situations they face, and their feelings about their stepmothers and stepfathers.

Name ______________________________ Date ______________

1–11

CHILDREN OR NO CHILDREN?

Enslaved African Americans did not reproduce themselves during the 1600s. In other words, the average number of children for each African American couple was one or less. Historians attribute this to the following reasons:

1. The ratio of African men to African women was 2 to 1.
2. African women who were brought to America were well advanced in their child-bearing years.
3. There was much disease.
4. There was a lack of desire to have children because of the extreme alienation of living as a slave in America.

DIRECTIONS: Put yourself in the situation of an enslaved African American of the 1600s. Would you have wanted to have children if you lived in this situation?

Complete the following:

I would/would not (circle one) have wanted to have children if I were an enslaved African American living in the 1600s.

My reasons are the following:

Reason 1 ______________________________

____

Reason 2 ______________________________

____

Reason 3 ______________________________

____

1-11 (continued)

Write a short essay explaining your point of view on this issue. Be sure to include an introduction, body, and conclusion in your essay. Also, be sure to elaborate on your reasons.

(Continue on the back.)

Name ________________________________ Date ____________

1–12
NEEDS/ECONOMIC INTERESTS

Have you ever thought about what you need to survive? Think of your life and write a list of at least six "survival needs" below.

I need:

______________________ ______________________

______________________ ______________________

______________________ ______________________

One way to think about late seventeenth-century American life for those living in Virginia and other southern colonies was in terms of eight groups of people with varying needs and economic interests: (1) large landowners, (2) wealthy merchants, (3) small farmers, (4) landless laborers, (5) artisans, (6) indentured servants, (7) slaves, (8) Native Americans. Each group had its own needs. Some of these needs were *mutual* with the needs of other groups. Other needs were *conflicting* with the needs of other groups. Read the following list of these needs. Based on your prior knowledge of seventeenth-century America, what can you add to this list?

a lot of land cheap labor livestock large house seed

tools plow wagon profit international market freedom

support from the English King pigs a job shelter food

clean drinking water peace fenceless land on which to hunt

protection of burial grounds small plots of farm land linen cloth leather

protection from Native Americans birds deer wool

protection from striking workers fish church roads

protection from rebelling slaves carriages cotton nails

wagons cloth protection from invading colonists pewter pots tea

protection from large European landowners trees cows ships corn

local markets high-priced products (tobacco, etc.) candles

low-priced products (tobacco, etc.) rain horses ducks chickens

ADDITIONS:

On the following page you will find a chart with boxes for each of the eight groups of people. Consider the words and phrases for each of these groups. Ask yourself the question—Does this group *need* this (trees, freedom, etc.) to survive? (A "need" can fit into more than one box!)

NEEDS/ECONOMIC INTERESTS

NEEDS OF LARGE LANDOWNERS:		NEEDS OF WEALTHY MERCHANTS:
NEEDS OF SMALL FARMERS:	NEEDS OF LANDLESS LABORERS:	NEEDS OF ARTISANS:
NEEDS OF NATIVE AMERICANS:	NEEDS OF INDENTURED SERVANTS:	NEEDS OF SLAVES;

Based on the information you have created with the chart, answer the following questions:

1. Which of these groups have *conflicting* needs and what exactly are the needs that are in conflict? (large landowners and slaves? large landowners and merchants?) Give at least three examples and explain *why* their needs are conflicting.

2. Which of these groups have *mutual* interests and what exactly are the needs that are mutual? (slaves and indentured servants? small farmers and artisans?) Give at least three examples and explain *why* their needs are mutual.

3. What events in history did the *conflicting* needs cause? (rebellions? laws? strikes? murders?) Give at least three examples and explain why conflicting needs caused these historical events.

4. What events in history did *mutual* needs cause? (treaties? tariffs? cooperation?) Give at least three examples and explain why mutual needs caused these historical events.

Name ______________________________ Date ______________

1–13

ECONOMIC CLASS TENSION?

Read the following quotations written by Virginia's Governor Berkeley in 1676 and look at the artist's drawing below. What do you think Governor Berkeley was saying about economic class tensions during the 1600s? What do you think the artist is expressing about economic class tensions during the 1600s? What do you think could be the repercussions of these tensions? (rebellions? strikes?) Write your answers in the space provided on the next page.

QUOTES FROM VIRGINIA'S GOVERNOR BERKELEY

"How miserable that man is that Governes a People where six parts of seaven at least are Poore Indebted Discontented and Armed."

". . . we cannot but resent that, forty thousand people should be impoverish'd to enrich little more than forty Merchants, who being the only buyers of our Tobacco, give us what they please for it, and after it is here, sell it how they please; and indeed have forty thousand servants in us at cheaper rates, than any other men have slaves. . . ."

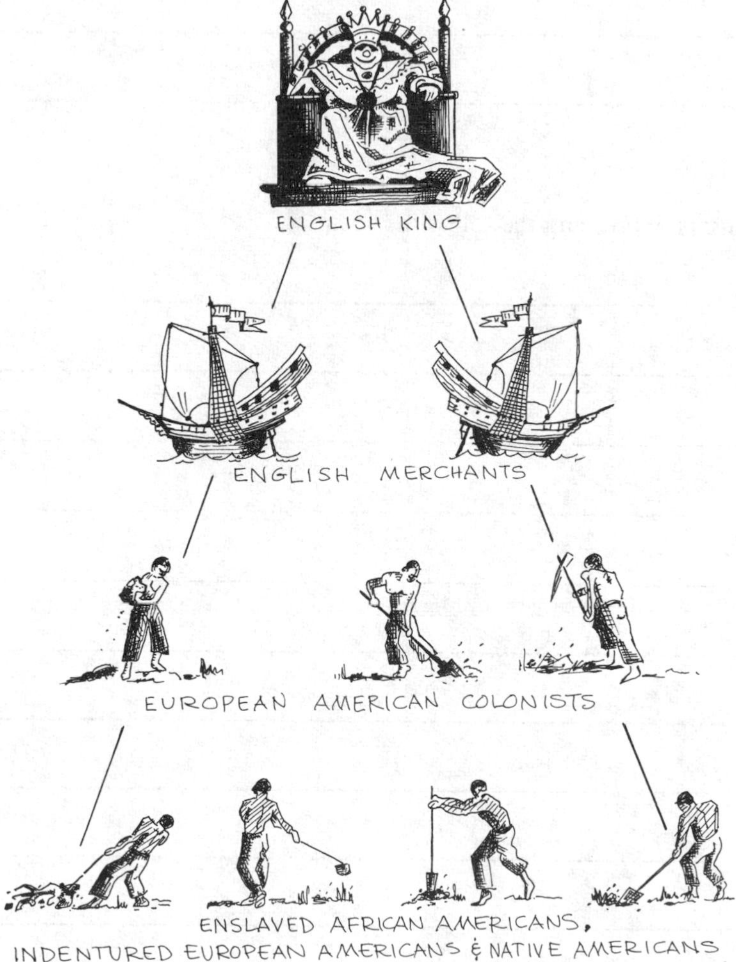

1-13 (continued)

Governor Berkeley was saying that

The artist's drawing is expressing the following idea:

Name ______________________________________ Date ______________

1–14

TIGHT QUARTERS (DAY 1)

The people we now refer to as the "Pilgrims" were actually called "Saints" or "Separatists" in the 1600s. When they were journeying across the Atlantic Ocean to North America in 1620, they each had a space approximately 2 1/2 feet by 7 feet in the hull of the Mayflower in which to keep all their belongings, eat, sleep, and live for 66 days. Using masking tape, mark off a space in the front of your classroom that is 12 1/2 feet wide and 7 feet long. Divide this space into five equal spaces that are each 2 1/2 feet by 7 feet. It should look like this:

Divide your class into five teams. Each team should make a list of what a passenger would need to survive the 66-day journey—that *can fit into these tight living quarters.*

MY TEAM'S LIST OF SURVIVAL NECESSITIES ARE THE FOLLOWING:

____

____

____

____

____

____

____

Tomorrow, bring in as many of these things as possible (e.g., suitcase, pillow, water bottle, medicines) to class. Remind your teacher to bring five onions and five lemons to class tomorrow.

Name ______________________________ *Date* ____________

1–14

TIGHT QUARTERS (DAY 2)

Each team should choose one person to be the team representative on the ship, and which 2 1/2-foot-by-7-foot space your representative will occupy. Place in this space all the survival necessities you brought to class. Finally, you also must choose which of the following people on the Mayflower your representative will be:

1. Female Saint who is nine months pregnant
2. Male Saint
3. Indentured servant
4. Orphan
5. Murderer

Before you place your representative on board the Mayflower, review the following facts about the journey:

1. It was the year 1620.
2. One-half of the passengers are Saints who are leaving England to escape religious persecution by King James.
3. The other half of the passengers are referred to as "the strangers" by the Saints and are looking for adventure, happiness, or freedom from jail. They include 10 indentured servants, a professional soldier, a barrel maker, four orphans, and a man who will be convicted of murder.
4. No one is allowed up on the deck.
5. There is little fresh air.
6. Many people are sick.
7. You have only hard bread and wet, moldy meat to eat.
8. You must eat onions and lemon (straight!) to avoid getting scurvy (a disease, resulting from a lack of Vitamin C, that makes you bleed easily and your teeth fall out).
9. During the journey, the pregnant passenger gives birth to a baby she names Oceanus.

ALL ON BOARD! For the rest of the class period (approximately 30 minutes) have the representative from your team occupy his or her space on the Mayflower. Your representative's job is to interact with the other passengers and see what it feels like to be in such a confined space. The job of the other team members is to take notes in the space below on what they observe. (This can include spoken comments, body language, and spacial arrangements.)

I observed the following on board the Mayflower:

____

____

____

____

At the end of class, share these observations with each other!

Name ______________________ Date ____________

1–15

INDENTURED SERVANTS

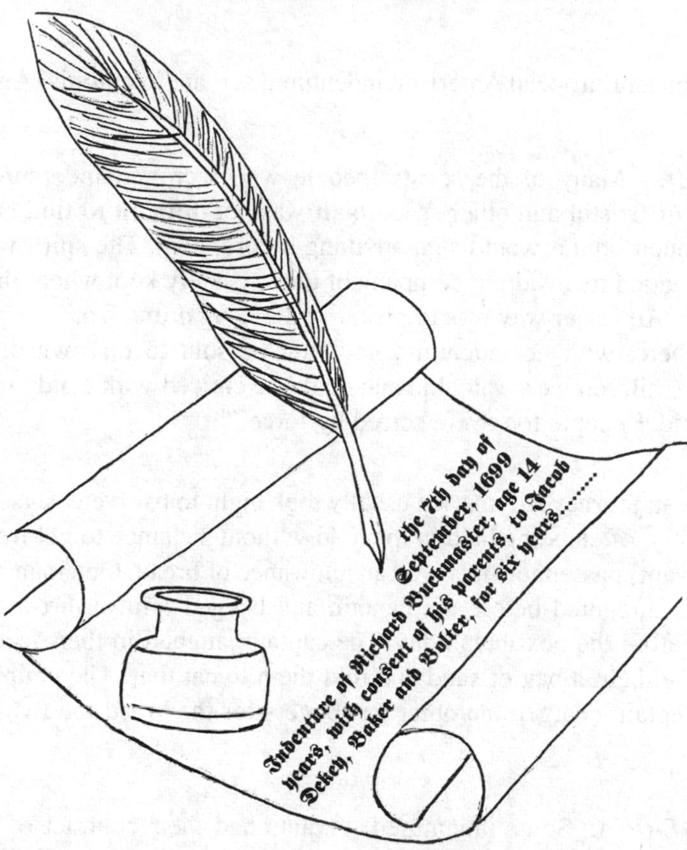

If you are an American of European descent and your ancestors came to this continent during the 1600s or 1700s, there is a 50 percent chance they came as indentured servants. It is estimated that one out of every two European colonists came to America under this condition. Think about the two words "indentured" and "servants." What do you associate with these two terms? Write whatever words come to your mind around the two encircled terms below.

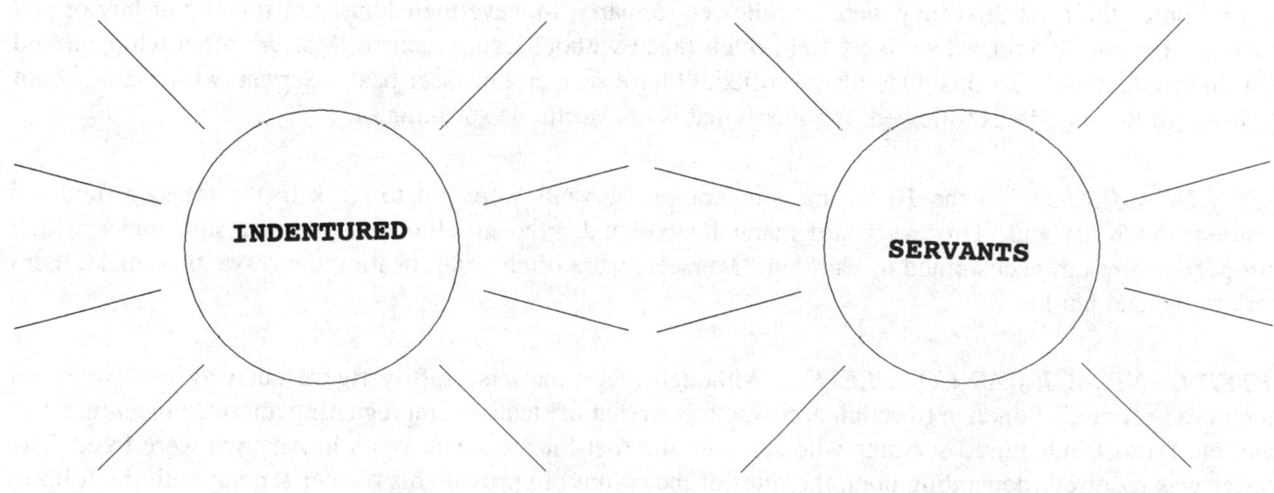

Now, look up the definition of "indenture" in the dictionary and write it below.

INDENTURE

What was it like to be an European American indentured servant in colonial America? Read the excerpts that describe their lives.

BEFORE THE JOURNEY: "Many of the spirits [people who recruited indentured servants] haunted the London slums and those of Bristol and other seaports. It was not difficult to find hungry and thirsty victims who, over a dinner and much liquor, would sign anything before them. The spirit would then hustle his prey to his headquarters to be added to a waiting company of others, safely kept where they could not escape until a ship was ready for them. An easier way was to pick up a sleeping drunk from the gutter and put him aboard a vessel for America, where, with no indenture, he could be sold to his own disadvantage and with the American planter's gain. Children were valuable and could be enticed with candy to come along with a spirit. Sometimes they, and older people too, were seized by force."[(1)]

THE JOURNEY: The ocean journey to America usually took eight to twelve weeks. Indentured servants were packed into the ships tightly, often being held in the hold without a chance to get fresh air. "Every two weeks at sea the [indentured servant] passengers received an allowance of bread. One man and his wife, having eaten their bread in eight days, staggered before the captain and begged him to throw them overboard, for they would otherwise starve before the next bread day. The captain laughed in their faces, while the ship's mate, even more of a brute, gave them a bag of sand and told them to eat that. The couple did die before the next ration of bread, but the captain charged the other passengers for the bread the two would have eaten if they had survived."[(2)]

UPON ARRIVAL IN AMERICA: Some indentured servants had their contract of service worked out with waiting American colonists who would be their masters for four to seven years. Others, upon arrival, were bought and sold much in the same manner as slaves. An announcement in the *Virginia Gazette* read, "Just arrived at Leedstown, the Ship Justitia, with about one Hundred Healthy Servants, Men Women and Boys. . . . The Sale will commence on Tuesday the 2nd of April."

TREATMENT BY THEIR MASTERS: Indentured servants had few rights. They could not vote. Without the permission of their masters, they were not allowed to marry, to leave their houses or travel, nor buy or sell anything. Female indentured servants were often raped without legal recourse. Masters often whipped and beat their indentured servants. One man testified: "I have seen an Overseer beat a Servant with a cane about the head till the blood has followed, for a fault that is not worth the speaking of. . . ."

WORK IN AMERICA: In the 1600s, most indentured servants were put to work in the tobacco fields of Virginia and Maryland. This was hard manual labor under the grueling hot summer sun, under which Europeans were not accustomed to working. Overseers were often cruel, beating the servants to make them work faster and harder.

AFTER CONTRACT WAS COMPLETED: Although many masters craftily figure out ways to extend an indentured servant's bondage (through accusing the servant of stealing, impregnating a female indenture servant, etc.), most indentured servants who survived the first four to seven years in America were freed. The master was required (depending upon the rules of the colony) to provide his former servant with the following: clothing, two hoes, three barrels of corn, and fifty acres of land.

Some historians argue that the life for European American indentured servants in America was very similar to that of African American slaves. Other historians disagree, arguing that there were significant differences. Based on the information given here about indentured servants and your prior knowledge of slavery, create a Venn diagram on the following page that visually shows the similarities and differences of the lives of indentured servants and slaves in early America.

DIFFERENCES AND SIMILARITIES BETWEEN EUROPEAN AMERICAN INDENTURED SERVANTS AND AFRICAN AMERICAN SLAVES IN EARLY AMERICA

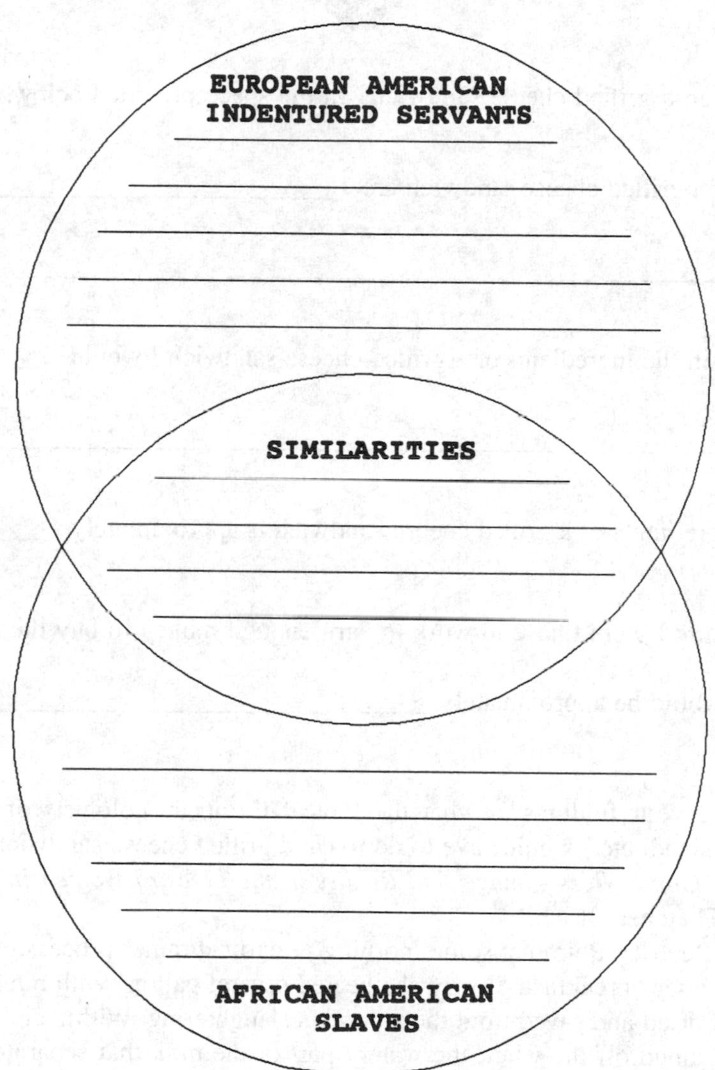

Write a short essay, based on the information you have outlined in the Venn diagram, stating your opinion—whether you agree with (1) the historians who believe the lives of African American slaves and European American indentured servants were more *similar* than different, or (2) the historians who believe the lives of African American slaves and European American indentured servants were more *different* than similar. Be sure to have an introduction, body, and conclusion to your essay.

Name ______________________________ Date ______________

1–16

GRILLED CHEESE SANDWICH

Have you ever eaten a grilled cheese sandwich? In the space provided below, complete the following sentences:

1. The ingredients of a grilled cheese sandwich are ______________________________
____.

2. If I wanted to obtain the ingredients of a grilled cheese sandwich I would ______________
____.

3. The cost of the ingredients of a grilled cheese sandwich is approximately ______________.

4. The number of hours I would have to work to earn enough money to buy the ingredients for a grilled cheese sandwich would be approximately ______________________________.

Now let's compare your findings to what the typical European colonists of northern America (i.e., Massachusetts, Rhode Island, etc.) would have to do to eat a grilled cheese sandwich in the 1600s. Read the excerpts from the book *Good Wives—Image and Reality in the Lives of Women in Northern New England 1650–1750*, by Laurel Thatcher Ulrich.

"We can imagine Beatrice Plummer some morning in early summer processing the milk which would appear as cheese in a January breakfast. Slowly she heated several gallons with rennet [extract from the lining of a calf's stomach] dried and saved from the autumn's slaughtering. Within an hour or two the curd had formed. She broke it, drained off the whey, the watery part of the milk that separates from the curds or fat, then worked in a little of her own fresh butter. Packing this rich mixture into a mold, she turned it in her wooden press for an hour or more, changing and washing the cheesecloth frequently as the whey dripped out . . . drying it, and placing it in the cellar or dairy house to age. . . . Judging from the grain in the upstairs chamber, the bread she baked was 'maslin', a common type made from a mixture of wheat and other grains, usually rye. She began with the sieves nearby, carefully sifting out the coarser pieces of grain and bran. Soon after supper she could have mixed the 'sponge', a thin dough made from warm water, yeast and flour. . . . Warmth from the banked fire would raise the sponge by morning, when Beatrice could work in more flour, knead the finished dough, and shape the loaves, leaving them to rise again . . . to produce bread in any quantity required an oven. . . . Moving about her kitchen, she would have kept an eye on this fire, occasionally raking the coals to distribute the heat evenly, testing periodically with her hand to see if the oven had reached the right temperature. When she determined that it had, she would have scraped out the coals and inserted the bread. . . ."[1]

Finish the following sentence:

5. If I had lived as a European American colonist in northern New England during the seventeenth century, the number of hours I would have to work to obtain the ingredients for a grilled cheese sandwich would be approximately ____________________.

   Compare the answer you computed in sentence 5 to that you gave in sentence 4. How much more time would it take for you to obtain the ingredients for a grilled cheese sandwich if you lived in the seventeenth century as compared with today? Compute your answer below:

6. Time it would take for me to obtain a grilled cheese sandwich in:

   1675: ____________________ Hours

   Today: ____________________ Hours

If preparing something as simple as a grilled cheese sandwich took such a considerable amount of time, what activities did European colonists have to forgo to accomplish these tasks? Think about your own life. What activites would you have to omit from your life to accomplish the things you needed to do to survive. Write your answer below:

____

____

____

____

____

____

____

____

____

____

____

____

____

(Continue on the back.)

1-16 (continued)

Let's consider another aspect of eating during the 1600s. First complete the following sentence:

The eating utensils I use when I eat food are ____

____.

During the 1600s, forks were considered a luxury. Most people ate all their meals with a wooden spoon and a dull knife. In the spaces below, hypothesize as to why this was so.

I think the reason the people of seventeenth-century America did not use forks was because

____

____

____

____

Now, for one entire day, eat all of your food with only a wooden spoon and a dull knife. (No forks allowed!) Be sure to eat a variety of food including salad, chicken, broccoli, beef, potato, rice, and pizza. Then, fill in the hair, eyes, and clothes of the person below so that it looks like you. Also, record in the bubbles some of your thoughts, feelings, comments, and conversation while you have this "forkless" experience.

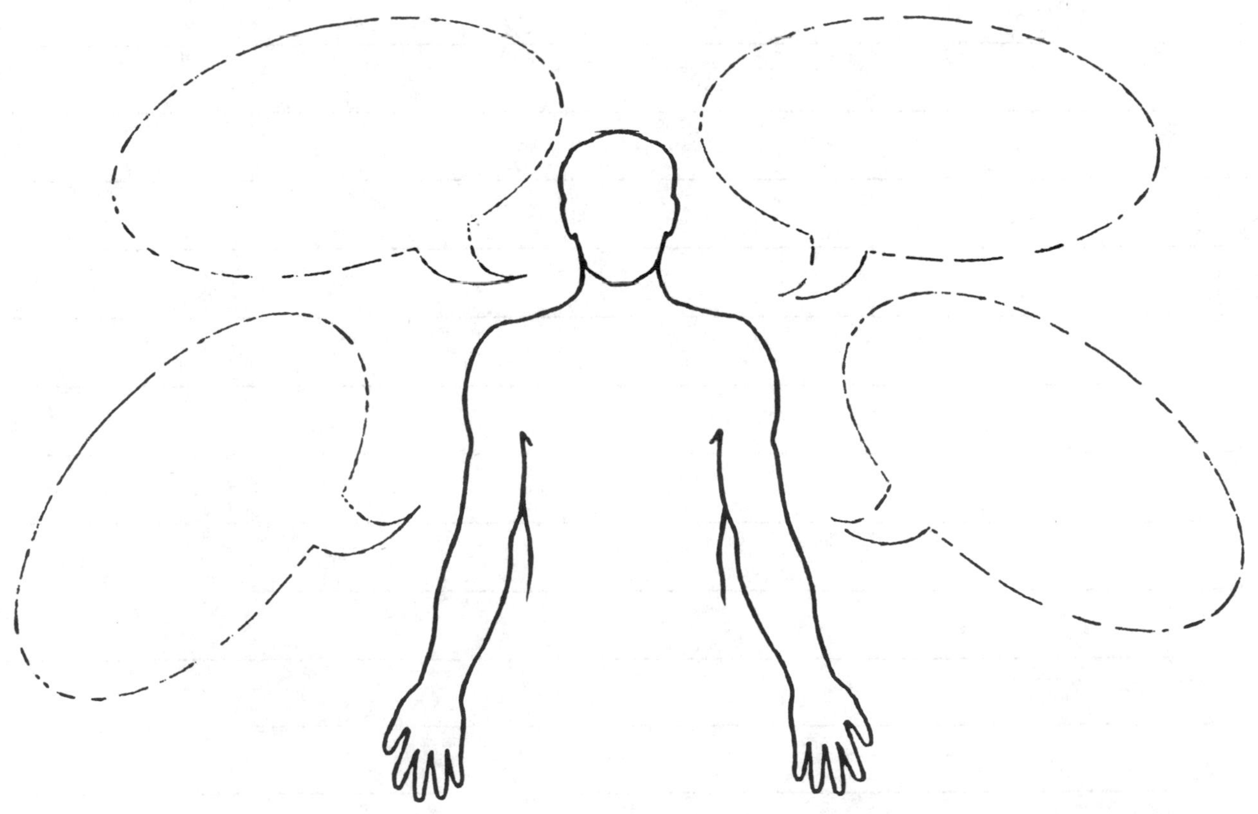

Name ______________________________ Date ______________

1-17

EUROPEAN AMERICAN WOMEN'S POSITION IN SOCIETY

How were women viewed in seventeenth-century New England society? Read the following information to see what you can surmise regarding this question.

1. European American boys and girls were taught to read; however, for the most part, only boys were taught to write.
2. European American women who could write often signed letters to their husbands as "your faythfull and obediant wife" or "your lovinge and obediant wife."
3. European American women who could write often signed letters to their brothers "your sister to command."
4. John Winthrop, governor of Massachusetts, called Anne Hutchinson, a European American religious leader, "a woman of a haughty and fierce carriage, of a nimble wit and active spirit and a very voluble tongue, more bold than a man, though in understanding and judgement, inferiour to many women." He suggested that if she "had attended her household affairs and such things as belong to women and not gone out of her way and calling to meddle in such things as are proper for men, whose minds are stronger, etc. she had kept her wits and might have improved them usefully and honorably in the place God had set her."
5. According to law, European American women were regarded as "chattel," private property, of their husbands.
6. According to law, European American women could not own private property or run a business while married.

Why were European American women relegated to a low position in seventeenth-century American colonial society? Hypothesize your answer to the question below.

Women were relegated to a low position in seventeenth-century American society because:

Hypothesis 1: ______________________________

____

Hypothesis 2: ______________________________

____

Hypothesis 3: ______________________________

____

Keeping in mind what you have just read, would you want to have been a seventeenth-century European American woman? Explain your answer to this question in the space provided below.

____

____

(Continue on the back.)

Name ______________________ Date __________

1–18
GUNS!

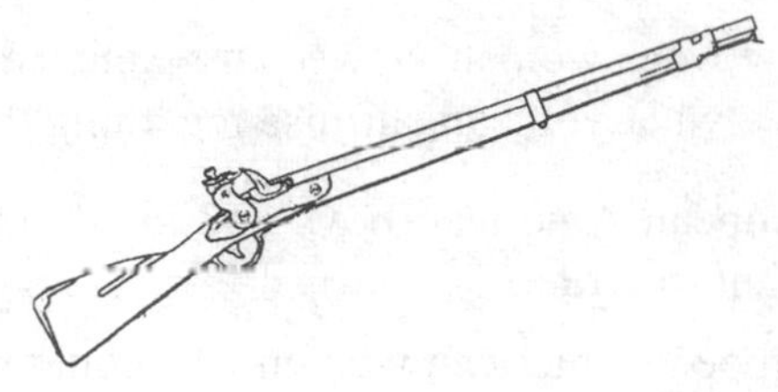

Can you solve this riddle—if the word "sylvania" means woods, what does the word "Pennsylvania" mean? Write your answer below.

I think the word "Pennsylvania" means ______________________

William Penn, a European American Quaker, was given the land for Pennsylvania by King Charles II to pay off a debt the king owed his father. The land was bigger than the country of England.

The Quakers believed all war was wrong because the Bible says "Thou shalt not kill." They believed in treating all people as equals and respecting all religions. They objected to slavery and tried to make peace with the Native Americans. They founded a colony, led by William Penn, that tried to live up to these ideals.

William Penn paid dearly for his beliefs. He was jailed often in England for his beliefs and was kicked out of college when he refused to attend the Church of England prayers. He felt strongly about his view and was willing to vocally oppose those who disagreed with him.

As you probably know, there is currently a debate about gun control in America. Read some of the following arguments in this debate and add your own arguments pro and con.

For Gun Control (1)	*Against Gun Control*
1. A total of 15,377 Americans were slain with guns in 1992.	1. The second amendment protects Americans' right to bear arms.
2. There are an estimated 200 million guns today in America and 1.5 million manufactured each year.	2. Because there are so many guns, you need one to protect yourself.
3. Guns were used in approximately 540,000 robberies and aggravated assaults during 1992.	3. The U.S.A. should just build more prisons to house criminals.
4.	4.
5.	5.

1-18 (continued)

Imagine you are William Penn and are alive today. Which side of the gun debate would you (Penn) be on and why? Write a speech in which you (Penn) express your opinion on this issue and how you defend your position. Begin your (Penn's) speech below:

(Continue on the back.)

Name ______________________________ *Date* ______________

1–19

ENGLISH AMERICAN NAMES

People who are partially or fully of English descent form the third largest ancestral group in the United States English culture and tradition are the basis of much of our American culture, from the language most Americans speak every day (English) to many holidays such as Thanksgiving and Halloween. A large number of traditional English names were introduced into the American colonies. These names were handed down from generation to generation and have become the most commonly used family names in American society. These names fall into six basic categories: (1) derived from forenames (first names such as James); (2) derived from places in England (Walsh); (3) derived from occupations (Miller); (4) derived from rank in the church, military, or police (Bishop); (5) derived from descriptive adjectives (Brown); (6) derived from topographical features (Rivers). Read the names below and try to decide into which category they fall. Place them in the correct category box on the next page. For extra credit, look in your local phone book and find out (1) how many of these names are in your area; and (2) what other names would fit into one of these categories:

Williams	Smith	Roberts	Tanner
Long	York	Rivers	Little
Short	Taylor	Hill	Miller
Weaver	Phillips	Farmer	Bishop
Davies	Strong	Martin	Dale
Kent	Priest	Armstrong	Rector
Allan/Allen	Lake	Shore	Brooks
Chaplain	Reid (Red)	Elder	Deacon
Thomas	Ford	Earl	Banks
English	Black	Woods	Squire
Sheriff	Park	Brown	Glenn
Major	Forest	Sergeant	Prentice
Charles	Masters	Young	David
Scott	Walsh (Welsh)	James	

1-19 (continued)

English American names based on topographical features:	*I found the following number of these names in the phone book:*

1.

2.

3.

4.

5.

6.

7.

8.

9.

10.

11.

12.

EXTRA CREDIT! Other English American names I found in the phone book based on topographical features:

13.

14.

15.

1-19 (continued)

English American names derived from forenames (first names):	*I Found the following number of these names in the phone book:*

1.

2.

3.

4.

5.

6.

7.

8.

9.

10.

EXTRA CREDIT! Other English American names I found in the phone book derived from forenames:

11.

12.

1-19 (continued)

English American names based on descriptive adjectives:	*I found the following number of these names in the phone book:*
1.	
2.	
3.	
4.	
5.	
6.	
7.	
8.	
9.	
10.	

EXTRA CREDIT! Other English American names I found in the phone book based on descriptive adjectives:

11.

12.

English American names related to rank (military, church, etc.)	*I found the following number of these names in the phone book:*
1.	
2.	
3.	
4.	
5.	
6.	
7.	
8.	
9.	
10.	
11.	
12.	

EXTRA CREDIT! Other English American names I found in the phone book based on rank:

13.

14.

English American names based on common occupations:	*I found the following number of these names in the phone book:*

1.
2.
3.
4.
5.
6.

EXTRA CREDIT! Other English American names I found in the phone book based on common occupations:

7.
8.
9.
10.

English American names derived from places in England:	*I found the following number of these names in the phone book:*

1.
2.
3.
4.
5.

EXTRA CREDIT! Other English American names I found in the phone book derived from places in England:

6.
7.

Name ______________________________ Date ____________

1–20
PEOPLE TO REMEMBER

In the blanks provided, write the letter of the description that matches each name on the column on the left.

______ 1. ANNE HUTCHINSON	A. first African American child born in America
______ 2. MASSASOIT	B. European American woman who founded a colony on Long Island
______ 3. JOHN SMITH	C. European American woman who was exiled by the Puritans because of her outspoken views
______ 4. MARY DYER	D. Native American male leader of the Algonquians who lived in what is now Virginia
______ 5. LORD BALTIMORE	E. European American who founded the colony of Pennsylvania
______ 6. ISABELLA	F. mother of the first African American child
______ 7. ANNE BRADSTREET	G. Native American girl who befriended the Jamestown colonists
______ 8. WILLIAM PENN	H. European American man who founded Baltimore, Maryland
______ 9. POWHATAN	I. European American male dissenter from the Puritans who founded Providence, R.I.
______10. ROGER WILLIAMS	J. European American woman who was hanged by the Puritans because of her religious beliefs
______11. POCAHONTAS	K. Native American male leader of the Wampanoags who lived in what is now Rhode Island
______12. THOMAS HOOKER	L. European American man who was the leader of Jamestown
______13. LADY DEBORAH MOODY	M. European American woman who published the first book of poetry in America
______14. WILLIAM	N. European American man who founded Hartford, Conn.
______15. SQUANTO	O. Native American man who taught the Pilgrims many survival techniques (planting corn, etc.)

Section *Two*

The 1700s

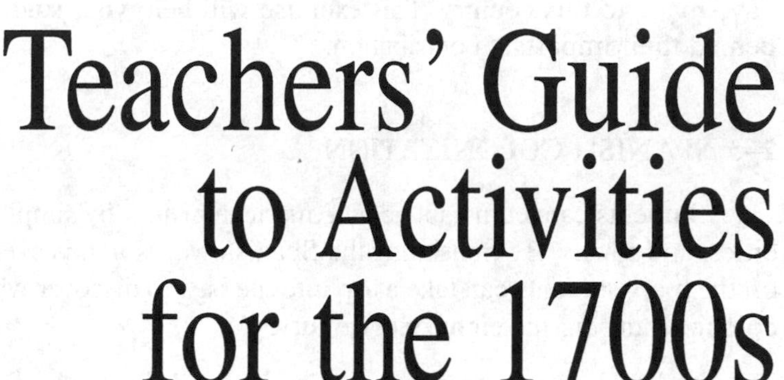

Teachers' Guide to Activities for the 1700s

2–1 DRAW!

Because English is the official language of the United States, our students often forget the impact other European cultures had on the formation of our country. This exercise will familiarize them with the extent to which the French, Spanish, and English colonized and controlled sections of North America. It will also give them an idea of the encroachment Native Americans felt upon land they had been living upon for centuries before the Europeans arrived.

2–2 HOW MUCH DO WE KNOW?

Before students launch into studying a subject area anew, it is important to review their *prior knowledge*. It is also important to see what biases and misconceptions we may bring to the subject area. This is a survey exercise to ponder what we do and do not know about the 1700s and hypothesize as to why we may have these misconceptions. ANSWERS: (1) John Hansen (2) the U.S. Constitution (3) less than 50% (4) True (5) views on women's rights (6) True (7) Sequoya (8) True (9) European Americans, African Americans, Native Americans (10) Phillis Wheatley, woman

2–3 STEREOTYPES

Many students have learned misconceptions regarding eighteenth-century Native Americans from many sources. This exercise helps them analyze their misconceptions and reform their concept of Native American culture.

2–4 THE ENVIRONMENT

An appreciation for the environment is an important contribution Native Americans have made to this country. This exercise will help your students understand the philosophy behind their important contribution.

2–5 SPANISH COLONIZATION

Students can learn a lot about American history by simply studying a U.S. map of states, cities, and towns. By translating the Spanish words in this exercise and finding their location on the map, students can take a trip into the past to discover where the Spaniards traveled and colonized during the eighteenth century.

2–6 FRENCH COLONIZATION

Students can learn a lot about American history by simply studying a U.S. map of states, cities, and towns. By translating the French words in this exercise and finding their location on the map, students can take a trip into the past to discover where the French traveled and colonized during the colonial period.

2–7 HATS AND LINGO

Most teenagers enjoy wearing or looking at hats. They also enjoy communicating by using the latest teenage vocabulary. Put these two ideas together and you have the ingredients for an unusual "hook" at the beginning of a lesson or for a homework assignment.

2–8 THREE CULTURES

Often history books emphasize the *differences* between cultures that create the great American melting pot rather than their similarities. This exercise is designed to help students see that it is valuable to study the differences *and* similarities people had.

2–9 EUROPEAN AMERICAN MEDICAL CARE

It is difficult to imagine life without antibiotics, anesthesia, or even aspirin! This exercise offers information regarding health care during the 1700s and an opportunity for students to reflect on what it would be like to be ill during that time period.

2–10 CHILDBIRTH AND MIDWIFERY

Interviewing family members or friends that are older than your students is an important way to learn history as well as a valuable skill to acquire. This exercise provides an opportunity for your students to teach as well as learn from an older woman.

2–11 POINT OF VIEW

Looking critically at research sources is an important skill for your students to acquire. This exercise looks at one event in American history—the Boston Massacre of 1770—and examines how much historians' viewpoints can differ on one event.

2–12 WHOSE SIDE ARE YOU ON?

Some students will be surprised that support for the Patriot cause was not 100 percent! By stepping into the shoes of other Americans, your students will better understand the many conflicting issues surrounding the War of Independence.

2–13 WHAT DID THEY SAY TO EACH OTHER?

Often history books emphasize the conflicts between cultural groups rather than meetings of the minds. This exercise provides an example of a positive step toward cultural understanding. It also will engage your students in creative thinking and writing.

2–14 SHOULD WOMEN BE SOLDIERS?

Your students may be shocked to learn that women actually fought in the War of Independence. By writing these diary accounts, they will imagine themselves in this unusual situation.

2–15 FOLLOW THE ARMY

Women have often been "invisible" in American history books. This exercise will help your students understand the role women played during the War of Independence and the important contribution they made.

2–16 HOME ALONE (WITH ALL THE WORK!)

Wars have often played an important part in changing ingrained societal attitudes. The War of Independence placed many women in roles they had previously not been encouraged to assume. This exercise will help your students understand one impetus for the women's movement that was to develop in the nineteenth century.

2–17 INSPIRATION

The contribution Native Americans have made to the American concept of government is often overlooked. This exercise will offer an opportunity for your students to reflect on how Native American philosophy interfaced with European American thought to help form the U.S. Constitution.

2–18 ABIGAIL ADAMS WRITES A LETTER

How would it feel to be a woman living in eighteenth-century America? This exercise explores the situation and introduces your students to a woman who spoke her mind—Abigail Adams.

2–19 TOO FAR OR NOT FAR ENOUGH?

The Constitution and the Bill of Rights were highly controversial during their time of creation. This exercise offers your students the opportunity to step into the shoes of eighteenth-century Americans to see how they would view this document.

2–20 THE IROQUOIS CONSTITUTION

This exercise offers a glimpse into the eloquence of Native American language and depth of Iroquoian thought.

2–21 WHICH SIDE OF THE ROAD?

History is a series of decisions. This dramatic exercise will place your students ino the situation of people who were forced to make history during the eighteenth century—the militia who were sent to put down Shays' Rebellion.

2–22 THE CAJUNS

By studying this unique cultural group, your students will learn the power that traditions and language from three centuries ago still have on our society today.

2–23 BENJAMIN BANNEKER

This exercise will acquaint your students with a leading thinker of eighteenth-century America—Benjamin Banneker—as they "translate" one of his writings into present-day English and analyze his analogy.

2–24 EVERYDAY LIFE

This exercise offers the opportunity for your students to compare and contrast their everyday activities with that of an eighteenth-century woman.

2–25 WHAT IF?

It is often difficult for our students to understand how a single invention can influence history. This exercise encourages them to use their creativity to imagine how history could have taken a completely different turn!

2–26 SAGOYEWATHA

Sagoyewatha was one of the great Native American orators. This exercise combines the use of social studies and English skills.

2–27 TRAGEDY

Creating hypotheses and deciding if research sources support or refute these hypotheses is an important skill for your students to develop. This exercise, which also provides information regarding one of the great tragedies of American history—the destruction of Native American Indian tribes—will develop the skill and sensitize your students to the plight of Native Americans living during the eighteenth century.

2–28 THE DU SABLES

The eighteenth century was one of great intermingling of three cultures in America—African, Native American, and European. This exercise helps your students reflect on their cultural heritage and introduces them to a truly *multicultural* couple—the Du Sables.

2–29 BENJAMIN FRANKLIN'S PARODY

This exercise introduces your students to one of the eighteenth century's greatest European American thinkers! It will also encourage them to use their creative writing skills!

2–30 PEOPLE TO REMEMBER

Women, men, Native Americans, European Americans, African Americans are all on this list! Divide your class into small groups and have them use the school library resources (encyclopedias and other references) to see which group can complete the list first! ANSWERS: (1) B (2) G (3) E (4) H (5) J (6) D (7) A (8) K (9) I (10) C (11) L (12) F

Name ______________________ *Date* __________

2–1

DRAW!

The map below shows what parts of the present-day continent U.S.A. that France, England, and Spain colonized and controlled at the beginning of the 1700s. Using a larger piece of paper (legal size or larger construction paper), a pencil and your eyes, redraw this map. Do not trace or use an overhead projector to enlarge the image! You can do it! Now, using four differently colored pencils or markers, highlight each colonized area. Your finished map will give you an idea of the impact European colonization had on the Native Americans who had been living there for thousands of years.

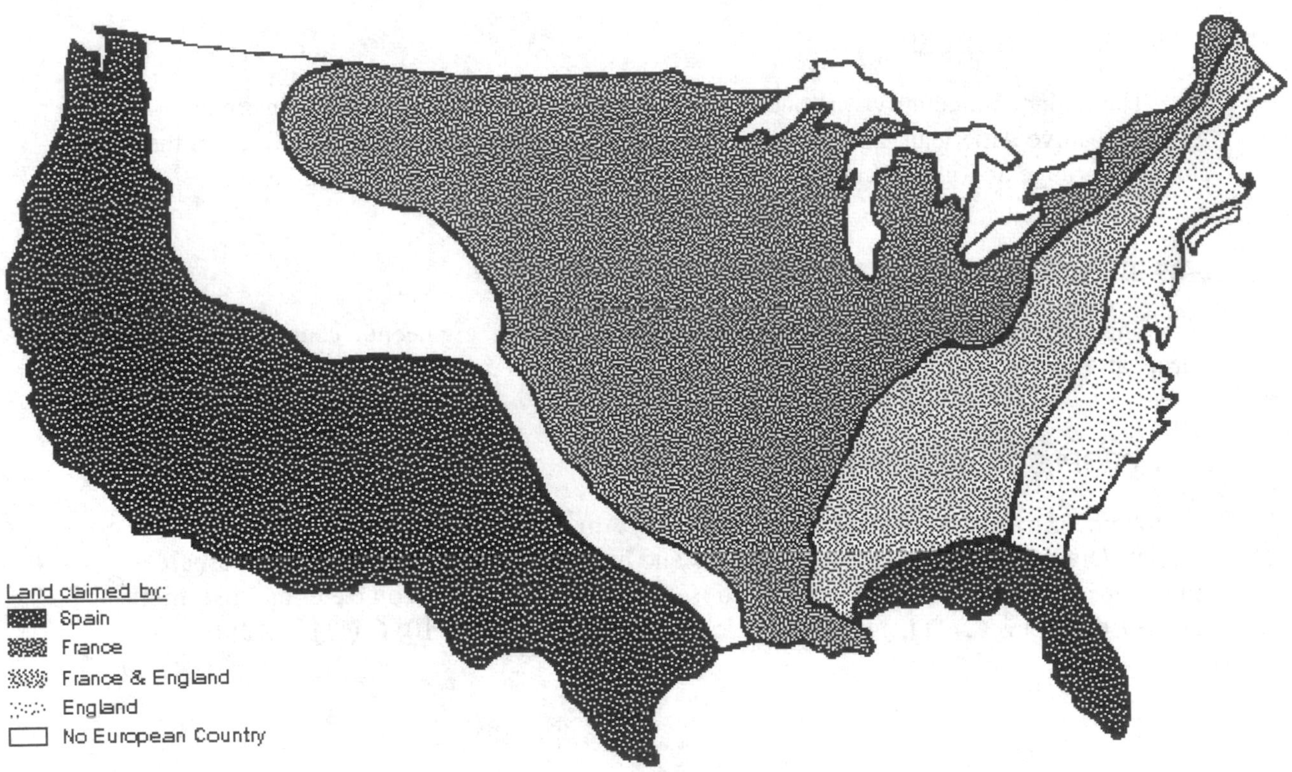

Name ______________________________ *Date* ____________

2–2

HOW MUCH DO WE KNOW?

How much do we Americans know about the early history of our country? There are many myths and misconceptions that people have accepted as truths. Put your name in the first box of this survey and answer the questions to the best of your knowledge. Then, review the correct answers with your teacher. Finally, choose five people (neighbors, relatives, friends, other teachers, anyone!) and ask them the questions, recording their answers on the chart.

NAMES							
1. The first president of the American Confederation was: a. George Washington b. John Hansen c. Benjamin Franklin							# correct _____ # incorrect ____
2. The constitution of the Iroquois Confederation was an inspiration for: a. the slaughter of Native Americans b. the U.S. Constitution c. the King of England							# correct _____ # incorrect ____
3. The percentage of colonists who supported the Patriots during the War of Independence is estimated to have been: a. approximately 10% b. less than 50% c. more than 75%							# correct _____ # incorrect ____

2-2 (continued)

NAMES							
4. In 1798 the U.S. Congress passed the Sedition Act, which made it a crime to criticize the government: a. True b. False							# correct _____ # incorrect ____
5. Abigail Adams, the wife of the second U.S. president, was known for her: a. views on women's rights b. White House decorations c. possession of slaves							# correct _____ # incorrect ____
6. Women served as soldiers in the Continental Army: a. True b. False							# correct _____ # incorrect ____
7. The Cherokee language was written down in a syllabary by: a. Christian missionaries b. Daniel Boone c. Sequoya							# correct _____ # incorrect ____
8. One of the first drafts of the U.S. Constitution outlawed slavery: a. True b. False							# correct _____ # incorrect ____

NAMES							
9. The following groups served in the Continental Army: a. only European Americans b. European Americans and African Americans c. European Americans, African Americans, and Native Americans							# correct ____ # incorrect ____
10. The first African American poet to publish in America was: a. Phillis Wheatley, a woman b. Benjamin Banneker, a man							# correct ____ # incorrect ____

Use your math skills to answer the questions below:

1. How many responses did you receive? (Add up the total number of people who took the quiz and multiply by 10.)

   ____

2. How many responses were correct? What percentage of the total responses was this number?

   ____

3. How many responses were incorrect? What percentage of the total responses was this number?

   ____

Why do you think people do not know all the answers to these questions? Write two hypotheses below: Many people have myths and misconceptions about the early history of our country because:

Hypothesis 1 ______________________________

____

Hypothesis 2 ______________________________

____

Name ______________________________ Date ______________

2–3
STEREOTYPES

Have you watched any old Western movies on TV? How are the Native Americans in these movies usually portrayed? Are they portrayed as warlike or peaceful? Are they portrayed as intelligent or ignorant? Write your answer in the space provided below.

____

____

____

____

____

____

____

____

____

Read the following excerpt from the Constitution of the Iroquois Confederation (a union of five Native American tribes of the Northeastern woodlands).

"I am Dekanawidah (considered the founding father of the Iroquois Confederation) and with the Five Nations confederate lords (representatives) I plant the tree of the Great Peace. . . . I name the tree the Tree of the Great Long Leaves. Under the shade of this Tree of the Great Peace we spread the soft white feather down of the globe thistle as seats for you, Atotarho, and your cousin lords. There shall you sit and watch the council fire of the confederacy of the Five Nations. Roots have spread out from the Tree, and the name of these roots is the Great White Roots of Peace. If any man of any nation shall show a desire to obey the laws of the Great Peace, they shall trace the roots to their source, and they shall be welcomed to take shelter beneath the Tree of the Long Leaves. The smoke of the confederate council shall pierce the sky so that all nations may discover the central council fire of the Great Peace. I, Dekanawidah, and the confederate lords now uproot the tallest pine tree and into the cavity thereby made we cast all weapons of war. Into the depth of the earth, down into the deep underearth currents of water flowing into unknown regions, we cast all weapons of war. We bury them from sight forever and plant again the Tree."[1]

What information does this excerpt give you about these Native Americans? How does this differ from the stereotype usually portrayed in American Western movies? Write your answer below.

(Continue on the back.)

Name ______________________ Date ______________

2–4
THE ENVIRONMENT

How have the natural environment of North America and the attitude of Americans toward their environment changed over the past 300 years? Read the excerpt below from the constitution of the Iroquois Confederation. It expresses these Native Americans' attitude toward the natural environment in the eighteenth century.

"The Onondaga Lords (Iroquois representatives) shall open council by expressing their gratitude to their cousin lords, and greeting them, and they shall make an address and offer thanks to the earth where men dwell, to the streams of water, the pools, the springs, the lakes, to the maize and the fruits, to the medicinal herbs and the trees, to the forest trees for their usefulness, to the animals that serve as food and who offer their pelts as clothing, to the great winds and the lesser winds, to the Thunderers, and the Sun, the mighty warrior, to the moon, to the messengers of the Great Spirit who dwells in the skies above, who gives all things useful to men, who is the source and the ruler of health and life. Then shall the Onondaga Lords declare the council open."(1)

Now, visit your school or local library and find a magazine article, newspaper article, or book about an environmental problem in your area. Compare the content of your reading to what you have read above. How has the American environment changed in the past 300 years? What has changed? What can we learn about caring for the environment by reading the Iroquois Constitution? Write an essay incorporating these questions on a separate piece of paper. Be sure to write an introduction, body, and conclusion!

____

____

____

____

____

____

____

(Continue on the back.)

Name ______________________ Date ____________

2–5

SPANISH COLONIZATION

Have you ever looked at a map and wondered where states, towns, and cities got their names? If you noticed that some names sound like English words and others sound as if they come from another language, you are right! Many of our states, towns, and cities were named by other European colonizers (other than Englishmen and -women) or Native Americans. You can learn a lot about American history by using maps and foreign language dictionaries. In this exercise you will discover where the Spanish originally colonized America. You will need a Spanish-English dictionary and an atlas of the United States. You can find these in your school or local library. Look at the names of towns, cities, and states listed below and find out what they mean in English by looking them up in your dictionary. Then look at the map with the dots on the next page and, using your atlas, figure out which dot each name represents. This will give you a good idea of the area in America that the Spanish originally colonized. (If you find additional Spanish names while looking for these, add them to your list and to the map!)

Name	*It means the following in English*
Los Angeles, California	
Las Cruces, New Mexico	
Amarillo, Texas	
La Mesa, Texas	
Laredo, Texas	
Port La Vaca, Texas	
Rio Grande City, Texas	
Mexia, Texas	
Las Vegas, Nevada	
Casa Grande, Arizona	
Sierra Vista, Arizona	
Cortez, Colorado	
Pueblo, Colorado	
Salida, Colorado	
Las Animas, Colorado	

2-5 (continued)

La Junta, Colorado

Montrose, Colorado

El Mirage, Arizona

Santa Fe, New Mexico

Sacramento, California

Fresno, California

Mission Viejo, California

Salinas, California

Corpus Christi, Texas

Yuma, Arizona

El Paso, Texas

Boca Raton, Florida

I found the following additional names and they mean the following:

2-5 *(continued)*

SPANISH COLONIZATION

Name ______________________________ *Date* ______________

2–6

FRENCH COLONIZATION

Have you ever looked at a map and wondered where states, towns, and cities got their names? If you noticed that some names sound like English words and others sound as if they come from another language, you are right! Many of our states, towns, and cities were named by other European colonizers (other than Englishmen and -women) or Native Americans. You can learn a lot about American history by using maps and foreign language dictionaries. In this exercise you will discover where the French originally colonized America. You will need a French-English dictionary and an atlas of the United States. You can find these in your school or local library. Look at the names of towns, cities, and states (which come from French words) listed below and find out what they mean in English by looking them up in your dictionary. Then look at the map with the dots on the next page and, using your atlas, figure out which dot each name represents. This will give you a good idea of the area in America that the French originally colonized. (If you find additional names that are derived from French, add them to your list and to your map!)

Name	*It Means the Following in English*
Des Moines, Iowa	
Fond du Lac, Wisconsin	
La Crosse, Wisconsin	
Conneaut, Ohio	
Portage, Michigan	
Presque Isle, Pennsylvania	
Cloquet, Minnesota	
Carthage, Illinois	
Eau Claire, Wisconsin	
Minot, North Dakota	
Marinette, Wisconsin	
Bassett, Nebraska	
Superior, Nebraska	
Beaumont, Texas	
Cape Girardeau, Missouri	

Chaumont, New York

Prairie du Chien, Wisconsin

Champaign, Illinois

Des Plaines, Illinois

Bourbonnais, Illinois

Terre Haute, Indiana

Belleville, Illinois

La Porte, Indiana

Louisville, Kentucky

Joliet, Illinois

Bottineau, North Dakota

La Moure, North Dakota

Marquette, Wisconsin

Belle Fourche, South Dakota

Traverse City, Michigan

Baton Rouge, Louisiana

Montpelier, Vermont

I found these additional names and they mean the following:

FRENCH COLONIZATION

2-6 (continued)

Name ______________________________ Date ______________

2–7
HATS AND LINGO

What kind of hats are in fashion today? Make a small collage below of pictures of hats. You can cut them out from magazines, newspapers, or photographs you have of yourself wearing your favorite hat.

Now, think of some of your favorite lingo or slang (no profanity, of course!) used today by teenagers. Write these words below:

1.   3.

2.   4.

Between 1600 and 1800 beaver skin hats were very fashionable in Europe. In fact, they were so fashionable that obtaining beaver pelts was one of the main reasons some Europeans came to America. You could say that beaver skin hats caused two cultures—Native Americans and Europeans—to come face to face. The two cultures exchanged many things; Europeans wanted beaver pelts to sell in Europe and Native Americans wanted to have European manufactured items such as iron axes, guns, cloth, shirts, copper kettles, bells, glass beads, bottles, jugs, and liquor.

Something else they exchanged was vocabulary—WORDS! We use many Native American words in our everyday English language today. Listed below are 16 words common in the English language that originally came from the Algonquian language spoken by many Northeastern Woodland Native Americans. Read them and make certain you know what they all mean. If you do not, look them up in a dictionary. Then create a short story using all 16 words. Write it on the back of this page. After you have written it, underline all the Algonquian words.

toboggan
skunk
husky (type of dog)
caribou
moccasin
pecan
hominy
Manhattan
moose
raccoon
succotash
squash
hickory
persimmon
Illinois
opossum

Name ______________________________ Date ______________

2–8
THREE CULTURES

During the 1700s, people from three continents came face to face in North America—Native Americans, European Americans, and African Americans. These people had many differences. They also had many similarities. Read the passages below that describe the farming methods each group brought to this meeting of cultures. As you read these passages, think about their similarities and differences.

THE SENECAS (who lived near Lake Ontario): "The Seneca women worked together in the fields under the direction of a field matron, generally a respected older woman whom they all elected in the spring and agreed to obey. They started work in one woman's field, labored there until the necessary tasks were completed and then went on to another woman's field. It was the field matron's job to see that all the women work together so that there would be no complaints that some of the women had to work harder than others. She also supervised the rest periods when the women sang, played games and told stories. Harvesting too was a communal effort. Each mutual-aid society divided into three groups; the first group husked the corn and threw the ears into baskets, others carried the corn to storage places, and the rest of the women cooked a feast for the field workers."[(1)]

EUROPEAN PEASANTS (of the early 1700s): "The greatest accomplishment of medieval agriculture was the open-field system of village agriculture developed by the European peasants. That system divided the land to be cultivated by the peasants of a given village into several large fields, which were in turn cut up into long narrow strips. The fields were open and the strips were not enclosed into small plots by fences or hedges. An individual peasant family—if it were fortunate—held a number of strips scattered throughout the various large fields. The peasants farmed each large field as a community, with each family following the same pattern of plowing, sowing, and harvesting in accordance with tradition and the village leaders."[(2)]

WESTERN AFRICANS (which comprised the majority of Africans who were enslaved and brought to America): "Though the men are expected to do much of the clearing for new fields, agricultural work is primarily the task of women. They work together to harvest the grain, singing as they toil and usually carrying a small child on their back. The grain is cut and then pounded in the ground with a large mallet. Then it is sifted to extract the hulls from the seed. Again the grain is pounded, this time in a large hollowed out container. The women work well together; all appear to know their particular responsibility to harvest the grain collectively."[(3)]

Comparing these three passages, create a chart on the next page of similarities and differences between the farming methods practiced by the three cultures.

DIFFERENCES AND SIMILARITIES OF SENECA, WEST AFRICAN, AND EUROPEAN FARMING METHODS

	SENECAS:	
WEST AFRICANS:	SIMILARITIES TO ALL THREE:	EUROPEANS:

America in the 1700s was, for the most part, a rural, agricultural society. Most of the farming was not done communally, for America had quickly became a country of individualized farms. Why did this occur? Did it have to do with technology? available land? international commerce? Write your hypotheses below.

America became a country of individualized farms because:

Hypothesis 1 ____

____

Hypothesis 2 ____

____

Name ______________________________ Date ____________

2–9

EUROPEAN AMERICAN MEDICAL CARE

In the space provided below, list the various illness (flu, headaches, etc.) and other health problems (e.g., broken bones) you have experienced in your lifetime.

____

____

____

____

Most of the medical treatments that European Americans used during the eighteenth century were transferred from Europe. Below are some of the common medical beliefs and methods used widely at that time on both sides of the Atlantic Ocean.

1. "Bloodletting" or "bleeding" was considered a medical cure-all. "Bad blood" was removed by physicians to remove the cause of the illness and recover the "balance of humors." One Philadelphia doctor wrote in 1799 that bleeding was appropriate treatment for "asthma, sciatic pains, coughs, head-aches, rheumatism, apoplexy, epilepsy, and the bloody fluxes (diarrhea)."(1)
2. Most people believed that disease was caused by bad odors. Physicians often carried canes that had heads containing smelling salts; they would use these salts to "protect" themselves from illness when visiting hospitals.
3. Operations were performed without anesthesia, which was considered dangerous. Amputations were common; a surgeon believed that a smooth surface would heal better because it could be cauterized with fire. Therefore, if a person broke an arm or a leg and the bone stuck out, an amputation was often performed.
4. Surgery was performed in the midst of filth and dirt because there was no knowledge of bacteria and the nature of infection. In fact, surgeons encouraged wounds to fester believing that pus would beneficially remove the base portions of the body.
5. There was no isolation of patients in hospitals. Beds were often shared by patients. Operations were performed in the patient's bed. Fresh air was considered harmful.
6. Regular purging of the bowels by strong laxatives and induced vomiting was considered essential to good health and the treatment of illness.

2-9 (continued)

DIRECTIONS: Imagine you lived in the eighteenth century. Take one of the illnesses or health problems you have had in your life and write a one page short story describing the experience of living through the treatment of this problem. Begin your story in the space provided below and continue it on the back.

Name ______________________________ Date ____________

2–10

CHILDBIRTH AND MIDWIFERY

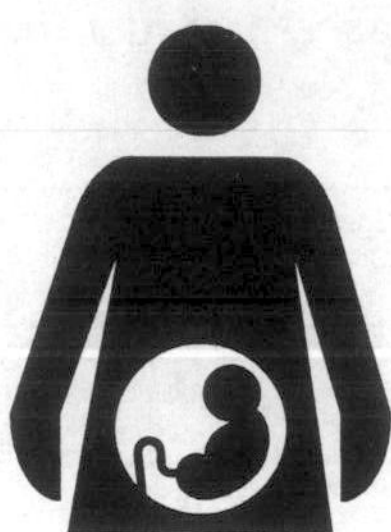

How has childbirth changed over the last three centuries? To answer this question, find a woman (your mother, aunt, neighbor, grandmother, or friend) who has given birth. Read the following information to her regarding New England European American women who gave birth during the 1700s.

1. Childbirth occurred in the home, usually in the bed the woman slept in every night. Childbirth linen was usually inherited from the woman's mother and was embellished with embroidery and lace.
2. Midwives assisted the mother in giving birth to her child. One midwife professed to having assisted in over 700 births.
3. Usually many other women were present as well. Sarah Smith of Falmouth Neck, Maine, had all the married women of her settlement present at the birth of her second son in June of 1731.
4. Men were rarely present at a birth. Only very occasionally would a pastor or physician be called in to render services.
5. During the first stage of labor there was a partylike atmosphere. The mother-to-be was expected to provide refreshments for her attendants. These refreshments were called "groaning beer" and "groaning cakes," which suggest that some of this food was eaten by the woman in labor.
6. Women in labor were encouraged to eat light, nourishing foods such as broth, poached eggs, or toasted bread in wine. They were also encouraged to walk around.
7. Herbs were gathered from the garden and field to relieve the discomfort of the woman in labor. Nicholas Gilman collected the herb "betony" in May of 1740 to prepare for his wife's labor. Mary Gilman crushed the herb, clarified the herb juice, and then made it into a syrup with double its weight in sugar to use at her birth.
8. Other natural ingredients such as newly laid eggs and butter were used in different aspects of the birthing process.

DIRECTIONS: In the space below, record the reactions of the woman to whom you read this information. Was she surprised at some of these facts? Does she have any questions? Did her experience in childbirth differ from that of the New England European American women of the 1700s? How did it differ?

____

____

____

(Continue on the back.)

Name ______________________________ Date ______________

2–11

POINT OF VIEW

Have you ever noticed how a historical figure will be considered a hero by some historians and a villain by others? Or how an action will be considered constructive by some historians and destructive by others? This reflects different points of view. One important American historical event that is seen from many points of view took place on March 5, 1770. This was the first conflict between the American colonists and the British army, and it eventually led to the American War of Independence. Crispus Attucks, a colonist of African and European descent, was part of the group of people engaged in this conflict. Let's see some different historians' points of view toward Attucks, these people, and this historical event:

Point of View 1: "That started things. Soon a noisy, jeering group of mischief-makers gathered in front of the Boston Custom House. They began pushing and shoving and throwing stones and pieces of ice at the British sentry. . . . There is some confusion about what happened next. The mob is said to have taunted the redcoats, yelling 'Fire! Fire!' Captain Preston is said to have yelled, 'Hold your fire!' Then a British soldier was hit with a big stick. He claimed he heard the word 'fire' so he fired his gun into the crowd. The street gang moved forward; the redcoats panicked and fired at unarmed people. Five Americans died; seven were wounded. None of them was a hero. The victims were troublemakers who got worse than they deserved. The soldiers were professionals (the British army was supposed to be the best in the world) who should not have panicked. The whole thing should not have happened."(1)

Point of View 2: "On March 5, 1770, grievances of ropemakers against British soldiers taking their jobs led to a fight. A crowd gathered in front of the customhouse and began provoking the soldiers, who fired and killed first Crispus Attucks, a mulatto worker, then others. This became known as the Boston Massacre."[(2)]

Point of View 3: "On March 5, 1770, the lawless behavior of a colonial mob erupted into tragic violence. A crowd of boys and men confronted some British soldiers, jeering and throwing snowballs at them. The soldiers panicked and opened fire on the crowd. Five colonists were killed and six were wounded."[(3)]

Point of View 4: "His name was Crispus Attucks and he was a Massachusetts native who had escaped from slavery and sailed the seas. Tall, brawny, with a look that was 'enough to terrify any person'. . . . He was a proper rebel, a drifter, a man who loved freedom and knew what it was worth. He was about 47 on this memorable night, and he had that undefinable quality called presence. When he spoke, men listened. When he commanded, men acted. . . . It was Attucks, according to eyewitnesses, who shaped and dominated the action on the night of the event known to history as the Boston Massacre. And when the people faltered, it was Attucks, according to almost all contemporary reports, who rallied them and urged them to stand their ground."[(4)]

Now that you have read the four points of view, go back and reread them, underlining the nouns, adjectives, verbs, and adverbs that describe Crispus Attucks, the group of people who were part of the conflict with the British soldiers, and their actions. Make a list of these words you have underlined, placing them under the POSITIVE column or the NEGATIVE column below:

POSITIVE WORDS	*NEGATIVE WORDS*
______________________	______________________
______________________	______________________
______________________	______________________

Hypothesize in the space provided below as to why these two groups of words differ so greatly. How could historians disagree so strongly? What important lessons can we learn from doing this exercise about point of view?

Historians have different points of view regarding the Boston Massacre because:

HYPOTHESIS 1 ____

____

HYPOTHESIS 2 ____

____

Lessons we can learn from this exercise about point of view are:

____

____

(Complete on the back.)

Name ______________________ Date ____________

2–12
WHOSE SIDE ARE YOU ON?

BRITAIN

Most historians agree that, at best, 50 percent of people living in colonial America supported the Patriots (colonists who wanted independence from England) during the American War of Independence; some historians believe that a more accurate breakdown was the following: 33 percent supported the Patriots, 33 percent supported the Tories (colonists who did *not* want independence from England), and 33 percent were neutral. This is sometimes hard for us to believe today! There were many issues for Americans to consider when contemplating which side to support or whether to remain neutral. Much depended upon your status in society and this status depended much on race, gender, and class. Below are listed many different kinds of Americans living in 1776. Imagine you are each of these people and consider the issues facing you at that time. Then in the space provided, write whether, if you had been this American, you would have been a Patriot, a Tory, or neutral, and why.

1. *ENSLAVED AFRICAN AMERICAN MAN*
   a. In 1776, the British announced that any enslaved African American man would be granted freedom if he fought for the Tories.
   b. Though many African Americans fought on the side of the Patriots in the beginning battles of the War of Independence, the Continental Congress forbade their enlistment from July 1776 to January 1777; as the war continued, African Americans were allowed to serve in the Continental Army.

If I had been an enslaved African American man during the American War of Independence, I would have (circle one) supported the Patriots/supported the Tories/remained neutral because

____

____

____.

2. *EUROPEAN AMERICAN WOMAN*
   a. Women were not allowed to vote or participate in politics.
   b. Upon marriage, all property owned by a woman would become the possession of her husband.
   c. Women were sometimes taught to read but rarely taught to write.

2-12 (continued)

If I had been a European American woman during the American War of Independence, I would have (circle one) supported the Patriots/supported the Tories/remained neutral because

____

____

____.

3. *INDENTURED EUROPEAN AMERICAN MALE SERVANT*
   a. Indentured servants typically had to serve their masters four to seven years before they gained their independence.
   b. Indentured servants were not allowed to vote.
   c. Fifty percent of the Europeans who came to America during the colonial period were indentured servants.
   d. A wealthy colonist who was being drafted into the Continental Army could pay another man (very often an indentured servant) to do his term of service.

If I had been an indentured European American male servant during the American War of Independence, I would have (circle one) supported the Patriots/supported the Tories/remained neutral because

____

____

____.

4. *NATIVE AMERICAN MAN*
   a. The King of England (King George III) had proclaimed in 1763 that colonists were not to settle land west of the Appalachian mountains; this area was reserved for the Native Americans.
   b. The Native Americans and European American colonists had often clashed between the years of 1619 and 1776; these were often bloody confrontations with much loss of life on both sides.
   c. Many Native Americans had fought with the French, against the English during the French and Indian War of 1754–1763.

If I had been a Native American male during the American War of Independence, I would have (circle one) supported the Patriots/supported the Tories/remained neutral because

____

____

____.

5. *WEALTHY EUROPEAN AMERICAN MALE PLANTATION OWNER*
   a. Growers of sugar, tobacco, and indigo (all which was grown in the southern colonies) were required to sell their products to England although they could often get higher prices from Continental European buyers.

b. Many wealthy Southerners were related to the upper class of England, often distantly related to English royalty.

c. The new taxes required by the 1767 Townshend Acts placed new levies on many English imports that wealthy colonists desired such as paper, glass, paint, and tea.

If I had been a wealthy European American male plantation owner, I would have (circle one) supported the Patriots/supported the Tories/remained neutral because

____

____

____.

6. *WEALTHY EUROPEAN AMERICAN MALE MERCHANT*

a. English mercantilism laws prohibited American colonists from manufacturing and exporting goods such as hats, iron, and wool cloth.

b. Navigation Acts passed by the English Parliament prohibited merchants from shipping their goods on any ships other than English or colonial ships.

c. The English parliament increased taxes on many goods imported to the colonies and called for strict enforcement.

If I had been a wealthy European American male merchant during the American War of Independence, I would have (circle one) supported the Patriots/supported the Tories/remained neutral because

____

____

____

____.

7. *EUROPEAN AMERICAN FEMALE SHOP OWNER AND INNKEEPER*

a. Unmarried women were allowed by the British government and colonial law to run small businesses on a very limited basis.

b. Colonists were required to provide food and housing for British soldiers upon demand.

c. The colonial economy depended greatly on smooth trade relations with England.

If I had been a European American female shopowner and innkeeper during the American War of Independence, I would have (circle one) supported the Patriots/supported the Tories/remained neutral because

____

____

____.

Name ______________________ Date ____________

2–13
WHAT DID THEY SAY TO EACH OTHER?

2-13 (continued)

Do you know who Phillis Wheatley and George Washington were? Wheatley was the first African American woman to publish poetry in America. George Washington was the European American head of the Continental Army during the War of Independence and the first president of the United States. Did you know that Washington and Wheatley had a half-hour conference in 1776? Before their meeting, African Americans were not allowed to serve in the Continental Army; shortly after their meeting, Washington issued an order to allow African Americans into the Continental Army. No one knows exactly what was said at this meeting. If you were to imagine the content of their conversation, what do you think it would be?

Write a short one-act play based on what *you* think transpired between Washington and Wheatley at this meeting. Here are a few facts about both Wheatley and Washington that you can use to develop your characters.

PHILLIS WHEATLEY'S LIFE

1. Wheatley was born in Africa and brought with her mother to America in 1761. She remembered that on board the ship her mother poured out water each morning "before the sun at its rising."
2. Wheatley was deposited by the slave ship on a Boston slave block where John Wheatley, a rich merchant and tailor, found her shivering and stark naked except for a dirty piece of carpet around her loins.
3. John's wife, Susannah Wheatley, taught Wheatley how to read and write, and within 16 months she was fluent in English.
4. Within six years of arriving in America, Wheatley was writing poetry: her first poem was written at age 14 and was a eulogy of Harvard University.
5. In 1773, Wheatley visited England and was hailed as a prodigy.
6. Wheatley was short and slim, and she had great glimmering eyes.
7. When Susannah Wheatley died, Phillis subsequently had an unhappy marriage with a grocer named John Peters.
8. Wheatley died penniless in December of 1784.
9. The following is an excerpt from one of her most famous poems:

   I, young in life, by seeming cruel fate
   Was snatch'd from Afric's fancy'd happy seat:
   What pangs excruciating must molest
   What sorrows labour in my parent's breast?
   Steel'd was that soul and by no misery mov'd
   That from a father seiz'd his babe belov'd
   Such, such my case. And then can I but pray
   Others may never feel tyrannic sway?

GEORGE WASHINGTON'S LIFE

1. Washington was born in Westmoreland County, Virginia, on February 11, 1732. His father, Augustine Washington, was a middle-income tobacco farmer. His mother was Mary Ball; she had nine children, George being the firstborn.
2. Washington's father died when he was 11 years old and left his son a 10,000 acre farm and 10 enslaved African Americans.
3. Washington received only brief and local schooling. Upon reaching adulthood he learned the trade of surveying, becoming an official surveyor of Culpeper County, Virginia, in 1749.
4. Washington served the English army as a colonel during the French and Indian War.

5. Washington ran and won a seat in the Virginia House of Burgesses in 1758.
6. Washington married one of the wealthiest women in Virginia, Martha Curtis, in 1759. Because her property immediately passed, in accordance with law, into Washington's hands, he became one of the richest men in Virginia. They had no children.
7. Washington was chosen to lead the Continental Army during the American War of Independence.
8. Washington owned enslaved African Americans throughout his lifetime.
9. In 1786 he wrote "There is not a man living who wishes more sincerely than I do to see a plan adopted for the gradual abolition of it [slavery]." To another correspondent he revealed his determination never "to possess another slave."
10. Washington did not fight to have slavery abolished in the U.S. Constitution.
11. Before Washington died in 1799, he freed all of his enslaved African Americans.

Write your "faction" play below:

Wheatley: ______________________________

____

____

Washington: ______________________________

____

____

Wheatley: ______________________________

____

____

Washington: ______________________________

____

____

Wheatley: ______________________________

____

____

(Continue on the back.)

Name ____________________ Date ____________

2–14
SHOULD WOMEN BE SOLDIERS?

If the U.S. were to enter a war tomorrow, do you believe men and women should be drafted to fight, only men should be drafted to fight, or no one should be drafted to fight? Write your opinion in the space provided below.

I think men and women/only men/no one (circle one) should be drafted to fight because

____

____

____

____.

During the American War of Independence, only men were officially allowed to serve in the army. However, some women felt so strongly about the Patriots' cause that they disguised themselves as men and fought along with the male troops. Using the information listed below, write a short "faction" (a combination of fact and fiction) diary excerpt to describe the experience of one of these women named Deborah Sampson.

1. Soldiers seldom bathed and usually slept in their clothes.
2. Sampson served in the army for three years.
3. Food rations were meager; one army surgeon described it in his diary as the following: "Here comes a bowl of beef soup—full of burnt leaves and dirt—sickish enough to make a Hector spew."
4. Sampson was injured two times but took care of herself to avoid being discovered as a woman.
5. "Yankee Doodle" was one of the soldiers' favorite songs.
6. Sampson was finally discovered by an army doctor who cared for her when she fell ill with a fever.
7. Doctors did not understand the need for sterilization because the "germ theory" was not discovered until the mid-nineteenth century; if one of your limbs was injured, surgeons tended to amputate because it was believed that "smooth surfaces" would heal better. Amputations and other operations were done with no anesthesia other than smelling salts or liquor.
8. Soldiers lived outdoors during all seasons of the year, including winter, and had to survive brutally cold conditions.
9. Soldiers were paid the following salaries:

Privates – $ 6.66 per month
Sergeants – $ 8 per month
Captains – $20 per month
Colonels – $75 per month

10. Soldiers had to pay for their own guns and uniforms.
11. The average length of service was three months.
12. The War of Independence: April 19, 1775, to October 17, 1781.

DIRECTIONS: Write at least three entries in your diary. You can either imagine you are Deborah Sampson or you can imagine you are a soldier who knows her. Write your three entries as follows:

Dear Diary, Date:

Dear Diary, Date:

Dear Diary, Date:

(Continue on the back.)

Name ______________________________ Date ______________

2–15
FOLLOW THE ARMY

American women contributed in many ways during the War of Independence. Some chose to stay home during the war; they organized boycotts of British goods, collected money for the Patriot cause, and took care of their husbands' farms and businesses. Other women decided *not* to stay home during the war; a few women actually disguised themselves as men (Deborah Sampson was one!) and fought along with the men. Other women decided to follow the army. In the space provided below, hypothesize as to why a woman would choose to follow the army.

Evidence that* supports *this hypothesis:	***Some women chose to follow the army during the War of Independence because:***	***Evidence that* refutes *this hypothesis:***
	HYPOTHESIS 1 ________ ____________ ____________	
	HYPOTHESIS 2 ________ ____________ ____________	
	HYPOTHESIS 3 ________ ____________ ____________	

2-15 (continued)

It is said that George Washington felt very conflicted about having a large group of women follow the army. In the space provided below, hypothesize as to why George Washington (1) wanted or needed the women to follow his army; (2) did *not* want or need women to follow his army.

Evidence that **supports** *this hypothesis:*	*Washington* **wanted** *women to follow the army because:*	*Evidence that* **refutes** *this hypothesis:*
	HYPOTHESIS 1 ____________ ____________ ____________ HYPOTHESIS 2 ____________ ____________ ____________	

Evidence that **supports** *this hypothesis:*	*Washington* **did not** *want women to follow the army because:*	*Evidence that* **refutes** *this hypothesis:*
	HYPOTHESIS 1 ____________ ____________ ____________ HYPOTHESIS 2 ____________ ____________ ____________	

The following are facts about the women who followed the Continental Army. These facts will help you determine if your hypotheses are correct or incorrect. Read each fact and decide if it *supports* or *refutes* each hypothesis. Write the number (1, 2, 3) under the SUPPORT or REFUTE columns next to your hypothesis. You can do additional research in your local or school library to explore your hypotheses.

FACT 1: The American Revolution was the last of the group of wars categorized as the "early modern wars" (wars that occurred between the 1500s and 1700s). In all of these wars, thousands of women, with their children, had followed the armies—functioning as nurses, laundresses, and cooks.

FACT 2: The British army, upon which Washington's army modeled itself to a large extent, had always had its own allocation of women. These women were usually the soldiers' wives and occasionally their mothers.

FACT 3: Some single women attached themselves to the troops and followed the armies because they had fallen in love and become impregnated by soldiers whom they had met while the army was stationed near their homes.

FACT 4: Some of the wives of wealthy soldiers came for a taste of adventure. Generals' wives, such as Martha Washington and Catherine Greene, spent the winters at Valley Forge and Morristown with their husbands.

FACT 5: Most of the approximately 200,000 women who followed the army were impoverished. They were, for the most part, wives and children of the soldiers, and they could not support themselves while their husbands and fathers were drawn into the service.

FACT 6: The administration of the Continental Army was notoriously bad. The office of the quartermaster (administrator responsible for supplying the food, clothing, and equipment) was run poorly. Hospital and nursing services were marginal at best.

FACT 7: The women who followed the army processed and cooked most of the food for the soldiers. They also did most of the necessary cleaning. Molly Pitcher, one of the most famous women who followed Washington's army, and many other American women made themselves useful hauling water for teams that fired cannons, and bringing food to men under fire.

FACT 8: "Even the most respectable women represented something of a moral challenge; by embodying an alternate loyalty to family or lover, they could discourage reenlistment or even encourage desertion in order to respond to private emotional claims. They were a steady reminder to men of a world other than the controlled one of the camp; desertion was high throughout the war and no general needed anyone who might encourage it further."(1)

FACT 9: Washington was constantly issuing contradictory orders regarding the women who followed his army. Sometimes he ordered the women to get into the wagons and ride so as not to slow down the troops. At other times he ordered them to walk so as not to take up valuable space in the wagons.

FACT 10: Women who followed the army had to be fed. Washington had to supply these women with full rations and their children with half-rations—in the midst of inadequate supplies of food even to feed the soldiers.

FACT 11: Women who followed the army were not orderly, disciplined, or professional. They could not be controlled by the usual military devices. They were often accused of theft and spying for the enemy.

FACT 12: "Great numbers of women, who seem to be the beasts of burden, having a bushel basket on their back, by which they were bent double, the contents seem to be Pots and Kettles, various sorts of Furniture, children peeping thro' gridirons and other utensils, some very young Infants who were born on the road, the women bare feet, cloathed in dirty raggs, such effluvia filled the air while they were passing, had they not been smoaking all the time, I should have been apprehensive of being contaminated by them."(2)

FACT 13: A woman who cooked for Washington and his troops and even brought them food when they were under fire was quoted as saying "it would not do for men to fight and starve too."(3)

FACT 14: Washington expressed his shock at the appearance of his soldiers at Bunker Hill who, because they thought that washing clothes was women's work, "wore what they had until it crusted over and fell apart."(4)

FACT 15 ". . . American [men], not being used to doing things of this sort, choose rather to let their linen etc. rot upon their backs than to be at the trouble of cleanin' 'em themselves."(5)

Now that you have read the facts and decided if they support or refute your hypotheses, can you think of some new hypotheses? Perhaps you learned something from the above information that you did not know beforehand. Write your new hypotheses below.

Evidence that supports *this hypothesis:*	*Washington wanted women to follow the army because:*	*Evidence that* refutes *this hypothesis:*
	HYPOTHESIS 1: ____________ ______________________ ______________________ HYPOTHESIS 2: ____________ ______________________ ______________________	

Evidence that supports *this hypothesis:*	*Washington did* not *want women to follow the army because:*	*Evidence that* refutes *this hypothesis:*
	HYPOTHESIS 1: ____________ ______________________ ______________________ HYPOTHESIS 2: ____________ ______________________ ______________________	

Name ______________________________ Date ______________

2–16

HOME ALONE (WITH ALL THE WORK!)

When their husbands left to serve in the Continental Army, many European American and free African American women were left home alone to take care of all the responsibilities. Because 95 percent of these women lived on farms and made their living from agriculture, this meant most women not only had to take care of children and elderly parents, but also had to run a house (without running water, refrigerators, washing machines, etc.!), plus take care of the crops and livestock. This was an extremely challenging task and, certainly, women had many strong emotions concerning this task as they bade farewell to their soldier husbands. Imagine that you are one of these women who lives on a small farm in Pennsylvania. What kinds of feelings would you have had about seeing your spouse leave and why would you have those feelings? Record them below.

Feeling	***The reason I would have those feelings is that:***
1. ______________	______________________________
2. ______________	______________________________
3. ______________	______________________________

Indeed, surviving on a farm without a mate was a formidable task. The challenge changed many women who had been conditioned to assume a role subservient to their husbands before the war due to cultural conditioning and legal limitations (married women could not own property or run their own business; women were not allowed to vote). Still imagining that you are the woman who lived on a small farm in Pennsylvania, how do you think this experience of independence would have changed you? Write your thoughts below:

Change	***I would have changed in this way because:***
1. ______________	______________________________
2. ______________	______________________________
3. ______________	______________________________
4. ______________	______________________________

Name ____ *Date* ______________

2–17

INSPIRATION

Benjamin Franklin had the idea that it would be beneficial to unite the colonies into a single nation long before the War of Independence. He had studied the Iroquois Confederation, a union of six Native American tribes. This Confederation originally included the Senecas, Oneidas, Onondagas, Mohawks, and Cayugas of the Northeastern Woodlands and was later joined by the Tuscaroras of the Southeast during the mid-1700s. He greatly admired their unity and their constitution. Franklin wrote in 1754:

"It would be a strange thing if Six Nations of ignorant savages should be capable of forming a scheme for such a union, and be able to execute it in such a manner that it has subsisted for ages and appears indissoluble; and yet that a union should be impracticable for ten or a dozen English colonies, to whom it is more necessary and must be more advantageous, and who cannot be supposed to want an equal understanding of their interests."[(1)]

What do you think he meant by these words? Do you agree with his term "ignorant savages"? Write your answers below.

____

____

____

____

____

____

____

____

____

____

____

____

____

____

(Continue on the back.)

Name ______________________ *Date* ______________

2–18

ABIGAIL ADAMS WRITES A LETTER

Women in eighteenth-century America were expected to remain silent on most matters and defer to men. One famous European American woman, Abigail Adams, refused to do this. She was the wife of the second president of the United States, John Adams. She was a prolific letter writer to her husband, who was often away on governmental business. Read the excerpts below of some of these letters to understand her views on women's position in eighteenth-century American society. She used very complicated English of the times to express herself. After each excerpt, explain what Mrs. Adams was saying in words that a teenager would understand today.

". . . and by the way in the new Code of Laws which I suppose it will be necessary for you to make [referring to the Constitution] I desire you would Remember the Ladies, and be more generous and favourable to them than your ancestors. Do not put such unlimited power into the hands of the Husbands. Remember all Men would be tyrants if they could. If perticuliar care and attention is not paid to the Ladies we are determined to foment a Rebelion, and will not hold ourselves bound by any Laws in which we have no voice, or Representation."(1)

Abigail Adams is saying in the letter to her husband:

____

____

____

____

____

"I cannot say that I think you very generous to the Ladies for whilst you are proclaiming peace and good will to Men, Emancipating all Nations, you insist upon retaining an absolute power over Wives. But you must remember that Arbitrary power is like most other things which are very hard, very liable to be broken—and notwithstanding all your wise Laws and Maxims, we have it in our power, not only to free ourselves but to subdue our Masters, and without violence throw both your natural and legal authority at our feet. . . ."(2)

Abigail Adams is saying in the letter to her husband:

____

____

____

____

____

Below is a list of women's legal limitations during the eighteenth century. Read this list and think about how *you* would feel living in a society like the following:

1. Women were not allowed to vote.
2. When a woman married, all of her property became a legal possession of her husband. She no longer had control over it.
3. Women were allowed only to run small businesses (inns, shops, etc.) on a very limited basis.
4. Men were allowed to use corporal (physical) punishment on their wives.
5. If a divorce occurred, the husband would retain custody of the children. Women had no rights with regard to the children.

Imagine you are Abigail Adams and write a letter to your husband, who is creating the new laws of a new country. Express your opinion on at least one of the facts listed above.

1776

Dear John Adams,

____

____

____

____

____

____

____

____

(Continue on the back.)

Name ______________________________ Date ____________

2–19

TOO FAR OR NOT FAR ENOUGH?

When the Constitution (1788) and the Bill of Rights (1791) were ratified, they were considered too radical by some Americans and not radical enough by other Americans. Much of this viewpoint depended upon your status in society; and this status depended much upon your race, gender, and class. Read the list below of many different kinds of Americans living in 1791. Imagine you are each of these people and consider the situation in which you were living. In the space provided decide: (1) Did the Constitution and the Bill of Rights go too far, not far enough, or just the right amount to protect your rights? (2) What amendments would you add or subtract to make these documents better reflect your interests?

1. *NATIVE AMERICAN (IROQUOIS) FEMALE*

   a. Native Americans were not counted in the 1790 American census; they were not considered U.S. citizens, although many were living close to or among African Americans and European Americans.

   b. The U.S. Constitution did not give Native Americans the right to vote.

   c. Though Iroquois men were the chiefs of their tribes, they were nominated by women who could impeach them. Women were organized under their own formal leaders, the matrons, who were elected to represent all women.

If I had been a Native American (Iroquois) woman in 1791, I would have thought the Bill of Rights and the Constitution: went too far/ did not go far enough/were just right (circle one) to protect my rights. I would have proposed adding or subtracting the following amendments:

____

____

____

2. *LOW-INCOME EUROPEAN AMERICAN (MASSACHUSETTS) MALE FARMER*

   a. The U.S. Constitution did not give all European American males the right to vote; only European American males with significant property holdings could vote in 1791.

   b. It is estimated that only approximately one-fifth of European American males were allowed to vote on ratification of the Constitution.

   c. Many poor Massachusetts farmers, who were also war veterans, had been thrown off their farms when they returned home from fighting in the War of Independence—because of their indebted financial situation. The federal and state government had done little to alleviate their financial problems.

If I had been a low-income European American (Massachusetts) male farmer in 1791, I would have thought the Constitution and the Bill of Rights: went too far/did not go far enough/were just right (circle one) to protect my rights. I would have proposed adding or subtracting the following amendments:

____

____

____

3. *FREE AFRICAN AMERICAN WOMAN*
   a. The U.S. Constitution did not give women the right to vote.
   b. In 1790, approximately 59,000 African Americans were free and 697,000 African Americans were enslaved.
   c. Some free African Americans were artisans and merchants who lived comfortably; most free African Americans were relegated to low-paying jobs.
   d. Women were not allowed to serve on juries.

If I had been a free African American woman living in 1791, I would have thought the Constitution and the Bill of Rights: went too far/did not go far enough/were just right (circle one) to protect my rights. I would have proposed adding or subtracting the following amendments:

____

____

____

4. *ENSLAVED AFRICAN AMERICAN MALE*
   a. The U.S. Constitution counted slaves as three-fifths of a person.
   b. The U.S. Constitution allowed importation of slaves to America until the year 1808; from that date on slavery could continue to exist but no other Africans were allowed to be brought as slaves to America.
   c. Slaves were not allowed to vote or serve on juries.

If I had been an enslaved African American male in 1791, I would have thought the Constitution and the Bill of Rights: went too far/did not go far enough/were just right (circle one) to protect my rights. I would have proposed subtracting or adding the following amendment(s):

____

____

____

5. *WEALTHY EUROPEAN AMERICAN FARMER*
   a. The Bill of Rights gave rights that had not existed previously to *all* citizens, wealthy and poor—such rights as freedom of speech and freedom of the press.
   b. Before the Constitution and Bill of Rights, courts and juries were controlled by upper-class European American males.
   c. Only European males with significant amounts of property were allowed to vote.

If I had been a wealthy European American farmer, I would have felt the Constitution and the Bill of Rights: went too far/did not go far enough/were just right (circle one) to protect my rights. I would have proposed subtracting or adding the following amendments:

____

____

____

Name ______________________________ Date ______________

2–20

THE IROQUOIS CONSTITUTION

The Iroquois Confederation united five Native American Nations (Senecas, Mohawks, Oneidas, Onondagas, and Cayugas) of the Northeastern Woodlands. (The Tuscaroras of the Southeast later joined this Confederation in the mid-1700s.) They had a written constitution that guided their union. This constitution framed values and expected conduct among Iroquois Confederation members. It was said that Thomas Jefferson studied this constitution when it came time to frame the U.S. Constitution. Read the excerpt from the Iroquois Constitution below that describes what is expected of the men who represent their respective Iroqouis Nation at the council meetings. Then imagine you are Jefferson and write an entry into your personal diary about how this passage prepared you for the long, hot Philadelphia summer in 1787 when 55 European Americans met and argued over what should be the content of the U.S. Constitution.

"We now crown you with the sacred emblem of the antlers, the sign of your lordship, You shall now become a mentor of the people of the Five Nations. The thickness of your skin will be seven spans, for you will be proof against anger, offensive action, and criticism. With endless patience you will carry out your duty, and your firmness shall be tempered with compassion for your people. Neither anger nor fear shall find lodgement in your mind and all your words and actions shall be tempered with calm deliberation. In all your official acts, self interest shall be cast aside. You shall look and listen to the welfare of the whole peoplc, and have always in view, not only the present but coming generations—the unborn of the future Nation."[1]

June 1, 1787

Dear Diary,

____

____

____

____

____

(Continue on the back.)

Name ______________________________ Date ______________

2–21
WHICH SIDE OF THE ROAD?

Sometimes history books make the birth of our nation sound like everything went so smoothly—as if there were no problems! Of course, this was not true. After the War of Independence, the American Confederation (as it was called then) faced serious financial problems. In this exercise, you will ask a group of people (it could be a group of four or more friends, family members, or classmates) to imagine they lived in 1786. They are going to be in the position that members of the Massachusetts militia were actually placed in and asked to make a decision about these financial problems. Find a large space (such as a classroom, living room, or the front lawn) and ask your group of people to sit or stand in the middle of this space. Then ask them to imagine they are in the middle of a road in Great Barrington, Massachusetts, in 1786. They are members of the militia who have been called out to quell a protest of poor Massachusetts farmers who are pressuring the courts to delay the foreclosure of their farms. Here is some background information your "militia" needs to know:

1. The American economy was seriously damaged during the War of Independence. In the South, crops such as rice and tobacco were destroyed. In the North, merchants lost many foreign markets. This also affected small farmers of the North who were impacted by the general downturn of the economy.

2. After the War of Independence, the American government was deeply in debt. There was a national currency—the continental dollar—but it was practically worthless. State governments were allowed to print their own paper money, but people in one state often did not accept money printed in another state. This did not help the national economy.
3. The American government did not have enough money to pay the Continental Army soldiers at the end of the war. The soldiers were issued "certificates of future redemption" instead of cash. This meant many soldiers returned to their farms penniless.
4. Many Massachusetts small farmers had borrowed money before the War to buy their land, houses, and livestock. When the economy took such a downturn after the war, the people who had lent them money demanded repayment. These small farmers were often war veterans who could not pay.
5. Many Massachusetts small farmers wanted their state to print a large amount of paper money; then the small farmers could use the paper money to pay their bills. But Massachusetts refused to print more money because when a lot of paper money is printed, its value goes down and inflation goes up.
6. A group of small farmers-veterans petitioned the General Court (legislature) of Massachusetts, asking them to reconsider their policy of issuing paper money to make it easier for them to pay off their debts.
7. Before the General Court could hear the petition, creditors moved to foreclose on many small farmers who were in debt. Before a creditor could seize land or livestock from a debtor-farmer, a judge had to authorize the seizure in court proceedings.
8. To stop these procedures from taking place, small poor Massachusetts farmers started organizing themselves, under the leadership of Daniel Shays, in towns such as Springfield, Northampton, Worcester, Athol, and Great Barrington. They organized hundreds of farmers and war veterans to attempt to stop these proceedings until after the General Court of Massachusetts ruled on their petition.
9. To stop the farmers-veterans from closing down the courts, the local militia would be called together. In one of the towns, Great Barrington, the head of the militia realized that the group of men he had assembled were not united in their resolve to stop the farmers-veterans. Many of the men in the militia were also farmers-veterans and empathized with the demonstrators. Therefore, this militia leader decided he would take a "vote with their feet" of his militia members; he asked those who thought they *should* stop the demonstrators from closing down the court to sit on the right side of the road and those who thought they *should not* stop the demonstrators to go to the left side of the road.

Ask your group of people to think for several minutes, discuss the decision among themselves, and then "vote with their feet." They must decide whether they will go to sit on the right or the left side of your imaginary road. After they all "vote with their feet," interview them. Ask them what information influenced their decision. Write their responses in the space provided below.

____

____

____

____

____

(Continue on the back.)

Name ______________________________ Date ______________

2–22
THE CAJUNS

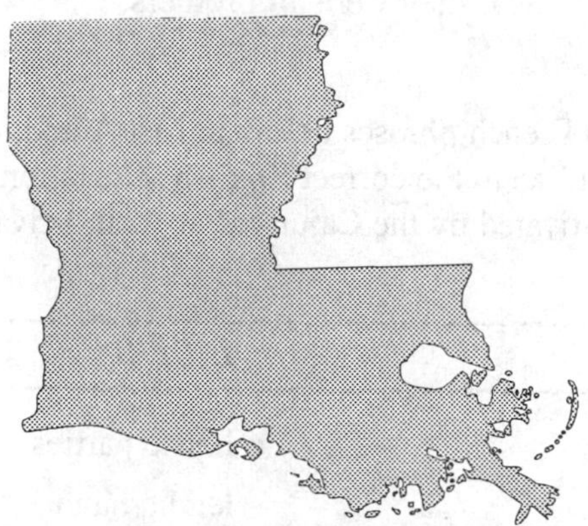

One of the largest European American ethnic communities still intact in America is that of the Cajuns, short for "Acadians." They live primarily in two areas—northern Maine, which has approximately 200,000 Cajuns; and Louisiana's "French Triangle" (the 22 southernmost parishes of the state), which has approximately 800,000 Cajuns. Read the excerpts that describe where the Cajuns originated.

"Originally, the Acadians came from rural areas of western France. In the early 17th century, they immigrated to New France [known today as Canada] and settled in the eastern coastal area known as Acadia and its neighboring regions, becoming farmers, fishers, hunters, and trappers. Large, close-knit families and communities helped insure the Acadians survival. Cut off from their mother country, living in a harsh, isolated land, the Acadians quickly developed a separate cultural identity. . . . The Acadian strong sense of kinship proved to be their salvation following 1713 when the Acadian homeland . . . passed into British hands. In 1755, [English] Governor Charles Lawrence sought to end the threat of Acadian-inspired subversion against the British. . . 6,000 out of a total of 15,000 Acadians were expelled in the first wave of a deportation program that lasted more than 10 years. . . . Upon arriving in Louisiana the Acadians settled north and west of New Orleans on the banks of the Mississippi, along the Bayou Teche and in the LaFourche Basin."[1]

On the map below, draw the route the ancestors of the Cajuns traveled from France, to New France to Louisiana. Be sure to include the approximate dates of their arrival on your map!

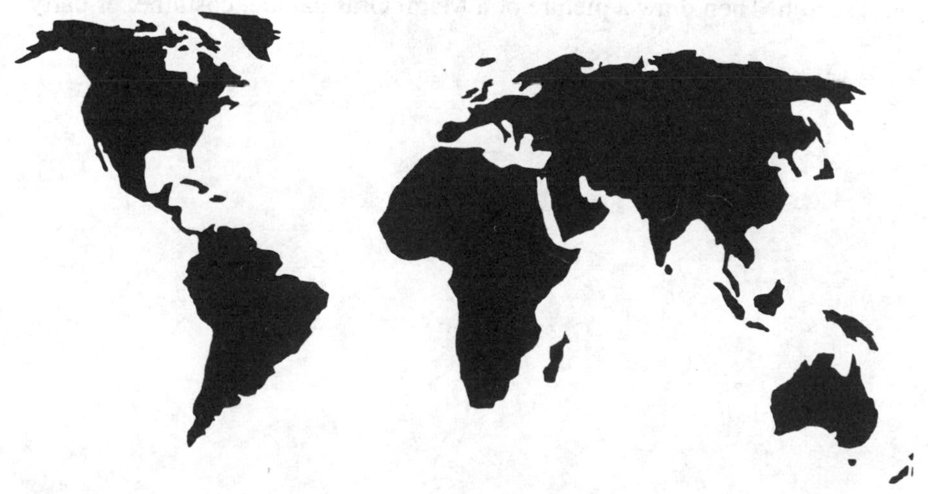

2-22 (continued)

Even after more than 200 years of living in the United States, Cajuns still claim French as their first or second language. The Cajun culture is still very much intact, perhaps due to the fact that, as one Spanish colonial governor of the Louisiana area stated, the Acadians are "a people who live as if they are a single family . . .; they give each other assistance . . . as if they were all brothers."[2]

DIRECTIONS: Read the Cajun French phrases below in List A and, using a French dictionary, discover what they mean in English. Draw a line to the correct English translation in List B. These phrases will give you an idea of the kind of culture cultivated by the Cajuns after their arrival in the eighteenth century:

LIST A	*LIST B*
coup de main	house parties
ramassaerie	lend a hand
boucherie de campagne	a two-time waltz
veillee	communal harvest
bals de maison	evening family hour
valses a deuz temps	hog butchering
contredanses	Fat Tuesday
Mardi Gras	"against" dances

The last phrase in List A, Mardi Gras, is a celebration held in New Orleans during late winter. Tourists from all over the United States and the world come to participate in the celebration of Mardi Gras. Its origins date back to Catholic celebrations held in Latin countries (such as France and Spain) and mark the period of eating and partying before the somber fasting period of Lent. It is known as a time of music, food, costumes, parades, and cookouts. Perhaps you have read about the Mardi Gras celebrations in your newspaper or seen pictures of it on television.

EXTRA CREDIT! Look up "Mardi Gras" in your school or local library in books, magazines, and newspapers. How is this celebration portrayed? Write a short description using quotes from the books, magazines, and newspapers you research. Then draw a picture of a Mardi Gras parade, costume, or party.

Name ______________________________ Date ______________

2–23
BENJAMIN BANNEKER

One of the most famous eighteenth-century Americans was of African and European descent. Benjamin Banneker was an acclaimed astronomer, mathematician, inventor, scientist, writer, and surveyor. Listed below is some information about his life.

BENJAMIN BANNEKER

1. was born November 9, 1731 in Ellicott's Mills, Maryland.
2. had a grandmother named Molly Welsh, who was an English indentured servant.
3. had a grandfather who was originally a slave of Molly Welsh, but whom she freed and then married.
4. had a mother named Mary—one of four children.
5. had a father who was an African native.
6. wrote a dissertation on bees.
7. designed and constructed what was probably the first wooden clock made in America.
8. attended a Quaker school in Maryland with European American and African American children.
9. farmed land ten miles outside Baltimore.
10. washed his own clothes, cooked his own meals, and cultivated gardens around his cabin.
11. was a "confirmed bachelor" who studied all night, slept all morning, and worked all afternoon.
12. wrapped himself in a great cloak at night, lay under a pear tree, and meditated on the revolutions of the heavenly bodies.

13. always had standing, in the middle of his cabin, a large table covered with books and papers.
14. played the violin.
15. was constantly in correspondence with other mathematicians in the United States, exchanging questions and seeking solutions.
16. from 1792 to 1802, wrote a series of annual almanacs that were widely read.
17. was named to the commission that surveyed the land upon which Washington, D.C., was built.
18. proposed that the cabinet have a Secretary of Peace as well as a Secretary of War.
19. worked for free public education and an end to capital punishment.
20. died on October 9, 1806, in Ellicott's Mills, Maryland.

Read the following excerpt of a 1791 letter Banneker wrote to European American leader Thomas Jefferson, who—though in theory opposed to slavery—himself owned slaves and accepted a U.S. Constitution that allowed slavery. While reading it, try to find the analogy (comparison of two sets of relationships) Banneker is making.

"Suffer me to recall to your mind that time, in which the arms of the British crown were exerted, with every powerful effort, in order to reduce you to a state of servitude; look back, I entreat you. . . . You were then impressed with proper ideas of the great violation of liberty, and the free possession of those blessings, to which you were entitled by nature; but sir, how pitiable is it to reflect, that although you were so fully convinced of the benevolence of the Father of Mankind, and his equal and impartial distribution of these rights and privileges which he hath conferred upon them, that you should at the same time counteract his mercies, in detaining by fraud and violence, so numerous a part of my brethren under groaning captivity and cruel oppression, that you should at the same time be found guilty of that most criminal act, which you professedly detested in others."

Banneker writes in a 1790 style that is very different from the style in which most of us write today. Take Banneker's letter and break it down into phrases (i.e., "suffer me to recall to your mind that time") and try to express what he is saying in words that would be understood by teenagers today (i.e., "please allow me to remind you of the time"). Write your reworded Banneker letter to Thomas Jefferson in the space provided below.

____

____

____

____

(Continue on the back.)

Now go back and reflect on what you have written. Banneker is making an *analogy* using four groups of people (An analogy is a comparison between two sets of relationships or four things . . . for example one analogy is "a paddle is to a canoe as a motor is to a ship"; another analogy is "love is to marriage as a horse is to a carriage.") Fill in the blanks for Banneker's analogy below.

____________________ curb the liberty of ____________________ as

____________________ curbed the liberty of ____________________.

Name ______________________________ Date ______________

2–24

EVERYDAY LIFE

Have you ever tried to describe your everyday life activities in a poem? Ruth Belknap of Dover, New Hampshire, did in 1782. Read her poem below.

Up in the morning I must rise
Before I've time to rub my eyes.
With half-pinned gown, unbuckled shoe
I haste to milk my lowing cow.
But, Oh! it makes my heart to ake,
I have no bread till I can bake.
And then, alas! it makes me sputter,
For I must churn or have no butter.
The hogs with swill too I must serve;
For hogs must eat or men will starve.
Besides my spouse can get no cloaths
Unless I much offend my nose
For all that try it know its true
There is no smell like colouring blue.
Then round the parish I must ride
And make enquiry far and wide
To find some girl that is a spinner,
Then hurry home to get my dinner. . . .

All summer long I toil & sweat,
Blister my hands, and scold & fret.
And when the summer's work is o'er,
New toils arise from Autumn's store.
Corn must be husk'd and pork be kill'd,
The house with all confusion fill'd.
O could you see the grand display
Upon our annual butchering day,
See me look like ten thousand sluts,
My kitchen spread with grease & guts,
You'd lift your hands surpris'd & swear
That Mother Trisket's self were there.

Ye starch'd up folks that live in town,
That lounge around your beds till noon,
That never tire yourselves with work,
Unless with handling knife & fork,
Come see the sweets of country life,
Display'd in Parson Belknap's wife.[1]

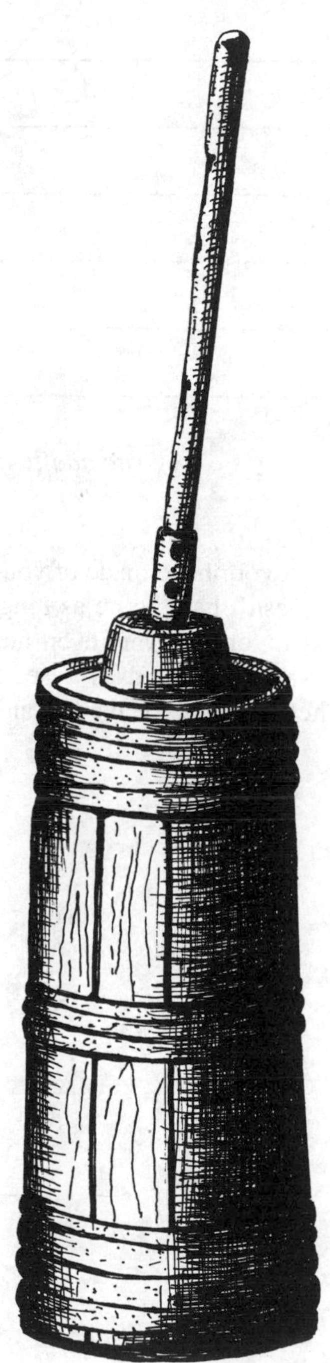

2-24 (continued)

MAKE A LIST OF RUTH BELKNAP'S EVERYDAY LIFE ACTIVITIES IN 1782:

1. ______________________________
2. ______________________________
3. ______________________________
4. ______________________________
5. ______________________________
6. ______________________________
7. ______________________________
8. ______________________________

MAKE A LIST OF YOUR EVERYDAY LIFE ACTIVITIES:

1. ______________________________
2. ______________________________
3. ______________________________
4. ______________________________
5. ______________________________
6. ______________________________
7. ______________________________
8. ______________________________

(Write additional activities on the back of this sheet.)

Using the list your have made of your own everyday activities, make a short poem (at least four lines!) out of them. It doesn't have to be as long as Ruth Belknap's poem, but try to use her A/B form of poetic measure. (The last word of every even-numbered line rhymes with the last word of the previous odd-numbered line; for example, Ruth uses "rise" and "eyes," or "ake" and "bake.") Use the space below or write it on a separate sheet of paper. Have fun and be ready to read it tomorrow in class!

Name ______________________________ Date ____________

2–25

WHAT IF?

During the 1700s an institution most people today consider very destructive, took hold in America; this was the institution of slavery. Over 50 million Africans were wrenched from their homeland and brought across the Atlantic Ocean to be sold. This institution would never have been possible without one invention. Read the following excerpt from a speech by Malcolm X, an African American leader of the 1960s, to find out what this invention was:

"He [the African] was only defeated when the Europeans invented, or got access to, gunpowder. I started to say invented gunpowder, but they didn't invent it, the Chinese invented it. . . . But they never defeated the African armies until they got gunpowder. Then with their gunpowder, they came in."[1]

Have you ever thought about how history might have turned out differently if another group had gotten the advantage of this invention first? Let's try to use our imaginations and rewrite history. Below is the beginning of an imaginary history book. The sentences are full of blanks. You probably know the "correct" information to fill in the blanks; but I want you to use your imagination and *change history*. In other words, *don't* fill in the correct answer; purposely fill in another person, continent, or group of people instead of the "right" one. Let's see where history could have taken another turn!

THE HISTORY OF THE WORLD: 1500–1800

The year 1492 was pivotal for the world; this was the year that ______________, a ______________ from the continent ______________________ crossed the ocean and began to explore the continent of ______________. ______________ was an excellent sailor and navigator but was quite inhumane because this ______________ was responsible for the deaths of many people in the continent of ______________. Before long many other people from the ______________ continent began crossing the ocean to form new settlements. They farmed, created towns and cities, and prospered in the new land. However, this was very difficult for the original inhabitants, the ________________, because they were pushed off their land, forced into many new wars, and died from the new diseases brought by the settlers from the continent ________________. In fact, between the years 1500 and 1800 the population of ________________ dropped from 5+ million to under 600,000.

Another tragic development at this time in world history was the increase in the number of slaves. The people from the continent of ______________ had invented gunpowder. Some people from the continent ____________ used this new invention to force over 50 million people from the continent of ____________ to cross the ocean and live in slavery in the continent of ____________. This caused many of the ____________ to revolt *against their masters or run away.*

EXTRA CREDIT! Keep adding to this imaginary history book on other sheets of paper. Add as much information as you would like. What other events (wars, inventions, etc.) might have occurred? Be sure to describe what the world would be like today if your imaginary history book had been true.

Name ______________________ Date ______________

2–26
SAGOYEWATHA

One of the most talented Native American orators of the eighteenth century was Sagoyewatha of the Senecas, who lived in the area we now know as New York. He was well respected among European Americans, African Americans, and Native Americans. Not only did he argue for Native American rights, but he also spoke with great eloquence. He is particularly remembered for his use of metaphors in his speeches.

DIRECTIONS: Read the excerpt from one of Sagoyewatha's speeches and, in the space provided, explain the metaphor he is using. What is he trying to say?

"We first knew you to be a feeble plant which wanted a little earth whereon to grow. We gave it to you: and afterward, when we could have trod you under our feet, we watered and protected you: and now you have grown to be a mighty tree, whose top reaches the clouds, and whose branches overspread the whole land, whilst we, who were the tall pine of the forest, have become a feeble plant and need your protection."

Sagoyewatha uses:

1. "a feeble plant" as a metaphor for ______________________
2. "we watered and protected you" as a metaphor for ______________________
3. "a mighty tree" as a metaphor for ______________________
4. "branches overspread the whole land" as a metaphor for ______________________
5. "tall pine of the forest" as a metaphor for ______________________

Sagoyewatha is saying in this speech that

____

____

____.

EXTRA CREDIT! On a separate piece of paper, draw two pictures to illustrate what Sagoyewatha is saying in words. Write the words of the speech under your drawings so they may be displayed.

Name ______________________________ Date ______________

2–27
TRAGEDY

One of the most tragic results of European American expansion into the Americas was the impact it had on the Native Americans. At the beginning of the sixteenth century, the Native American population was estimated to be 5+ million people; by the end of the eighteenth century, the population had dropped to approximately 600,000. In the space provided below, hypothesize why this occurred.

Evidence that **supports** *this hypothesis:*	***The Native American population decreased during the eighteenth century because:***	*Evidence that* **refutes** *this hypothesis:*
	Hypothesis 1 ______________ ______________ ______________	
	Hypothesis 2 ______________ ______________ ______________	
	Hypothesis 3 ______________ ______________ ______________	
	Hypothesis 4 ______________ ______________ ______________	

On the following pages you will find facts about Native Americans of the eighteenth century. These facts will help you determine if your hypotheses are correct or incorrect. Read each fact and decide if it *supports* or *refutes* each hypothesis. Write the number (1,2,3) under the *support* and *refute* columns next to your hypothesis. You can do additional research in your local or school library to further explore your hypotheses.

FACT 1: "... Since these Englishmen have seized our country, they have cut down the grass with scythes, and the trees with axes. Their cows and horses eat up the grass, and their hogs spoil our bed of clams; and finally we shall all starve to death."

MIANTONOMO (NARRAGANSETT)

FACT 2: "Native American Indian leaders pleaded to colonial leaders to curb the spread of alcohol. The arguments they used were two: their people were dying in excessive numbers from drinking-related murders (and we know also from exposure and increased susceptibility to colds, pneumonia, and other diseases), and the temperance issue."(1)

FACT 3: On June 24, 1763, Captain Ecuyer, of the royal Americans noted in his journal: "Out of our regard for them [i.e., two Indian chiefs] we gave them two blankets and a handkerchief out of the smallpox hospital. I hope it will have the desired effect."(2)

FACT 4: ". . . Colonel Cresap, in cold blood and unprovoked, murdered all the relations of Logan, not even sparing my women and children."

LOGAN (MINGO)

FACT 5: "Having converted the Illinois to monogamy and Catholicism, the French could more or less respectably intermarry with the Indians. This further depopulated the Illinois [Native Americans] through racially mixed offspring, some of whom were perhaps not considered as Illinois."(3)

FACT 6: Sioux pictographs from Winter Counts (recording the most significant events of the year) show: (a) Measles (b) Whooping Cough (c) Smallpox (d) Starvation (e) Dropsy

a

b

c

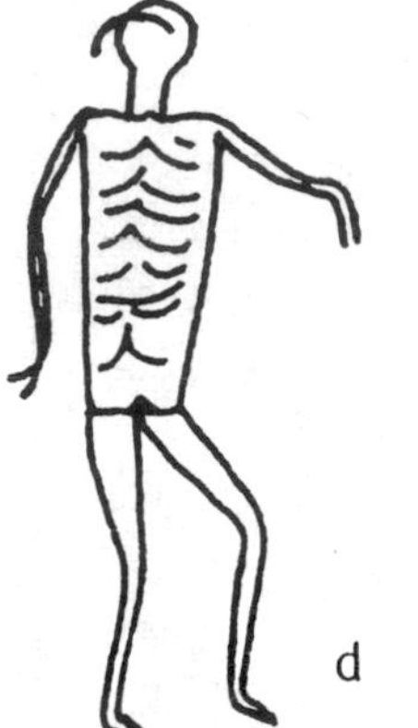
d

e

FACT 7: The Illinois Native Americans fought with the following Native American groups during the 1600s and 1700s: Iroquois, Miami, Missouri, Pawnee, Osage, Chickasaw, Cherokee, Shawnee, Kaskinampo, Fox, Kickapoo, Mascouten, Sac, Potawatomi, Winnebago, Menominee, Ojibwa.

FACT 8: California Indians were brought into the [Christian] missions sometimes forcibly, sometimes voluntarily; but once there they were typically prevented from leaving and punished for attempted escapes. . . . The mission housing aggregated many people in a relatively small area with bad sanitation and minimal ventilation and heat, providing a favorable environment for the spread of contagious diseases.(4)

FACT 9: The following wars were fought between Native American groups and Europeans over land in the eighteenth century: the Tuscarora War of 1771–1712; the Yamasee War of 1715–1716; the Natchez War of 1731; the Apalachee War of 1703; the French and Indian War of 1754–1763.

FACT 10: The winter of 1779–1780 was known by the Sioux Native Americans as the "Smallpox Used Them Up Winter"; the winter of 1780–81 was known by the Sioux as the "Smallpox Used Them Up Again Winter."

FACT 11: A phenomenon called "social splintering" (the formation of groups that departed from the main tribal body) occurred among many Native American tribes after contact with the French, English, Spanish, and American colonizers. These intertribal splits developed as one part of a Native American tribe would become aligned with one or another non-Indian group. This was a factor contributing to the depopulation.

FACT 12: The following epidemics affected the Native Americans during the eighteenth century: smallpox, measles, influenza, plague, typhus, diphtheria, and scarlet fever. Tuberculosis, syphilis, and other sexually transmitted diseases were also present among them. Old world diseases were the primary killers of the eighteenth century Native Americans, with smallpox being the most deadly one.

Now that you have read the facts and decided if they support or refute your hypotheses, can you think of some new hypotheses? Perhaps you learned something from the above information that you did not know beforehand. Write your new hypotheses below.

Evidence that supports *this hypothesis:*	*The Native American population decreased during the eighteenth century because:*	*Evidence that* refutes *this hypothesis:*
	Hypothesis 5: ____________ ____________ ____________ Hypothesis 6: ____________ ____________ ____________	

Name ______________________________ Date ______________

2–28

THE DU SABLES

One unique American couple of the 1700s were Jean and Catherine Du Sable. They represent the intermarriage of people from different cultures that occurred during that century. Read the information about these two people.

1. Jean Baptiste Point Du Sable was born in Haiti in 1745 to a French mariner father and an enslaved African mother.
2. Catherine Du Sable was born in the area we today call Illinois to Potawatomi Native American parents.
3. Jean's mother died when he was very young and his father sent him to Paris to be educated.
4. Jean worked as a seaman on his father's ships and was shipwrecked near New Orleans in the 1780s. He headed north and became a fur trapper on the southern tip of Lake Michigan.
5. Jean and Catherine met during the 1780s near Lake Michigan and were married in 1788.
6. The Du Sables lived for sixteen years at the mouth of the Chicago River, creating the first permanent settlement—Chicago. They were the city's founders.
7. The Du Sables built a 40-foot by 22-foot log house, a bakehouse, a dairy, a smokehouse, a poultry house, a workshop, a stable, a barn, and a mill.
8. The Du Sables traded in furs, ran a mill to grind grain, traded livestock, made barrels, and grew their own food.
9. The Du Sables had a daughter and a son.
10. The Du Sables had 23 French works of art in their crude cabin.

DIRECTIONS: Imagine you are a sculptor who has been commissioned by the city of Chicago to create a sculpture depicting the founders of the city. What kind of statue would you create? What pose would the Du Sables be in and what would they have around them? What should the plaque that will be placed under the sculpture say about this unique couple? Write your answers to these questions in the space provided below. Use extra sheets of paper to draw an example of your statue, if you like!

____

____

____

____

____

____

____

(Continue on the back.)

Name ______________________________ Date ______________

2–29

BENJAMIN FRANKLIN'S PARODY

Slavery was a very controversial issue when the United States was first formed. There were many debates concerning slavery in the first U.S. Congress. One senator from Georgia made a speech saying that slavery was good for African Americans and that slave masters were just following the Christian Bible. Benjamin Franklin, someone whom we generally remember as an inventor and writer of the Constitution, was also an abolitionist and disagreed with this senator. To publicly express his disagreement, he wrote a parody—a humorous imitation that took the senator's ideas and turned them around. He published a made-up letter from an imaginary Muslim prince whom he named Sidi Mehemet Ibrahim. Ibrahim was the ruler of the imaginary African nation, Algiers, where supposedly captive European Christians were held as slaves. This pretend Muslim prince wrote in his letter that slavery was good for these white Christians and that the slave owners were just following the ideas of the Muslim holy book, the *Koran*. Read an excerpt from Ibrahim's (Franklin's) letter below:

"Is their condition then made worse by their falling into our hands? No; they have only exchanged one slavery for another, and I may say better; for here . . . they have an opportunity of making themselves aquainted with the true doctrine, and thereby saving their immortal souls. Those who remain at home have not had that happiness. . . . Let us then hear no more of this detestable proposition [the freeing of slaves], the adoption of which would, by depreciating our lands and houses and thereby depriving so many good citizens [slave owners] of their properties. . . ."

What is Benjamin Franklin saying in the above excerpt? Translate his writing into terms that a teenager today would understand in the space provided below.

____

____

____

EXTRA CREDIT! Imagine you are Benjamin Franklin and create a letter from the Muslim Prince Sidi Mehemet Ibrahim describing slavery of European Christians in your country and defending this institution's existence. Begin your letter with the salutation "Dear Georgian Senator," on the back of this page.

Name ______________________________ *Date* ____________

2–30

PEOPLE TO REMEMBER

In the blanks provided, write the letter of the description that matches each name on the column on the left.

_____ 1. ABIGAIL ADAMS	A. famous Iroquois male orator and chief born in 1725
_____ 2. BENJAMIN BANNEKER	B. European American woman who spoke for women's rights
_____ 3. SEQUOYA	C. European American woman who disguised herself as a man and fought in the War of Independence
_____ 4. DANIEL SHAYS	D. European American man who was first president of the United States
_____ 5. DU SABLES	E. Native American man who invented the Cherokee syllabary of 85 characters
_____ 6. GEORGE WASHINGTON	F. European American man who wrote the Declaration of Independence
_____ 7. SAGOYEWATHA	G. man of African and European descent who surveyed the land where Washington, D.C. was built
_____ 8. PHILLIS WHEATLEY	H. European American man who led a rebellion of farmers and war veterans in 1786
_____ 9. BENJAMIN FRANKLIN	I. European American male inventor and signer of the Constitution who opposed slavery
_____ 10. DEBORAH SAMPSON	J. the American couple of Native American, African, and European descent who founded Chicago
_____ 11. CRISPUS ATTUCKS	K. first African American poet to publish in America
_____ 12. THOMAS JEFFERSON	L. man of African and European descent who led the first rebellion against the British army

SECTION *Three*

THE 1800s

Teachers' Guide to Activities for the 1800s

3–1 DRAW!

Research shows that our students retain the most knowledge when it is "clustered" in their minds. This exercise, which breaks down the tremendous physical growth of the United States in the nineteenth century into seven "clusters," will help your students remember when various areas of the country became territories and states. ANSWERS: States from the Louisiana Purchase (Arkansas, Iowa, Missouri, Montana, Nebraska, North Dakota, South Dakota, Oklahoma, and parts of Louisiana, Colorado, Kansas, Minnesota, and Wyoming); from the Texas Annexation (Texas and parts of Colorado, Wyoming, New Mexico, Oklahoma, and Kansas); from the Oregon Country (Idaho, Oregon, Washington); from the Mexican Cession and Gladsden Purchase (California, Utah, Nevada, Arizona and parts of New Mexico, Wyoming, and Colorado); from the Florida Cession (Florida and parts of Louisiana, Alabama, and Mississippi); from the land ceded by Great Britain in 1818 (parts of North Dakota, South Dakota, and Minnesota).

3–2 HOW MUCH DO WE KNOW?

Interfacing with their friends, neighbors, and relatives will not only make history a more interesting subject for our students but will help them remember historical information. The more they discuss what they are learning in class *outside* the classroom, the more learning will be meaningful and fun! ANSWERS: (1) German (2) men, women, and children (3) European American men, African American men, and women (4) African American and

European American men and women (5) Wyoming (6) all of the above (7) all of the above (8) African Americans and European Americans (9) Sacagawea, a woman (10) Tecumseh

3–3 DECISIONS AND CHOICES

Part of becoming a teenager is taking responsibility—making your own decisions and choices. This exercise will connect this important developmental task with a true story in history. It will also shed light on the strength of African American families, even under the tremendous strain of slavery. (Correct answer: Morris chose to stay with his family!)

3–4 SACAGAWEA

Becoming this historical character will encourage your students to get into her shoes and empathize with this woman's strength and talents. Give your students a block of time to work on this by themselves and you will be surprised with the quality of work they produce!

3–5 YORK

There is a lot of information in our textbooks about the European American explorers Lewis and Clark. Few of our students know about this African American man's contribution to the exploration of the Louisiana Purchase.

3–6 SPELLING

Connecting history directly with an everyday activity such as spelling will not only help our students remember this important chapter of American history but empower our students to feel just as smart as the famous Meriwether Clark.

3–7 REWRITE HISTORY

It is difficult for our students to realize that history *could* have turned a very different path. They often believe it was set in stone! This exercise will aid them in imagining what if . . . ?

3–8 TRAIL OF TEARS

Making educated guesses, or hypotheses, is interesting for our students. Learning to make their way through historical facts and extract what supports and refutes their educated guesses is an important skill to attain. This exercise combines both of these activities and enriches our students' understanding of Native American history.

3–9 WORKING CONDITIONS

Industrialization in America was a messy process for American workers. Though it enhanced our lives in the long run, this exercise makes our students realize the price paid for our present-day life of manufactured clothes, cars, shoes, and other goods.

3–10 MEN, WOMEN, AND MONEY

Here is an exercise where our students can practice their math skills in history class! It is also a good motivator for a discussion on economic equality between men and women. Beware! They can discuss this for hours! (As of 1995, women earn, on the average, 72 cents for every dollar a man earns.)

3–11 FIGHT, AND IF YOU CAN'T FIGHT, KICK

Many students assume that enslaved African Americans were docile and meek. This exercise helps them realize that, with much courage and tenacity, slaves carved out their own spheres of influence.

3–12 FREDERICK DOUGLASS

Our students have many feelings about the institution of slavery, ranging from guilt to anger. It is important for them to express these feelings in a positive manner. This exercise will not only give them an appreciation for this important African American writer and speaker, but will also offer an outlet for those myriad feelings.

3–13 TELLING HER STORY

It is difficult for our students to fathom the lengths enslaved African Americans went to, to secure their personal dignity and independence. This unbelievable story will give them a glimpse into the struggle to attain these goals.

3–14 A WOMAN'S FATE

This exercise will give our students important information about the institution of slavery and sensitize them to the special situation in which African American women were placed.

3–15 ABOLITIONISTS WORKING TOGETHER

This exercise will give your students an introduction to some of the most important, but often overlooked, women who fed the flames of the Abolitionist Movement. It will also give your students insight to the problems these women had working together to form a movement!

3–16 SUSAN B. ANTHONY GOES TO JAIL

It is important to motivate our students to become active participants in our democracy. This exercise will help them understand the struggle women went through to gain the right to vote—something that should not be taken lightly!

3–17 DO YOU AGREE?

What jobs should women have? This debate still continues in our society today. This exercise will show our students that a job that is considered "female work" today, was once looked at differently!

3–18 THE STORY OF TIN FOOK

The history of racism against the Chinese immigrants is an important part of U.S. history for our students to learn. This exercise gives information about the various barriers set up to keep the Chinese immigrants from assimilating into American society.

3–19 I'VE BEEN WORKING ON THE RAILROAD

The enormous contribution made by the Chinese immigrants to the development of the transcontinental railroad is discovered in this exercise. Allow your students to step into the shoes of these important Americans.

3–20 LEE YICK

Fighting racism in the legal system at a time when Chinese were not even allowed to vote or serve on juries was a courageous act. This exercise will give your students a glimpse into this difficult process and serve as a positive example of how our justice system *can* work effectively.

3–21 THE MEXICAN WAR

This highly controversial war was a prelude to other highly controversial American wars. Understanding the parameters of the debate will guide our students to analyzing other American conflicts. (The language is very difficult in this exercise. It is designed for students with a high reading ability.)

3–22 JUAN NEPOMUCENO CORTINA

What would we do if this happened today? This exercise encourages students to understand the situation of 80,000 Mexican Americans in 1848.

3–23 MEXICAN AMERICANS

What does it feel like not to speak the language? Some of our students have had this experience; most of them have not. This exercise will help sensitize our students to the situation, and educate them about the difficulties faced by Mexicans when, overnight, they became American citizens.

ENGLISH TRANSLATIONS

1. (In English legal language) If grantor wishes to deny privity of estate due to improper execution of the deed or other cause determined by objective and subjective tests of the court, n.b., reversion is restricted by the applicable statute of limitations to eject a possessor forthwith to whosoever claims adversely to the owner and who shall be thereafter barred from bringing an action in ejectment. Under a claim of right, statutory requirements assert a claim of title which expresses the necessary adversity, discussed supra.
2. (In English everyday language) If the original owner wants to cancel the document that transfers ownership of his or her land to someone else, he or she must give good reasons that are acceptable to a judge and that show that he or she has been harmed. He or she must do this within the legal time limits, or else he or she will never be able legally to claim the land again. The law says you can claim the land is yours if it was taken in a wrongful way, as it says above.

3–24 THE CIVIL WAR

For Whom Would You Fight? This exercise will provide a vehicle for understanding what influenced Americans of various economic, gender, and cultural backgrounds to support, not support, or remain neutral toward the Civil War!

3–25 AFRICAN AMERICAN SOLDIERS

The movie *Glory* brought us a long way toward understanding the contribution African Americans made to the Civil War. This exercise attempts to move us even further.

3–26 ABRAHAM LINCOLN

History textbooks tend to reduce a historical figure to a "package deal," without exposing our students to the thinking processes and development that led to that figure's legend. This exercise will shed light on the conflicts inside Lincoln's head regarding the institution of slavery.

3–27 ROBERT BROWN ELLIOT

The debate that occurred between African American and European American Congressional representatives during the Reconstruction Era is an important chapter in American history. This exercise introduces your students to one of the most eloquent post–Civil War players.

3–28 CLOSE QUARTERS

TV often romanticizes the experience of Western pioneers. This exercise breaks down the myth and gives students a feeling for the real life of nineteenth-century homesteaders. (The woman is carrying buffalo dung which was used for fuel, in her wheelbarrow.)

3–29 AFRICAN AMERICAN PIONEERS

Most old West characters played in movies have white faces. This exercise breaks that myth and sensitizes your students to the hopes and dreams of African American homesteaders.

3–30 COWBOY QUIZ

This exercise will challenge your students' knowledge about an "all American" concept. (Answers: (1) c (2) c (3) c (4) b (5) c (6) a (7) c

3–31 CHEYENNE NATIVE AMERICAN GAME

This exercise is perfect for one of those Friday afternoons when you *know* that nothing else will "sink in." It is an entertaining and lively way to learn about Native American culture.

3–32 WHAT DO THEY HAVE IN COMMON?

Recognizing similarities in historical trends is an important skill to hone. This exercise will help your students make connections between disparate American experiences.

3–33 IMMIGRATION

The transfer of millions of human beings from varying continents to America had many motivating factors. This exercise will aid your students in learning some of the major influences that made people pack their bags and take the risk!

3–34 WORDS WE SPEAK EVERY DAY

We often do not understand the cultural roots of words we use in our everyday language. This exercise will encourage your students to use dictionaries and encyclopedias to take a closer look at their lingo! Answers: Germany (hamburger, seltzer, frankfurter), Ireland (paddywagon), Holland (Santa Claus, Yankee), France (dessert), Mexico (rodeo, ranch), China (ketchup), Yiddish (bagel), Italy (spaghetti), Sweden (troll).

3–35 GERMAN AMERICANS

How many of our students have attended kindergarten and never given a thought to what that word means in German? This, with many other words we use often, offers just a few examples of the enormous contribution German Americans have made to American society.

3–36 JEWISH AMERICANS

Teenagers generally chafe against limits. This exercise will be an unforgettable physical experience, helping them relate to the particular situation faced by many Jewish Americans from eastern Europe.

3–37 LITTLE BAGS OF IRISH EARTH

Creating a "faction" story about one of the largest ancestry groups in our country will allow your students to step into the shoes of these hard-working immigrants.

3–38 THE GROWTH OF THE CITIES

We take so many things for granted today—running water, elevators, sewage systems. This exercise will help our students understand how far our cities have come in just 100 years.

3–39 QUEEN LILIUOKALANI

The history of the Native Hawaiians is often lost in our history textbooks. This exercise places your students on the throne of this remarkable woman and requires them to make some important decisions. (Queen Liliuokalani chose *not* to fight the insurrection because she feared it would lead to too much bloodshed.)

3–40 PEOPLE TO REMEMBER

People from all cultural backgrounds contributed during the nineteenth century to the development of our country. This exercise touches on only a few of them. Divide your class into small groups and have them work with library resources (encyclopedias and other references) to see which group can complete the list first! ANSWERS: (1) C (2) G (3) A (4) F (5) J (6) L (7) K (8) E (9) H (10) I (11) B (12) D

Name ______________________ Date ____________

3–1
DRAW!

The 1800s was a century of great expansion for the United States. Look at the map on the next page, which shows the area the United States controlled by the end of the nineteenth century. Then, take a large piece of paper (legal size or larger construction paper) and a pencil and redraw this map. Do not trace or use an overhead projector to enlarge the image! You can do it! Using colored pencils, highlight the seven areas (Louisiana Purchase, Texas Annexation, Oregon Country, Mexican Cession, Gladsden Purchase, the Florida Cession, and land ceded by Great Britain in 1818). For extra credit, compare this map to 1) the map showing the original location of Native American tribes (exercise 1-1), and 2) a map showing the 48 states of the continental U.S. and answer the following questions:

1. List the Native American tribes who were affected by the annexation of the Louisiana Purchase, the Texas Territory, Oregon Country, Mexican Cession, Gladsden Purchase, the Florida Cession, and the land ceded by Great Britain in 1818 in the space provided below.

____

____

____

____

____

____

____

2. List the states that were eventually carved out of these seven areas of land in the space provided below.

Louisiana Purchase: ______________________

Land Ceded by Britain: ______________________

Florida Cession: ______________________

Texas Annexation: ______________________

Oregon Country: ______________________

Mexican Cession: ______________________

Gladsden Purchase: ______________________

3-1 (continued)

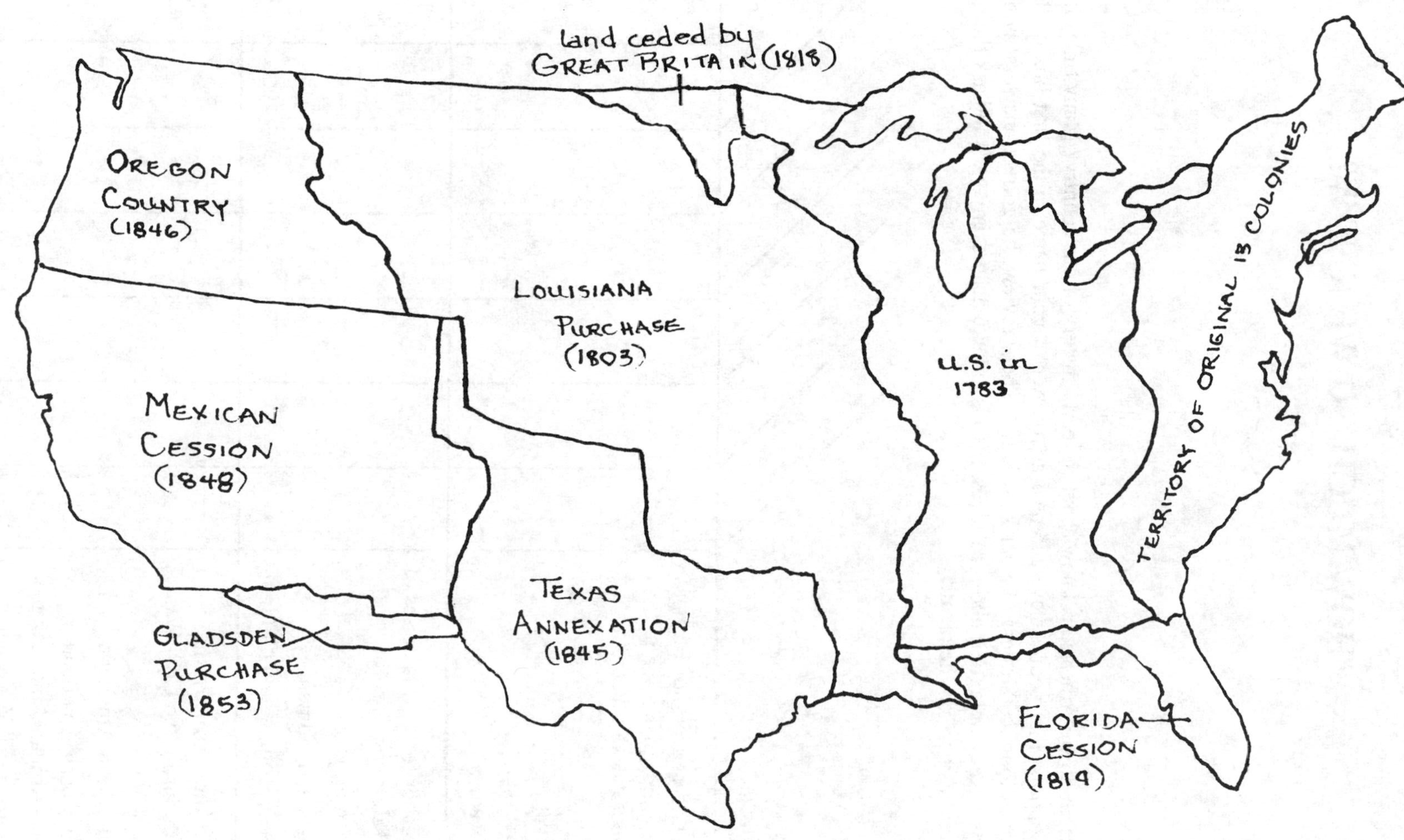

Name ______________________________ *Date* ____________

3–2
HOW MUCH DO WE KNOW?

How much do we Americans know about the early history of our country? Many times there are myths and misconceptions that people have accepted as truths. Put your name in the first box of this survey and answer the questions to the best of your knowledge. Then, review the correct answers with your teacher. Finally, choose five people (neighbors, relatives, friends, other teachers, anyone!) and ask them the questions, recording their answers on the chart.

NAMES							
1. The largest group of European immigrants that came to the United States in the 1800s were: a. Irish b. German c. Swedish							# correct ____ # incorrect ____
2. The labor force in factories of the 1800s consisted of: a. men only b. men and women c. men, women, and children							# correct ____ # incorrect ____
3. The Union Army of the North during the Civil War consisted of: a. European American men b. European American men and African American men c. European and African American men, and women							# correct ____ # incorrect ____

NAMES							
4. Members of the abolition movement were: a. African American men b. European American men c. African American and European American men and women							# correct _____ # incorrect ____
5. The first state in which women won the righ to vote (1869) was: a. Wyoming b. Massachusetts c. New York							# correct _____ # incorrect ____
6. Mexican Americans in the 1800s contributed: a. much of the cowboy lingo (ranch, lasso, etc.) b. copper, silver, and gold mining techniques c. all of the above							# correct _____ # incorrect ____
7. Asian immigrants to the United States in the 1800s contributed: a. many cooking techniques b. much of the labor to build the transcontinental railroad c. all of the above							# correct _____ # incorrect ____
8. Pioneers who moved West and formed small farming communities were: a. only European Americans b. European Americans and African Americans c. European Americans, African Americans, and Asian Americans							# correct _____ # incorrect ____

3-2 (continued)

NAMES							
9. The guide for the Lewis & Clark expedition was: a. Sacagawea, a woman b. Zebulon Pike, a man c. Sitting Bull, a man							# correct _____ # incorrect _____
10. The Native American who attempted to unite all the tribes east of the Mississippi to stem the tide of European expansion was: a. Tecumseh b. Sacagawea c. Sagoyewatha							# correct _____ # incorrect _____

DIRECTIONS: Do some math to answer the following questions:

1. How many responses did you receive? (Add up the total number of people who took the quiz and multiply by 10.)

____

2. How many responses were correct? What percentage of the total responses was this number?

____

3. How many responses were incorrect? What percentage of the total responses was this number?

____

Why do you think people do not know all the answers to these questions? Write two hypotheses below.

Many people have misconceptions about the early history of our country because:

Hypothesis 1 ____

____

Hypothesis 2 ____

____

Name ______________________ Date __________

3–3
DECISIONS AND CHOICES

What is the most difficult decision you have made in your life? Describe this decision in the space provided below.

Difficult decisions usually have to do with making a choice between several options. There are usually one or two major deciding factors in making that choice. What were your options and deciding factors for your most difficult decision? List them below:

Option 1 ______________________

Option 2 ______________________

Option 3 ______________________

Deciding Factor(s) ______________________

3-3 (continued)

Americans living in the 1800s also had to make some very difficult decisions. Read the following excerpt from *The Black Family in Slavery and Freedom 1750–1925*, written by Herbert G. Guttman.

"In 1804, the slave Morris superintended Pierce Butler's slaves on a small island north of St. Simon's Island in the Georgia Sea Islands. During a great storm, Morris's quick thinking saved many lives and prevented property damage. For a reward, Butler gave Morris the choice of either staying with his family as a slave and receiving cash and a silver goblet or receiving his freedom."(1)

If you were Morris, which option would you have chosen? Explain below.

____

____

____

Which option do you think Morris chose? (You can ask your teacher for the correct answer to this question.) What do you think was his deciding factor? What does this story tell us about the strength of enslaved African American families?

Write a short story (one page) using the information supplied above about the enslaved African American Morris and write two endings for it—one for each option. To make your story more realistic, look up the small island upon which Morris lived on a map of Georgia. Also, do some quick research on what a Georgian "great storm" is like by looking up newspaper articles about some of the recent hurricanes that have hit Georgia. Use information from these two sources in your story. Begin your story below.

TITLE ____

____

____

____

____

____

____

____

EXTRA CREDIT! Make a visual project about this true story on a 2-foot by 4-foot mat board. (You can buy this in your local stationery store or ask your teacher to secure one from the school supply closet.) You can make a collage of copied photographs of some recent storms or hurricanes in Georgia from newspapers or magazines to give your audience a feeling for the power of Georgian storms. You can also create a small hand-drawn map showing the island upon which Morris lived. Finally, rewrite or type your short story and display it on your project with the two endings. Ask your audience which ending they would choose for the story and what was their deciding factor. Then explain to your audience which choice Morris made.

Name ______________________________ Date ______________

3–4

SACAGAWEA (sak-uh-juh-we-uh)

One of the most famous Native American women of the nineteenth century was Sacagawea. She has an interesting life story that, in this exercise, you will turn into a short play. The text below summarizes parts of her life. Use your imagination and write a play with 11 short scenes that depict Sacagewea's life.

Scene 1: Sacagawea was born in approximately 1787 to a Shoshone woman who was part of a Native American tribe that lived in the Rocky Mountain area of Northwestern United States. Her name means "Bird Woman" in the language of the Shoshone.

Scene 2: When she was a young girl, she was captured by an enemy Native American tribe called the Hidatsas, and sold to a Missouri Mandan Native American.

Scene 3: Sacagawea was then sold to a French Canadian fur trader named Touissant Charbonneau. Charbonneau married Sacagawea (she was at this point 16 years old) and she became pregnant.

Scene 4: When Sacagawea was about nine months pregnant, her husband was hired by Lewis and Clark (sent by President Thomas Jefferson to explore the Lousianna Purchase) to be an interpreter. They were in the

North Dakota area in the winter of 1805 where they all settled down to wait out the long, cold winter before setting off west again.

Scene 5: Sacagawea's baby was born in this North Dakota camp during the winter of 1805. She named her little boy Jean Baptiste, for his father, but called him Pompey.

Scene 6: In the spring of 1805, Lewis and Clark set out west again. They were trying to find a water route to the Pacific Ocean and were following the Missouri River westward. Charbonneau and Sacagawea, with Pompey strapped to her back, traveled with them. Lewis and Clark soon found out that Sacagawea was much more help than her lazy husband!

Scene 7: The exploring party followed the Missouri River to its source in the foothills of the Rocky Mountains. By this time, it was late summer of 1805. Winter would soon set in and the explorers realized that there was no water route to the Pacific. They had to get out of the mountains or they would freeze and starve to death. They needed horses to do this!

Scene 8: A group of Shoshone Native Americans visited the explorers' camp. Could Lewis and Clark persuade the Shoshones to sell them some horses? As soon as Sacagawea saw the leader of these Native Americans, she burst into tears; this man, Ca-me-ah-wait, was her brother from whom she had been kidnapped many years ago. They embraced in joy.

Scene 9: Lewis and Clark got their horses from the Shoshones! They all were able to continue their expedition westward, cross the Rocky Mountains, and reach the Pacific Ocean.

Scene 10: On their way back, Sacagawea and her husband were left off at their Mandan village.

Scene 11: Sacagawea lived to be almost 100 years old! She died in Wyoming on April 9, 1884. Her son, Pompey, also became a famous guide for European American explorers.

Begin your play in the space provided below:

Title: ____

Scene 1:
(character)

____________________ : ____

____

____

____________________ : ____

____

____

____________________ : ____

____

____

Name ______________________ *Date* ____________

3–5
YORK

One of the most accomplished African American men of the nineteenth century was York. He has an interesting life story that, in this exercise, you will turn into a short play. The text below summarizes parts of his life. Use your imagination and write a play with 10 short scenes that depict York's life.

Scene 1: York was born around 1780 to enslaved African American parents who lived on a Virginia plantation owned by the Clark family.

Scene 2: One of the Clark children, William, was the same age as York. The two boys became good friends, sharing many boyhood adventures as they were growing up.

Scene 3: When York and William were 19 years old, William inherited the Clark estate; this meant that, officially, York was owned by William.

Scene 4: When the two men were 23 years old, President Thomas Jefferson bought the Louisiana Purchase from France. Jefferson chose his secretary, Meriwether Lewis, to lead an exploration party to map the new land. Lewis chose his good friend, William Clark, to accompany him. And Clark decided to bring along York.

Scene 5: In 1804, the expedition trained for the trip in the city of St. Louis. York was an imposing 6 feet in height and 200 pounds in weight. He began to pick up many French and Native American words while training in St. Louis. His physical strength and his linguistic abilities proved to be invaluable on the trip.

Scene 6: The expedition set out, traveling north on the Mississippi River and then west on the Missouri River. York was an important member of the exploring party with his hunting, fishing, and scouting talents.

Scene 7: York and the Native American woman scout, Sacagawea, worked together to convince the many Native American tribes they met on the trip that the 43 men and 1 woman came in peace.

Scene 8: The Native Americans were fascinated with York's physical appearance; most of them had never met anyone of African descent. They would sometimes rub his dark skin with a wet finger to see if his color would come off. One Native American described York in the following manner: "Those who had been brave and fearless, the victorious ones in battle, painted themselves in charcoal." The black man, they thought, had been the bravest in the party.

Scene 9: By the end of the expedition in 1805, York and Sacagawea were asked to lend an equal voice to an important decision; they were asked to vote on where the winter camp should be located.

Scene 10: After the expedition arrived back home, William Clark freed York. Legend has it that York returned West and became the chief of a Native American tribe.

Begin your play in the space provided below:

Title: ______________________________

Scene 1:
(character)

____________ : ______________________________

____

____

____________ : ______________________________

____

____

____________ : ______________________________

____

____

Name ______________________________ Date ______________

3–6
SPELLING

Do you like spelling challenges? Did you know that spelling words "correctly" has been practiced in America only since the mid-nineteenth century? Before that time, people spelled words the way that seemed right to them. It was not until 1828, when Noah Webster wrote the American dictionary, that people worried about spelling words correctly! Look at the excerpt from the diary of Meriwether Lewis (he was President Thomas Jefferson's secretary!) when he was exploring the Louisiana Purchase with William Clark. He is describing the Great Falls of the Missouri River on June 13, 1805. Take a red pen or a pencil and correct this famous European American's spelling!

"I had proceded about two miles . . . whin my ears were saluted with the agreeable sound of a fall of water and advancing a little further I saw the spray arrise above the plain like a collumn of smoke. . . . I hurryed down the hill which was about 200 feet high and difficult of acces, to gaze upon this sublimely grand specticle . . . the hight of the [right-hand] fall is the same of the other but the irregular and somewhat projecting rocks below receives the water in it's passage down and brakes it into a perfect white foam which assumes a thousand forms in a moment sometimes flying up in jets of sparkling foam to the hight of fifteen or twenty feet and are scarcely formed before large roling bodies of the same beaten and foaming water is thrown over and conceals them."

Name ______________________________ *Date* ____________

3–7
REWRITE HISTORY

A famous Native American of the nineteenth century, Tecumseh, worked very hard and came close to accomplishing his lifetime goal—uniting the Native American tribes east of the Mississippi River to keep the European Americans and African Americans from pushing westward. What if he had been successful? How would the history books read today? Read the beginning of Tecumseh's life story below.

Tecumseh was born in 1768. His parents were Native Americans of the Shawnee tribe—a tribe that lived in what we now call Ohio. His father named him Tecumseh, which means "Panther Passing Across," in honor of a shooting star that passed overhead on the night he was born. He was an agile boy, able to run, shoot arrows, and think better than the other boys in his village. When he turned 11 years old, a European American boy was adopted into his tribe; this boy taught Tecumseh how to speak, read, and write English.

As he grew older, Tecumseh learned to love many things such as the land, the animals, and the people in his village. He also learned to hate some things, especially the European Americans who were killing his people and taking his land. He did not believe the European American treaties, which promised that, if only the Native Americans would move a bit further westward, they would be left alone. He began to travel to the villages of many Native American tribes—the Winnebagos, the Ottawas, the Delawares, the Kickapoos (to mention only a few), attempting to build a league of Native American nations.

Tecumseh used the image of a braid to try to get the Native American tribes to unite. He said that a single strand of hair is easily broken, but a thick braid of hair is impossible to tear. He was a forceful speaker and many Native Americans agreed with him. He attracted many followers and persuaded many tribes to join his cause. . . .

Tecumseh was not successful. In fact, due to disease, war, and starvation, the Native American population decreased from 600,000 to 250,000 during the nineteenth century and Native Americans were pushed onto smaller and smaller pieces of land. What if Tecumseh *had* been successful? How would history books read today if he had achieved his goal? Use your imagination and, in the space provided below, *rewrite history*! Imagine you are the writer of Tecumseh's story, and write an alternative ending—what *could* have happened if Tecumseh had been successful.

____

____

____

(Continue on the back.)

Name ______________________ Date __________

3–8

TRAIL OF TEARS

One of the most tragic results of European American expansion into the Americas was the impact it had on the Native American population. At the beginning of the nineteenth century, the Native American population was estimated to have been 600,000 people. By the end of the nineteenth century, the population had declined to approximately 250,000. In the space provided below, hypothesize why this occurred.

Evidence that **supports** *this hypothesis:*	***The Native American population decreased during the nineteenth century because:***	*Evidence that* **refutes** *this hypothesis:*
	Hypothesis 1: ______	
	Hypothesis 2: ______	
	Hypothesis 3: ______	
	Hypothesis 4: ______	

3-8 (continued)

On the following pages you will find facts about Native Americans who lived during the nineteenth century. These facts will help you determine if your hypotheses are correct or incorrect. Read each fact and decide if it *supports* or *refutes* each hypothesis. Write the number (1, 2, 3) under the SUPPORT and REFUTE columns next to your hypothesis. You can do additional research in your local or school library to explore your hypotheses.

FACT 1:

The U.S.A. in 1800 **The U.S.A. in 1900**

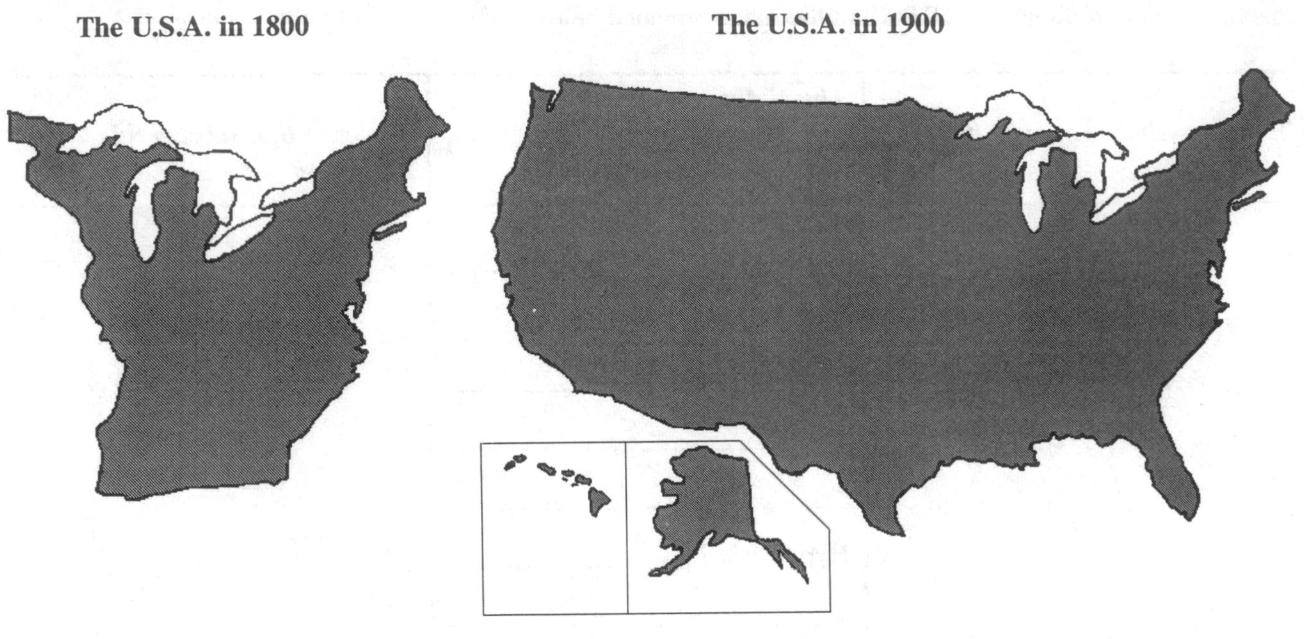

FACT 2: North American Buffalo Population History[(1)]

Date	**Population**
Aboriginal Times	60,000,000
1800	40,000,000
1850	20,000,000
1865	15,000,000
1870	14,000,000
1875	1,000,000
1880	395,000
1885	20,000
1889	1,091
1895	less than 1,000
1902	1,940
1983	50,000

FACT 3: The following trails were established by pioneering European Americans and African Americans during the nineteenth century: the Santa Fe Trail from Missouri to present-day New Mexico; the Oregon Trail from Missouri to present-day Oregon; the Mormon Trail from Iowa to Utah Territory; the Smokey Hill Trail from Arkansas to present-day Colorado; and the Boseman Trail from Nebraska Territory to Montana Territory.

FACT 4: The Indian Removal Act of 1830 made it legal for the President to remove Native Americans living east of the Mississippi River to designated areas west of the Mississippi River.

FACT 5: "The slaughter along the stream bed was terrible. . . . One poor woman, heavy with child, fell behind the others racing up the stream bed. Soldiers killed her too. Then one of them cut her open, and pulling out her unborn baby, he threw the little one down on the earth beside her. . . ."[2]

Peter Powell, witness of the 1864 Colorado Massacre of the Southern Cheyenne

FACT 6:

"Buffalo Bill, Buffalo Bill
Never missed and never will.
Always aims and shoots to kill
And the company pays his buffalo bill."

(NINETEENTH CENTURY SONG ABOUT BUFFALO HUNTER
WILLIAM F. CODY NICKNAMED "BUFFALO BILL")

FACT 7:

MORTALITY OF NINETEENTH CENTURY EPIDEMICS AMONG THE OMAHA INDIANS[3]

Date	*Epidemic*	*Mortality*
1801–1802	Smallpox	75% (over 1500)
1837	Smallpox	Over 300
1849	Cholera	Over 500
1874	Measles	76
1888	Measles	87
1889	Measles	50

FACT 8: In the 1830s, thousands of Cherokee Native American Indians were removed from their Southeast homelands (Georgia, North Carolina, Tennessee, Alabama) to west of the Mississippi River. During this removal, approximately 8,000 Cherokees died. They named this removal "Nunna daul Tsunyi" or "the trail where we cried." It is now known as "The Trail of Tears."

FACT 9: Before the expansion of Europeans into North America, there were many herds of buffalo. By the mid-nineteenth century, there were only two herds left. The southern herd was destroyed between 1870 and 1874; the northern herd between 1876 and 1883. The slaughter occurred because the economic value of the hides to Americans was high and because the animals were in the way of the rapidly westward-expanding American population.

FACT 10: There were an estimated 27 nineteenth century epidemics of Old World pathogens among North Americans: 13 of smallpox, 5 of measles, 3 of cholera, 2 of influenza, 1 each of diphtheria (in Canada), scarlet fever (in Canada), tularemia, and malaria. This total was more than had occurred during any of the three previous centuries. Other diseases, such as syphilis and tuberculosis, also devastated Native Americans during this century.

FACT 11: "I have fought through the Civil War and I have seen men shot to pieces and slaughtered by the thousands, but the Cherokee removal was the cruelest work I ever knew."[4]

CIVIL WAR VETERAN

FACT 12: The Sioux Reservations 1868–1889

FACT 13: The Native Americans relied on the buffalo for the following: a food source, clothing, housing, blankets and bedding, spoons, shoes, knives and tools, bowls, saddles, musical instruments, cosmetics, jewelry and charms, armor, masks, shields, and sleds. Buffalo dung was also used for fuel.

FACT 14: "Fully three miles from the scene of the massacre, we found the body of a woman completely covered with snow, and from this point on, we found them scattered along as they had been relentlessly hunted down and slaughtered while fleeing for their lives. . . . When we reached the spot where the Indian camp had stood, among the fragments of burned tents and other belongings we saw the frozen bodies lying close together or piled one upon another."[5]

EXCERPT FROM THE AUTOBIOGRAPHY
OF DR. CHARLES A. EASTMAN,
A SANTEE SIOUX PHYSICIAN

3-8 (continued)

Now that you have read the facts and decided if they *support* or *refute* your original hypotheses, can you think of some new hypotheses? Perhaps you learned something from the above information that you did not know beforehand. Write your new hypotheses below.

Evidence that **supports** *my hypothesis:*	***The Native American population decreased during the nineteenth century because:***	*Evidence that* **refutes** *my hypothesis:*
	Hypothesis 5: ______ ______ ______ ______ ______ ______ ______ ______ ______	
	Hypothesis 6: ______ ______ ______ ______ ______ ______ ______ ______ ______	

Name ______________________________ Date ____________

3–9
WORKING CONDITIONS

As a result of the industrial revolution, an increasing number of Americans began working in factories and mines in the mid-nineteenth century rather than on farms. Working conditions were far from ideal for these first industrial workers. American workers found it necessary to strike (refuse to work) to improve these conditions. In the space provided below, hypothesize as to why American workers went on strike.

Evidence that **supports** *this hypothesis:*	*American industrial workers went on strike during the nineteenth and twentieth centuries because:*	*Evidence that* **refutes** *this hypothesis:*
	Hypothesis 1: ______________ ______________ ______________ ______________ ______________	
	Hypothesis 2: ______________ ______________ ______________ ______________ ______________	
	Hypothesis 3: ______________ ______________ ______________ ______________ ______________	
	Hypothesis 4: ______________ ______________ ______________ ______________ ______________	

On the following pages you will find facts about the working conditions of nineteenth-century and early twentieth-century American factory and mine workers. Determine if your hypotheses are correct or incorrect. Read each fact and decide if it *supports* or *refutes* your hypotheses. Write the number (1, 2 ,3) under the SUPPORT and REFUTE columns next to your hypothesis. You can do additional research in your local or school library to explore your hypotheses.

FACT 1: " . . . The first petitioner who testified was Eliza R. Hemingway. She had worked 2 years and 9 months in the Lowell factories. Her employment is weaving—works by the piece. . . . She complained of the hours for labor being too many, and the time for meals too limited. In the summer season, the work is commenced at 5 o'clock A.M. and continued until 7 o'clock P.M. with half hour for breakfast and three quarters hour for dinner. . . ."(1)

MASSACHUSETTS HOUSE OF REPRESENTATIVES HEARINGS ON INDUSTRIAL CONDITIONS, 1845

FACT 2:

MY BOY

I have a little boy at home,
A pretty little son;
I think sometimes the world is mine
In him my only one . . . .

'Ere dawn my labor drives me forth
Tis night when I am free;
A stranger am I to my child;
And stranger my child to me. . . .
Morris Rosenfield, nineteenth century pants presser

FACT 3: One out of every six children (1,118,000 total) under 16 years of age in the United States were at work in factories and mines in 1880.

FACT 4: "What a glorious privilege we enjoy in this boasted republican land. Here I am a healthy New England girl, quite well behaved, bestowing just half of all my hours, including Sundays, upon a company for less than two cents an hour"(2)

FACTORY GIRL

FACT 5: "It is a subject of comment and general complaint among the operatives [factory workers] that while they tend three or four looms, where they used to tend but two, making nearly twice the number of yards of cloth, the pay is not increased to them, while the increase to the owners is great."(3)

FACTORY OWNER

FACT 6: "Upon accepting a position in her factory an employee is compelled to purchase a sewing machine from the proprietess, who is an agent for the S.M. Co. This must be paid for in weekly payments of 50 cents, provided the operative makes $3. . . . At any time before the machine is paid for, through a reduction of the already meager wages, or the enforcement of some petty tyrannical rule—sickness, anger or any cause, the operative leave her employ, she forfeits the machine and all the money paid upon it, and to the next applicant the machine is resold."(4)

REPORT OF THE GENERAL INVESTIGATOR
PROCEEDINGS OF THE GENERAL ASSEMBLY OF THE KNIGHTS OF LABOR, 1888

FACT 7: "Sadie is an intelligent, neat, clean girl who has worked . . . in embroidery factories. . . . In her work she was accustomed to use a white powder (chalk or talcum was usual) which was brushed over the perforated designs and thus transferred to the cloth. The design was brushed off when made of chalk or talcum. . . .Her last employer therefore commenced using white lead powder, mixed with rosin, which cheapened the work as the powder could not be rubbed off and necessitate restamping. None of the girls knew of the change in powder, nor of the danger in its use. The workroom was crowded and hot, the stampers' tables were farthest from the windows and the constant use of the powder caused them to breathe it continually and their hands were always covered with it. Sadie had been a very strong, healthy girl, good appetite and color; she began to be unable to eat, had terrible colic, but continued to go to work in spite of the fact that she felt miserable. Her hands and feet swelled, she lost the use of one hand, her teeth and gums were blue. When she finally had to stop work, . . . her physician advised her to go to a hospital. The examination revealed the fact that she had lead poisoning. . . ."[(5)]

REPORT OF THE NY STATE FACTORY INVESTIGATING COMMITTEE

FACT 8: "Pregnant women worked at the machines until a few hours before their babies were born. Sometimes a baby came right there in the mill, between the looms."[(6)]

FACT 9: ". . . dangerously broken stairways . . . windows few and so dirty. . . . The wooden floors that were swept once a year. . . . Hardly any other light but the gas jets burning by day and by night . . . the filthy malodorous lavatory in the dark hall. No fresh drinking water...mice and roaches. . . . During the winter months . . . how we suffered from the cold. In the summer we suffered from the heat. . . ."

FACT 10:

Weinstock: If a worker loses his life, are his dependents compensated in any way?

Osgood: Not necessarily. In some cases they are and some cases they are not.

Weinstock: If he is crippled for life is there any compensation?

Osgood: No sir, there is none . . . .

Weinstock: Then the whole burden is thrown directly on their shoulders?

Osgood: Yes, sir.

Weinstock: The industry bears none of it?

Osgood: No, the industry bears none of it.[(7)]

CONVERSATION BETWEEN COMMISSIONER HARRIS WEINSTOCK
OF THE COMMISSION ON INDUSTRIAL RELATIONS
AND PRESIDENT JOHN OSGOOD, HEAD OF A COLORADO COAL CO.

FACT 11: "Condemned to slave daily in the washroom in wet shoes and wet clothes, surrounded with foul-mouthed, brutal foremen . . . the poor girls work in the vile smell of sour beer, lifting cases of empty and full bottles weighing from 100 to 150 pounds. . . . Rheumatism is one of the chronic ailments and is followed closely by consumption. . . .The foreman even regulates the time the girls may stay in the toilet room . . . ."

MOTHER JONES, LABOR ORGANIZER

Now, you have read the facts and decided if they *support* or *refute* your hypotheses. Can you think of some new hypotheses? Perhaps you learned something from the above information that you did not know beforehand. Write your new hypotheses below:

Evidence that **supports** *this hypothesis:*	***American industrial workers went on strike during the nineteenth and twentieth centuries because:***	*Evidence that* **refutes** *this hypothesis:*
	Hypothesis 5: ________ ________ ________ ________ ________ ________ ________ ________	
	Hypothesis 6: ________ ________ ________ ________ ________ ________ ________ ________	

Name ______________________________ Date ______________

3–10

MEN, WOMEN, AND MONEY

To begin this exercise, answer the following questions regarding men, women, and money.

1. In today's society, do women earn more money, less money, or money equal to that earned by men in the same profession?

____

2. How much, on the average, does a woman in today's society earn for every dollar a man earns?

____

Ask your teacher for the correct answers to these questions!

Now, let's look back at the nineteenth century. Study the statistics below that are excerpted from *Women in the American Economy—A Documentary History, 1675–1929*, by Mary M. and W. Elliot Brownlee.[1] These statistics give information regarding jobs held by both men and women during the 1800s.

OCCUPATION	*HOURS OF LABOR PER DAY*	*AVERAGE DAILY WAGES* *Men*	*Women*
Farm Laborers	10–14	$1.58	$1.00
Store Workers	7–12	2.00	1.25
Boots and Shoes	10	3.50	1.50
Button Makers	10	2.37	.92
Hatters	9–10	2.35	1.00
Hosiery Workers	10	1.83	1.00
Rubber and Elastic Goods	10	2.12	1.25
Straw Workers	10	2.50	1.25
Cotton Workers	11–12	1.67	1.05
Print Workers	10	1.50	.87
Corset Makers	10	2.50	1.17
Woolen Workers	11–12	1.57	1.04
Cigar Makers	10	3.00	1.25
Pottery Workers	10	2.50	.92
Glass Makers	10	2.00	.75
Bookbinders	10	3.00	1.00
Paper Makers	10	1.87	1.87
Paper-collar Makers	10	2.50	1.00
Brush Makers	10	1.87	1.00

OCCUPATION	HOURS OF LABOR PER DAY	AVERAGE DAILY WAGES Men	Women
Comb Makers	11	2.30	1.12
Felting Makers	11	2.00	.83
Jewelry Makers	10	2.50	1.25
Watchmakers	10	3.00	1.50
Pocketbook Makers	10	2.62	1.15
Flax	10	2.00	1.00
Whips	10	2.75	1.25
Chair Makers	10	2.25	.87
Upholsterers	10	3.00	1.17
Cutlery Makers	10	2.25	1.00
Bakers	10-12	2.00	1.00
Tailors and Tailoresses	10	3.50	1.25

Using information from the chart above, complete the following sentence:

3. During the nineteenth century, female bakers earned _________ for every dollar earned by a male baker.

(*Hint!* to get the answer you must do the following equation:

$$\frac{\text{The female baker's daily wages}}{\text{The male baker's average daily wages}} \quad \text{or} \quad \frac{\$1.00}{\$2.00} = \frac{x}{\$1.00}$$

Now, using the equation in the example above, complete the following chart:

OCCUPATION	IN THIS OCCUPATION, WOMEN MADE:	FOR EVERY DOLLAR MADE BY A MAN
Farm Laborers		$1
Store Workers		$1
Boots and Shoes		$1
Button Makers		$1
Hatters		$1
Hosiery Workers		$1
Rubber and Elastic Goods		$1
Straw Workers		$1
Cotton Workers		$1
Print Workers		$1

OCCUPATION	IN THIS OCCUPATION, WOMEN MADE:	FOR EVERY DOLLAR MADE BY A MAN
Corset Makers		$1
Woolen Makers		$1
Cigar Makers		$1
Pottery Workers		$1
Glass Makers		$1
Bookbinders		$1
Paper Makers		$1
Paper-collar Makers		$1
Brush Makers		$1
Comb Makers		$1
Felting Makers		$1
Jewelry Makers		$1
Watchmakers		$1
Pocketbook Makers		$1
Flax		$1
Whips		$1
Chair Makers		$1
Upholsterers		$1
Cutlery Makers		$1
Bakers		$1
Tailors and Tailoresses		$1

Compute the *average* amount a nineteenth-century woman would earn for every dollar earned by a man. Add all the figures you have in the first column of your chart above. Then take this total and divide it by 31 (the number of occupations listed above). Write your answer below.

4. On the average, a nineteenth-century woman earned ________________ for every $1 earned by a man.

Hypothesize as to why men and women did not earn the same wages during the nineteenth century. Write your hypotheses in the space provided below.

During the nineteenth century, men and women did not earn the same wages for the same kind of occupation because:

HYPOTHESIS 1: ____

____

HYPOTHESIS 2: ____

____

3-10 (continued)

HYPOTHESIS 3: ____

____

Compare the nineteenth century with today. Compare the answer to question 4 of this exercise with that to question 2. Is there much difference between the two time periods? Do you think there has been sufficient change or not enough change? In the space provided below, write your answers to these two questions. What arguments would you use to back up your opinion?

____

____

____

____

____

____

____

____

____

____

____

____

____

____

____

(Continue on the back.)

EXTRA CREDIT: Using the information you have generated above, create a visual project on a large poster board! Choose at least five nineteenth-century occupations and make a visual representation (e.g., a drawing of a shoe or a book). Educate your audience on the differences between what a man and woman would make doing the *same* occupation. Do some research in your school and local library on the differences between what men and women would make doing the same occupation today (store manager, hospital administrator, etc.). Include this information in your project too! Be sure to give it an eye-catching title such as "Enough Change?" or "Are Men and Women Equal?–The Nineteenth Century and Today."

Name ______________________________ Date ____________

3–11

FIGHT, AND IF YOU CAN'T FIGHT, KICK

Though enslaved African Americans were severely restricted, it would be incorrect to assume they gave up all control of their lives to their masters. Often they used tenacity, creativity, and courage to carve out spheres of influence. The following is an excerpt from an oral history of a formerly enslaved African American. She describes her mother, who, though enslaved, used her strength to impose her will on her master.

"My mother was the smartest black woman in Eden. She was quick as a flash of lightning, and whatever she did could not be done better. She could do anything. She cooked, washed, ironed, spun, nursed and labored in the field. She made as good a field hand as she did a cook.

The one doctrine of my mother's teaching which was branded upon my senses was that I should never let anyone abuse me. 'I'll kill you, gal, if you don't stand up for yourself,' she would say, 'Fight, and if you can't fight, kick; if you can't kick, bite.' Ma was generally willing to work, but if she didn't feel like doing something, none could make her do it. At least, the Jennings couldn't make her or didn't make her.

One day my mother's temper ran wild. For some reason Mistress Jennings struck her with a stick. Ma struck back and a fight followed. Mr. Jennings was not at home and the children became frightened and ran upstairs. For half hour they wrestled in the kitchen. Mistress, seeing she could not get the better of ma, ran out in the road, with ma right on her heels. In the road, ma flew into her again. The thought seemed to run across my mother's mind to tear the clothes off her body. She suddenly began to tear Mistress Jennings' clothes off. She caught hold, ripped, pulled and tore. Poor mistress was nearly naked when the storekeeper got to them and pulled ma off.

Pa heard Jennings say that Fannie would have to be whipped by law. He told ma. Two mornings afterward, two men came to the big gate, one with a long lash in his hand. I was in the yard and I hoped that they couldn't find ma. To my surprise, I saw her running around the house, straight in the direction of the men. She must have seen them coming. I should have known that she wouldn't hide. She knew what they were coming for and she intended to meet them half-way. She swooped upon them like a hawk on chickens. I believe they were afraid of her or thought she was crazy. One man had a long beard which she grabbed with one hand, and the lash with the other. Her body was made strong with madness. She was a good match for them. Mr. Jennings came and pulled her away. I don't know what would have happened if he hadn't come at that moment, for one man had already pulled his gun out. Ma did not see the gun until Mr. Jennings came up. On catching sight of it, she said, 'Use your gun, use it and blow my brains out if you will' . . . .

That evening Mistress Jennings came down to the cabin.

'Well Fannie,' she said, 'I'll have to send you away. You won't be whipped and I'm afraid you'll be killed. . . .'

'I'll go . . . anywhere else, but I won't be whipped,' ma answered.

'You can't take the baby, Fannie, Aunt Mary can keep it with the other children.'

Thus my mother and father were hired out to Tennessee. The next morning they were to leave. I saw ma working around with the baby under her arms as if it had been a bundle of some kind.

'Fannie, leave the baby with Aunt Mary,' said Mr. Jennings very quietly.

At this, ma took the baby by its feet, a foot in each hand, and, with the baby's head swinging downward, she vowed to smash its brains out before she'd leave it. Tears were streaming down her face. It was seldom that Ma cried, and everyone knew that she meant every word. Ma took her baby with her. . . ."[1]

3-11 (continued)

DIRECTIONS: Now that you have read this oral history, think about what aspects of Fannie's life she controlled and what aspects she did not control. Then, look at the circle entitled "Fannie's Life," which is divided into ten parts. With a red crayon, marker, or pen, shade in the percentage of the circle (10%? 40%? 60%?) that best represents, in your mind, the percentage of Fannie's life that *Fannie* controlled. Then, with a blue crayon, marker, or pen, shade in the percentage of the circle (20%? 50%? 70%?) that best represents, in your mind, the fraction of Fannie's life that the *Jennings* controlled. In the space provided below the circle, write a justification for how you shaded your circle.

FANNIE'S LIFE

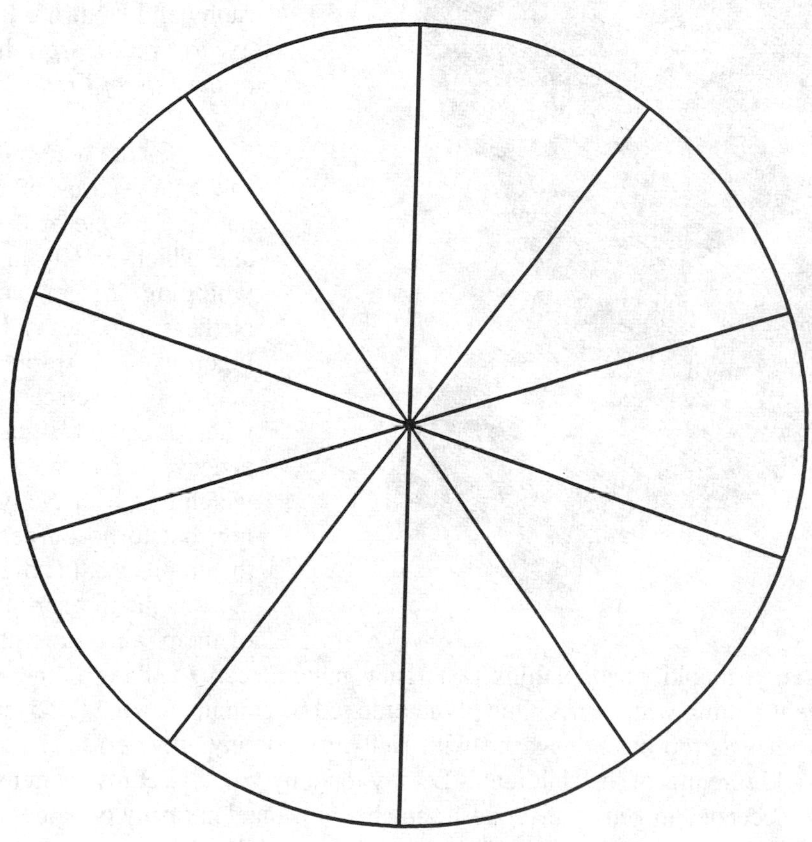

I think Fannie had control over _________ percent of her life and the Jennings had control over _________ percent of her life because:

____

____

____

____

(Continue on the back.)

Name ______________________________ Date ____________

3–12

FREDERICK DOUGLASS

One of the most eloquent nineteenth-century writers and speakers was an African American named Frederick Douglass. He was an influential abolitionist who had escaped from slavery but continued to expose the horrors of this institution by writing his autobiography and lecturing frequently. Read the excerpt below from his book, *Narrative of the Life of Frederick Douglass*.

". . . after the whipping of Aunt Esther, I saw many cases of the same shocking nature. . . . One of the first which I saw, and which greatly agitated me, was the whipping of a woman . . . named Nelly. . . . She was a bright mulatto . . . a vigorous and spirited woman. . . . Mr. Sevier, the overseer, had hold of Nelly, when I caught sight of them; he was endeavoring to drag her toward a tree, which endeavor Nelly was sternly resisting; but to no purpose, except to retard the progress of the overseer's plans. Nelly . . . was the mother of five children; three of them were present, and though quite small (from seven to ten years old, I should think,). . . . They gallantly came to their mother's defense, and gave the overseer an excellent pelting with stones. One of the little fellows ran up, seizing the overseer by the leg and bit him; but the monster was too busily engaged with Nelly, to pay any attention to the assaults of the children. . . . Amidst the wild screams of the children—'Let my mammy go!'—'Let my mammy go!' . . . he finally overpowered her, and succeeded in getting his rope around her arms, and in firmly tying her to the tree, at which he had been aiming. This done, and Nelly was at the mercy of his merciless lash; and now, what followed, I have no heart to describe. The cowardly creature made good his every threat; and wielded the lash with all the hot zest of furious revenge. The cries of the woman, while undergoing the terrible infliction, were mingled with those of the children, sounds of which I hope the reader may never be called upon to hear. When Nelly was untied, her back was covered with blood. The red stripes were all over her shoulders. She was whipped—severely whipped; but she was not subdued, for she continued to denounce the overseer, and to call him every vile name. He had bruised her flesh, but had left her invincible spirit undaunted. Such floggings are seldom repeated by the same overseer. They prefer to whip those who are most easily whipped. The old doctrine that submission is the best cure for outrage and wrong, does not hold good on the slave plantation. He is whipped oftenest, who is whipped easiest; and the slave who has the courage to stand up for himself against the overseer, although he may have many hard stripes at first, becomes in the end a freeman, even though he sustain the formal relation of a slave."[1]

DIRECTIONS: Write your reactions to this passage and other thoughts or feelings you may have about slavery inside the letters on the next page, which spell SLAVERY. You can use full sentences, phrases, or just single words to express yourself!

3-12 (continued)

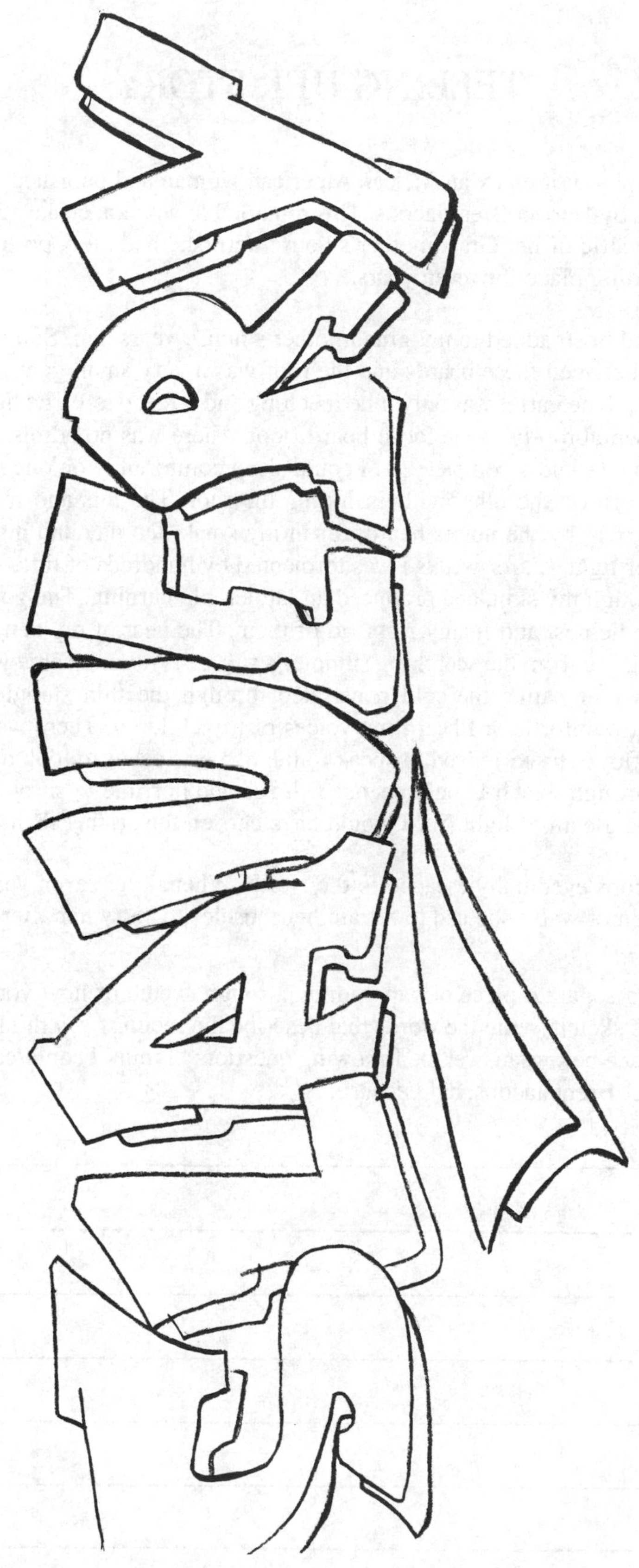

Name ______________________________ Date ______________

3–13

TELLING HER STORY

The first autobiography written by an African American woman and pubished in the U.S. was *Incidents in the Life of a Slave Girl*, by Harriet Brent Jacobs. This remarkable woman, enslaved in North Carolina, spent seven years hiding in the attic of her Grandmother's house until she had an opportunity to escape. Read the excerpt describing her hiding place for seven years.

"A small shed had been added to my grandmother's house years ago. Some boards were laid across the joists at the top, and between these boards and the roof was a very small garret, never occupied by anything but rats and mice. . . . The garret was only nine feet long and 7 feet deep. The highest part was only three feet high, and sloped down abruptly to the loose board floor. There was no admission for either light or air . . . the air was stifling; the darkness complete . . . I could sleep comfortably on one side; but the slope was so sudden that I could not turn on the other without hitting the roof. The rats and mice ran over my bed. . . . Morning came I knew it only by the noises heard; for in my small den day and night were the same. I suffered for air more than for light . . . for weeks I was tormented by hundreds of little red insects, fine as a needle point that pierced through my skin, and produced an intolerable burning. The good grandmother gave me herb teas and cooling medicines, and finally I got rid of them. The heat of my den was intense, for nothing but thin shingles protected me from the scorching summer's sun. . . . Autumn came with a pleasant abatement of heat. . . . But when winter came, the cold penetrated through the thin shingle roof, I was dreadfully chilled. . . . But I was not comfortless. I heard the voices of my children. There was joy and sadness in the sound. It made my tears flow. How I longed to speak to them! I was eager to look upon their faces; but there was no hole, no crack, through which I could peep. . . . It seemed horrible to sit or lie in a cramped position day after day, without one gleam of light. Yet I would have chosen this, rather than my lot as a slave. . . ."[1]

Harriet Brent Jacobs eventually escaped to the North. When, after seven years, she came down from the garret, her legs would not walk; she had to retrain her muscles to carry her after seven years of inaction.

DIRECTIONS: On a separate piece of paper, draw a rough sketch of how you imagine Jacob's hiding place looked. Around this sketch, write the words that describe the feelings *you* think Jacobs had while living in hiding. Then, in the space below, answer the following question: "I think I could/could not (circle one) have endured hiding, as Harriet Brent Jacobs, did because:

____

____

____

____

____

____

____

(Continue on the back.)

Name ______________________ Date ____________

3–14

A WOMAN'S FATE

Nearly all historians agree that the institution of slavery was a degrading and harsh experience for both enslaved African American men and women. However, some historians, also argue that the institution of slavery was particularly harsh for enslaved African American women. In the space provided below, hypothesize as to why these historians have come to this conclusion.

Evidence that **supports** *this hypothesis:*	***The institution of slavery was especially hard for African American women because:***	*Evidence that* **refutes** *this hypothesis:*
	Hypothesis 1: ____________ ____________ ____________ ____________ ____________	
	Hypothesis 2: ____________ ____________ ____________ ____________ ____________	
	Hypothesis 3: ____________ ____________ ____________ ____________ ____________	

A WOMAN'S FATE: "WOMAN WHIPPING FEMALE SLAVE" (1834) (LIBRARY OF CONGRESS, #LC-US262-80825).

Below you will find facts about enslaved African American women. These facts will help you determine if your hypotheses are correct or incorrect. Read each fact and decide if it *supports* or *refutes* your hypotheses. Write the number (1, 2 ,3) under the SUPPORT and REFUTE columns next to your hypothesis. You can do additional research in your local or school library to explore your hypotheses.

FACT 1: "Women are generally shown some little indulgence for three or four weeks previous to childbirth; they are at such times not often punished if they do not finish the task assigned to them. . . . They are generally allowed four weeks after the birth of a child, before they are compelled to go into the field. They then take the child with them, attended sometimes by a little girl or boy, from the age four to six, to take care of it while the mother is at work. When there is no child that can be spared, or not young enough for this service, the mother, after nursing it, lays it under a tree, or by the side of a fence, and goes to her task, returning at stated intervals to nurse it."[(1)]

FACT 2: "My brothers and sisters were bid off first, and one by one, while my mother, paralyzed with grief, held me by the hand. Her turn came and she was bought by Issac Riley of Montgomery County. Then I was offered . . . my mother, half distracted with the thought of parting forever from all of her children, pushed through the crowd while the bidding for me was going on, to the spot where Riley was standing. She fell at his feet and clung to his knees, entreating him in tones that a mother could only command, to buy her baby as well as herself, and to spare her one, at least one, of her little ones. . . . This man disengaged himself from her with . . . violent blows and kicks. . . . I must have been then between five and six years old."[2]

FACT 3: "I saw slaves sold. I can see the block now. My cousin Eliza was a pretty girl, really good looking. Her master was her father. When the girls in the big house had beaus coming to see them, they'd ask, 'Who is that pretty gal?' So they decided to get rid of her right away. The day they sold her will always be remembered. . . . The man who bought Eliza was from New York. The Negroes had made up 'nough money to buy her off themselves, but they wouldn't let that happen. There was a man bidding for her who was a big Swedelander. He always bid for the good-looking gals and bought 'em for his own use. He asked the man from New York, 'What you gonna do with her when you get her?' The man from New York said, 'None of your . . . business, but you ain't got money enough to buy her.' When the man from New York had done bought her, he said, 'Eliza, you are free from now on.'"[3]

FACT 4: "As I went out in the morning, I observed several women, who carried their young children in their arms to the fields. . . . One woman did not, like the others, leave her child at the end of the row, but had contrived a sort of crude knapsack, made of a piece of coarse linen cloth, in which she fastened her child, which was very young, upon her back; and in this way carried it all day, and performed her task at the hoe with the other people."[4]

FACT 5: "Fanny has had six children; all dead but one. . . . Leah has had six children; three are dead. Sophy . . . came to beg for some old linen. She is suffering fearfully; she has had ten children; five of them are dead. Sally . . . has had two miscarriages and three children born, one of whom is dead. She came complaining of incessant pain and weakness in her back. Sarah. . . . She had had four miscarriages, had brought seven children into the world, five of whom are dead, and was again with child. She complained of dreadful pains in the back, and an internal tumor which swells with the exertion of working in the fields; probably, I think, she is ruptured. . . . There was hardly one of these women . . . who might not have been a candidate for a bed in the hospital, and they come to me after working all day in the fields. . . ."[5]

FACT 6: "Patsey was slim and straight. . . . There was an air of loftiness in her movement, that neither labor, nor weariness, nor punishment could destroy. . . . She was a skillful teamster. She turned as true a farrow as the best, and at splitting rails, there was none that could excel her. . . . Such lightning-like motion was in her fingers . . . that in cotton picking time, Patsey was queen of the field. . . . Naturally she was a rejoicing creature, a laughing lighthearted girl, rejoicing in the mere sense of existence. Yet Patsey wept oftener, and suffered more, than any of her companions. . . . Her back bore the scars of a thousand stripes . . . because it had fallen her lot to be the slave of a licentious master and a jealous mistress. . . . In the great house, for days together, there were high and angry words . . . whereof she was the angry cause. Nothing delighted the mistress so much as to see her suffer. . . . Patsey walked under a cloud. If she uttered a word in opposition to her master's will, the lash was resorted to at once, to bring her to subjection; if she was not watchful while about her cabin, or when walking in the yard, a billet of wood, or a broken bottle perhaps, hurled from her mistress' hand, would smite her unexpectedly in the face. . . . To be rid of Patsey-to place her beyond sight or reach, by sale or death, or in any other manner—of late years, seemed to be the ruling thought and passion of my mistress."[6]

FACT 7: "Blackshear had them take their babies with them to the field and it was two or three miles from the house to the field. He didn't want them to lose time walking backward and forward nursing. They built a long trough like a great long old cradle and put those babies in it every morning when the mother come out to the field. It was set at the end of the rows under a big cottonwood tree. When they were at the other end of a row all at once a cloud no bigger than a small spot came up and it grew fast, and it thundered and lightened as if the world were coming to an end, and the rain just came down in great sheets. And when it got so they could go to the other end of the field, the trough was filled with water and every baby in it was floating around in the water, drowned."[7]

You have read the facts and decided if they *support* or *refute* your original hypotheses. Can you think of some new hypotheses? Perhaps you learned something from the above information that you did not know beforehand. Write your new hypotheses below.

Evidence that **supports** *this hypothesis:*	*The institution of slavery was especially hard for African American women because:*	*Evidence that* **refutes** *this hypothesis:*
	Hypothesis 4: ________________ ________________ ________________ ________________ ________________ ________________ ________________ ________________ ________________	
	Hypothesis 5: ________________ ________________ ________________ ________________ ________________ ________________ ________________ ________________ ________________	

Name ______________________________ Date ______________

3–15

ABOLITIONISTS WORKING TOGETHER

During the nineteenth century, many free African American women and European American women were part of the abolitionist movement; they wrote articles, gave speeches (at a time when most people viewed these activities as "radical" for women!), hid African Americans on the Underground Railroad, and raised money for African American schools and communities. Three female abolitionist organizations (in Salem, Boston, and Philadelphia, were biracial; European American and African American women worked together on the abolition movement projects. The rest of the abolitionist organizations were not biracial. Many African American women worked hard to change the attitude of European American women who, though sympathetic and involved in the abolitionist movement, would not accept fellow membership with African American women. The following are two excerpts: One is from a poem written by African American abolitionist Sarah Forten and the other is from a speech given by African American abolitionist Sojourner Truth. In the space provided below these excerpts, explain in your own words what these two women are saying to European American abolitionist women.

POEM BY SARAH FORTEN

We are thy sisters, God has truly said,
That of one blood the nations he has made
O, Christian woman! in a Christian land!
Canst thou unblushingly read this great command?
Suffer the wrongs which wring our inmost heart,
To draw one throb of pity on thy part!
Our skins may differ, but from thee we claim
A sister's privilege and a sister's name.

Sarah Forten is saying ______________________________

____

____

SPEECH BY SOJOURNER TRUTH

"Nobody ever helps me into carriages, or over mud puddles, or gives me any best place! And, ain't I a woman? Look at me! I have ploughed, planted and gathered into barnes, and no man could head me! And ain't I a woman? I could work as much and eat as much as a man—when I could get it—and bear the lash as well! And ain't I a woman? I have born thirteen children and seen most all sold into slavery. And when I cried out with my mother's grief, none but Jesus heard me! And ain't I a woman?"

Sojourner Truth is saying ______________________________

____

____

3-15 (continued)

DIRECTIONS: Read the descriptions of five women who played leadership roles in the abolitionist movement. As you read, think about how they would argue their opinions about the issue of biracial membership in abolitionist organizations.

SARAH FORTEN was the daughter of one of the wealthiest African American men in nineteenth-century America—James Forten who made his fortune as a sailmaker. She attended private school, where she studied art, music, French, and German as well as other academic subjects. Her parents' home was always a center of activity for the abolitionist movement. She and her sisters and mother were founding members of the biracial Philadelphia Female Anti-Slavery Society, founded in 1833.

SOJOURNER TRUTH, born Isabella Baumfree, was an enslaved African American woman who obtained her freedom in 1827 at the age of 30. Truth moved to New York City, where she worked as a domestic servant until 1843 when, with the help of European American abolitionists, she went on the abolitionist "lecture circuit" to educate Americans about the evils of slavery.

MARY SHADD was the daughter of a wealthy African American shoemaker of Delaware. Her entire family was involved in the abolitionist movement. Mary emigrated to Canada in 1851 when she was 28 years old. Especially after passage of the Fugitive Slave Act of 1850, she believed that it was nearly impossible to change racist American society attitudes and felt that African Americans should emigrate to Canada. Furthermore, she felt the abolitionist movement was dominated by European Americans, exhibited racist attitudes, and relied primarily on unsuccessful tactics.

LUCY STONE was the daughter of a poor European American farmer. Working as a housekeeper, laundress, and teacher, she earned her tuition and attended Oberlin College, the first American college to admit women and African Americans. She became a member and speaker for the Anti-Slavery Society of Massachusetts, an organization that was not biracial.

LUCRETIA MOTT, a European American woman, was one of the initiators of the first Women's Rights Conference of 1848. She was also a leader in the Philadelphia Female Anti-Slavery Society, a biracial organization.

Imagine that these five women had come together for a special meeting to discuss the issue of biracial membership in the abolitionist movement. Write a short, one-act play depicting the dialogue that occurred among these five women during this meeting. Below is a possible beginning for your play! Add to it—expressing the opinion of each of the above mentioned women!

SARAH FORTEN: Ladies, we have gathered here this evening to discuss a very delicate and controversial question of the abolitionist movement: Should European American and African American women belong to the same organizations? You know my opinion on this issue. I would like to hear some of your opinons.

____

____

____

____

(Continue on separate sheet of paper.)

Name ______________________________ Date ______________

3–16
SUSAN B. ANTHONY GOES TO JAIL

When you are 18 years old, do you plan to register to vote and participate in local, state, and federal elections? Why or why not? Write your answer to these questions in the space provided below.

____

____

____

Would you be willing to be arrested and go to jail to be able to vote in local, state, and federal elections? Why or why not? Write your answer to these questions in the space provided below.

____

____

____

A very famous European American woman, Susan B. Anthony, was willing to go to jail for the right to vote. Read the passage below, which gives you a bit of information about the *suffrage movement* or "the right to vote" movement during the nineteenth century:

> When the United States was first formed, only European American men and free African American men, both of whom owned significant amounts of property, could vote. Native Americans, enslaved African Americans, and women were not allowed to vote. All of these groups fought long and hard to have *suffrage* or the right to vote. African American males won the right to vote after the Civil War. Native Americans won the right to vote in 1924. Women won the right to vote in 1920. Susan B. Anthony was a woman who dedicated her life to the suffrage movement. She was willing to risk even going to jail for this cause. Read below what she did on November 1, 1872.
>
> November 1, 1872—Susan B. Anthony and 15 other women walked into their local barber shop in Rochester, New York. The barbershop was the location for male voter registation. The 16 women

demanded of the three men who were registering voters there, that they be allowed to register to vote. The men argued a bit with them but eventually were convinced that they should register the 16 women to vote. The next day the newspapers were aflame with the news that Susan B. Anthony and her friends had been registered. The women were called "lawbreakers."

November 5, 1872—The 16 women were at the polls at 7 A.M. to vote. The newspapers all over the country had headlines regarding the news.

November 28, 1872 (Thanksgiving Day)—A tall deputy marshall knocked on the door of Susan B. Anthony's house. He said, "I have a warrant for your arrest. You have broken an act of Congress." He led her to jail in handcuffs.

November 29, 1872—The government decided to prosecute Susan B. Anthony alone; she would represent the other 15 women. The three men were also to be brought to trial. The trial dates were set for June of 1873. During the six months before the trial, Susan B. Anthony went on the lecture circuit in the area where she lived to convince people that what she did was right. She said "We the people" does not mean "We the male citizens." She referred to the "unalienable rights" that belonged to *every* U.S. citizen, not just male citizens.

June 17, 1873—When the trial date arrived, Judge Ward Hunt would not allow Susan B. Anthony to speak for herself. He judged her "incompetent." At the end of the trial, Judge Hunt turned to the jurors and said, "Under the 15th Amendment, . . . Miss Anthony was not protected in the right to vote . . . . therefore I direct you that you find a verdict of guilty." The jurors said nothing. Judge Hunt then said "Gentlemen of the jury, I dismiss you." Judge Hunt then ruled that Susan B. Anthony was guilty, fined her and sentenced her to jail.

Imagine you are a reporter who is following Susan B. Anthony's story. Write headlines for each of the five dates mentioned above. Then choose one date and write a short editorial that describes your opinion of what Susan B. Anthony did or what happened to her on that date.

Headline 1:

Headline 2:

Headline 3:

Headline 4:

Headline 5:

Name ______________________________ Date ____________

3–17

DO YOU AGREE?

American women began to assert themselves more forcefully during the nineteenth century. Many participated in the suffrage movement, the abolitionist movement, and the temperance movement. More and more women began to take on occupations that were previously closed to women, such as factory work, teaching, and nursing. Below is a letter to the editor of the nineteenth-century magazine *American Medical Times.* It is written by a man concerning the issue of female nurses. While you read the letter, think about whether you *agree* or *disagree* with this man's opinion.

July 18, 1861

Dear Editor,

Our women appear to have become almost wild on the subject of hospital nursing. We honor them for their sympathy and humanity. Nevertheless, a man who has had experience with women nurses among male surgical cases, cannot shut his eyes to the fact that they, with the best intentions in the world, are frequently a useless annoyance. Cases are continually occurring in male surgical wards of such a character as require strong arms, and attentions which any reasonable medical man is loath to extract from female nurses. Imagine a delicate, refined woman assisting a rough soldier to the close-stool, or supplying him with a bedpan, or adjusting the knots on a T-bandage employed in retaining a catheter in position, or a dozen offices of a like character which one would hesitate long before asking a female nurse to perform, but which are frequently and continually necessary in a medical hospital. Besides this, women, as a rule, have not the physical strength necessary. . . .

Women, in our humble opinion, are utterly and decidedly unfit for such service. They can be used, however, as the regular administrators of the prescribed medicines, and in delicate soothing attentions which are always so grateful to the sick, and which at the same time none know so well how to give as do noble, sensible, tenderhearted women.

But as hospital nurses for wounded men, they [women] are by nature, education, and strength totally unfitted. . . .[1]

S.G.

3-17 (continued)

DIRECTIONS: In the space provided below, write another letter to the editor of the *American Medical Times* either supporting this man's position or refuting it. Be sure to give your reasons for your opinion!

Date:

Dear Editor,

In response to the July 18, 1861, letter written by S.G., I would like to offer the following opinion on the subject of female nurses:

Sincerely,

Now, let's consider the issue of "appropriate" jobs for women in today's society. Are there still jobs that some people consider "inappropriate" for women? If your answer is "yes," in the space provided below, write a list of these jobs, the reasons some people consider these jobs inappropriate for women, and whether you agree or disagree.

SOME PEOPLE CONSIDER THE FOLLOWING JOBS "INAPPROPRIATE" FOR WOMEN:	*THEIR REASONS FOR CONSIDERING THIS JOB "INAPPROPRIATE" FOR WOMEN ARE:*	*I AGREE/DISAGREE WITH THIS OPINION BECAUSE:*
1.		
2.		
3.		

Name ______________________________ Date ______________

3–18

THE STORY OF TIN FOOK

Among the many contributions made by Chinese immigrants to the United States was the hard labor that turned the land, what once was swampland, into the city of San Francisco and that built the transcontinental railroad. Unfortunately, many European Americans acted with prejudice against the Chinese Americans, who were often treated with disrespect and violence. Read the story below of a young Chinese boy written by Betty Lee Sung and excerpted from her book *The Chinese in America*. Tin Fook's story is typical of what the Chinese went through in the early days of the development of the American West.

"Tin Fook pressed his face against the cracks in the floorboard. His eyes were round with fear. Above him, the scuffling of heavy boots scraped back and forth accompanied by crashing thuds as the band of marauders pulled things from the shelves and overturned the wooden chests.

His heart sank when he saw the men had uncovered his father's little hoard of gold. He almost cried out in rage when the men pocketed it and left the little cabin in complete disorder. But Tin Fook had been warned by his father to hide beneath the boards and to keep still whenever the drunken white men came to plunder.

When the men were gone, Tin Fook sobbed until he was exhausted. . . . Tin Fook had come to this strange land known as the Mountain of Gold with his father, his elder cousin, and his uncles after one of their trips home to China. The men had spoken glowingly of their adventures in the land beyond the Pacific Ocean. Tin Fook had listened with rapt attention to stories of their ocean voyage, their search for gold, and their encounters with men from all corners of the globe. He had wanted to come with his father and uncles, although they had a hard time persuading his mother to let him go.

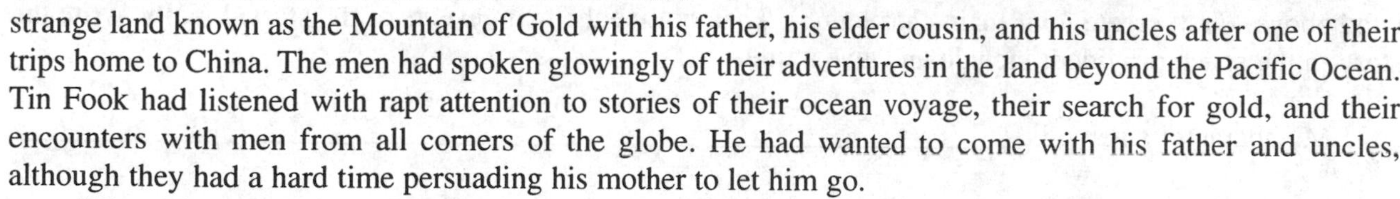

When Tin Fook's father and uncles came home that night, they shrugged their shoulders. 'We are helpless.' they sighed. 'The white men have turned against us. They come in to rob us, beat us, and kill us whenever they get drunk. If we resist, they go away and come back with more men. Public officials not only give us no protection, they even stir up trouble.'"[1]

Chinese immigrants began to come to America in 1848 during the California gold rush days. Their population quickly rose to over 100,000 by the 1880s. However, due to racial prejudice, many local, state, and federal laws were passed to discourage further Chinese immigration or assimilation into American culture. Read the list of these laws. As you are reading them, imagine some of the incidents, such as the story of Tin Fook, that occurred because of these laws.

ANTI-CHINESE LOCAL, STATE, AND FEDERAL LAWS

1850—CALIFORNIA FOREIGN MINER'S TAX—placed a heavy tax on miners who were not Americans by birth.

1863—Law passed that forbade Chinese witnesses to testify against European American men in court.

1870—CALIFORNIA SIDEWALK ORDINANCE—forbade walking on the sidewalk carrying merchandise on poles. (Chinese immigrants used this mode of carrying goods because they lacked wagons, horses, and other means of transporting their merchandise and belongings.)

1871—CUBIC AIR ORDINANCE—required at least 500 cubic feet of living space for each adult. Because Chinatown was severely overcrowded (as many as 10–12 people living in one room), hundreds of Chinese immigrants were jailed for breaking this ordinance until the jails were overflowing.

1871—QUEUE ORDINANCE OF SAN FRANCISCO—required all prisoners of the city jail to have their hair cut to less than one inch. This was cruel punishment for the Chinese men who wore their hair in a long braid down their backs (called a queue) and needed this braid, for cultural reasons, to return to their families in China without retribution by the ruling Manchu dynasty.

1873—CALIFORNIA LAUNDRY ORDINANCES—Anyone transporting laundry without horse-drawn wagons had to pay a high licensing fee. Because only the Chinese hand-carried their laundry, these ordinances were clearly directed against them.

1879—CALIFORNIA CONSTITUTION—forbade California corporations to hire Chinese immigrants.

1882—CHINESE EXCLUSION ACTS—suspended Chinese immigration for ten years.

1887—THE SCOTT ACT—prohibited Chinese laborers from entering the United States. Even those who had left the country for temporary visits to their home in China and who held reentry permit visas were not allowed to return. About 20,000 Chinese who had families, property, and businesses in America were not allowed to return.

1892—GREARY ACT—extended all bills in force against the Chinese for another ten years. It stripped the Chinese from any protection in court. Every Chinese immigrant had to get a certificate of eligibility to remain in the United States.

1913—ALIEN LAND ACT—forbade Chinese immigrants to own land; therefore they could not farm.

DIRECTIONS: Write a "faction" story (a combination of "fact" and "fiction") based on one of the laws cited above. First, create your main character(s). Then outline the main events of the story. Finally, write the story in the space provided; include and give a title.

My character's name is ______________________________

TITLE: ______________________________

____

____

____

____

(Continue on the back.)

Name ______________________________ Date ______________

3–19

I'VE BEEN WORKING ON THE RAILROAD

In 1869, America completed the first transcontinental railroad. Americans could then travel from one coast to the other by train. Though it made it possible for Americans to travel with greater ease, building the railroad was far from easy! Much of the construction work for the railroad was performed by Chinese immigrants. Most of these men had left their wives and families in China, traveled to the United States to work for several years, and intended to return home to China. Read the following facts and quotes describing their work.

1. "Fifty Chinese were hired [at first]. They were hauled to the end of the track. They disembarked, glanced without curiosity at the surrounding forest, then tranquilly established camp, cooked a meal of rice and dried cuttlefish, and went to sleep. By sunrise, they were at work with picks, shovels and wheelbarrows. At the end of their first twelve hours of plodding industry, Crocker [director of construction] and his engineers viewed the result with gratified astonishment."[(1)]
2. The Chinese workers organized themselves into labor crews of 12 to 20 men, often keeping a few extra workers so that even if someone got sick, they could turn out a full crew.
3. Each Chinese work crew set up tents or huts in which they lived. Each crew had its own Chinese head man who organized the work and kept discipline. They each also had their own cook who organized the food; dried oysters, abalone, bamboo shoots, bean sprouts, crackers, noodles, Chinese bacon and pork, poultry and tea were all imported by the Chinese to feed themselves.
4. Each night the Chinese workers bathed after work and changed into clean clothes before supper. These customs amazed the other workers who seldom bathed.
5. Cutting trees, rooting out stumps, breaking and carting rocks, grading roadbeds, putting down ties, spiking the rails, the Chinese soon earned a reputation as tireless, disciplined, and energetic workers.
6. The Chinese workers found a way to resolve the problem of the sheer Sierra Mountains. They gathered reeds in San Francisco Bay and wove waist-high baskets. With a rope and pulley, Chinese workmen were lowered in these baskets down the side of the steep cliff. After chipping holes for the blasting powder in the rock, they were pulled up to safety before the blast created a ledge for workers to enlarge into a road for the railroad.
7. Working day and night, Chinese construction crews tunneled through solid granite. They organized themselves into eight-hour shifts. Even when winter snowstorms hit and many of the other workers refused to work, many of the Chinese laborers went on working. By creating air shafts and access tunnels, they worked and lived completely under the snow. Between 500 and 1,000 Chinese workers were killed by rock and snow avalanches, falls, and other accidents.
8. "I want to remind you of the things that Chinese labor did for us in opening up the western portion of this country. I am the son of the man who drove the first transcontinental railroad across the American

Northwest, the first rail link from Minnesota to Oregon and the waters of Puget Sound. I was near him when he drove the last spike and paid an eloquent tribute to the men who had built that railroad by their manual labor for there were no road-making machines in those days.

He never forgot and never failed to praise the Chinese, of whom nearly 10,000 stormed the forest fastness, endured cold and heat . . . to aid in the opening up of our great Northwestern empire.

I have a dispatch from the chief engineer of the Northwestern Pacific telling how the Chinese laborers went out into eight feet of snow with the temperature far below zero to carry on the work when no American dared face the conditions."[2]

TESTIMONY BEFORE UNITED STATES CONGRESS BY OSWALD GARRISON VILLARD

DIRECTIONS: Imagine you are one of these Chinese immigrants, and write a letter to your family (mother, father, wife), describing your American experience. (Add a picture to help them understand what you are going through!)

1864

Dear

____

____

____

____

____

____

____

____

____

____

____

____

____

____

____

(Continue on the back.)

Name ______________________________ Date ______________

3–20
LEE YICK

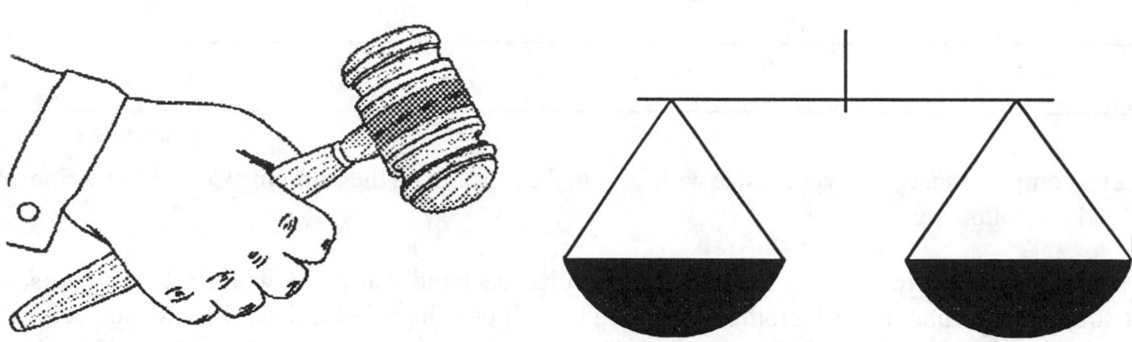

Between 1842 and 1882, approximately 300,000 Chinese immigrated to America. These Chinese immigrants worked as railroad laborers, agricultural workers, and factory workers, Many opened up their own small businesses—such as bakeries, restaurants, and laundries. Unfortunately, there was much racism exhibited toward the Chinese immigrants by the European Americans; this came in the form of institutional racism and mob violence (many Chinese were lynched, their housing and businesses burned during the nineteenth century). One important Chinese immigrant decided to fight back against this hatred. His name was Lee Yick and he ran a laundry named Yick Wo Laundry in San Francisco. Read the facts regarding a case he took all the way to the Supreme Court. Then hypothesize about how you think the Supreme Court ruled in his case.

THE CASE OF YICK WO VS. HOPKINS

1. In 1886, there were 310 laundries built of wood in San Francisco; 240 of these laundries were owned by Chinese immigrants and the rest were owned by European Americans.
2. A San Francisco ordinance was passed that said, due to fire hazard, all laundries must be built of brick.
3. Sheriff Hopkins arrested all of the Chinese laundry owners and one female European American laundry owner; the other 79 European American male laundry owners were not arrested.
4. The arrested laundry owners went on trial, were convicted, and fined. If they did not, or could not, pay the fine, they were jailed.
5. Lee Yick, one of the convicted laundry owners, had operated his laundry in San Francisco for 22 years. He thought the judgment by the local court was racist and unfair. With the help of the other Chinese launderers, he appealed his case to the California Supreme Court.
6. The California Supreme Court upheld the decision of the lower San Francisco court. Lee Yick appealed his case to the United States Supreme Court.
7. The United States Supreme Court agreed to hear the case.

Take a couple of minutes to determine how *you* think the U.S. Supreme Court ruled on this case. In the space below, hypothesize as to who you think won this case and what arguments the U.S. Supreme Court justices made to uphold their decision.

3-20 (continued)

I hypothesize that Lee Yick won/lost (circle one) the case entitled Yick Wo vs. Hopkins. The following is what I think the brief (the written legal argument) made by the Supreme Court justices outlining their reasoning was:

____

____

(Continue on the back.)

Let's compare what you hypothesize with an actual excerpt from the Supreme Court brief written on this case. Read the following:

"For no legitimate reason this body by its action has declared that it is lawful for 80-odd persons who are not subjects of China to wash clothes for hire in [wood] buildings, but unlawful for all subjects of China to do the same thing. . . . It was a law applied with an evil eye and an unequal hand. . . . The Fourteenth Amendment to the Constitution is not confined to the protection of citizens. [Chinese immigrants were not considered citizens.] It says, "Nor shall any state deprive any person of life, liberty or property, without due process of law; nor deny to any person within its jurisdiction the equal protection of the laws."

In the space provided below, state in your own words the Supreme Court brief quoted above. What was their decision? What was their reasoning?

____

____

____

____

____

Do you agree with the decision made by the U.S. Supreme Court on the case Yick Wo vs. Hopkins? Write your response to this question in the space provided below. Be sure to explain your reasoning.

____

____

____

____

____

____

____

Name ______________________________ Date ______________

3–21

THE MEXICAN WAR

The Mexican War (1846–1848) was highly controversial. Some Americans were extremely supportive of the war effort (PRO) and some Americans were adamantly opposed (CON). Look at the map below that shows the the U. S.A. before and after the Mexican War. From this map you can see that the United States gained nearly one-third of its present-day size by winning this war.

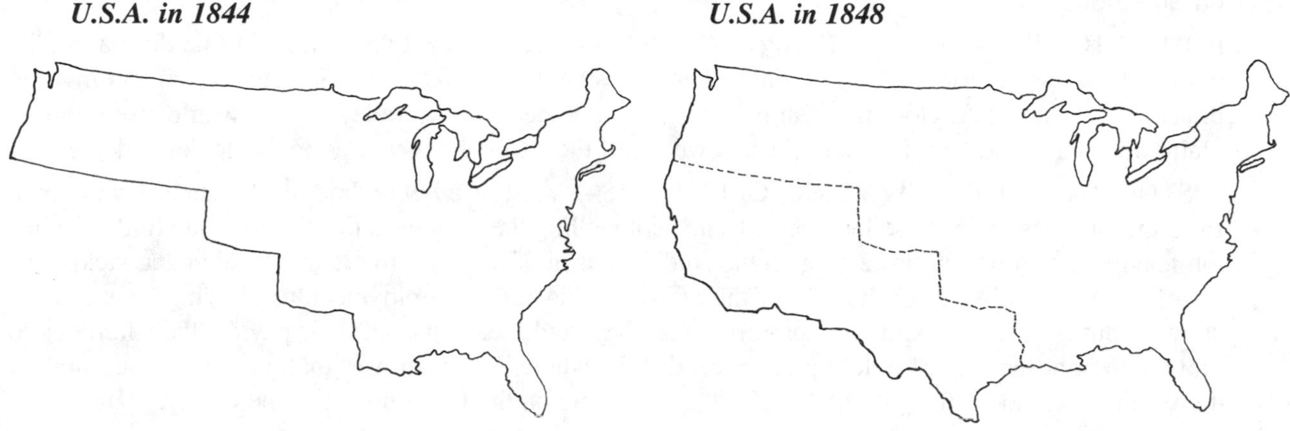

Read the following quotes of Americans who lived during this time period and decide if they were PRO or CON regarding the Mexican War. Place the number of these Americans in the chart below. After you have finished reading all the quotes, hypothesize in the space provided at the end of this exercise as to what you think were the main issues in this war.

PRO	*CON*

1. PRESIDENT POLK— "... Mexico has passed the boundary of the U.S., has invaded our territory, and has shed American blood upon American soil.... As war exists, notwithstanding all our efforts to avoid it, exists by the act of Mexico herself, we are called upon by every consideration of duty and patriotism to vindicate with decision, the honor, the rights, and the interests of our country."
2. ABRAHAM LINCOLN (then Illinois representative to the U.S. Congress)—"I challenge President Polk to specify the exact spot where American blood was shed on American soil."
3. JOSHUA GIDDINGS (Ohio Representative to the United States Congress)—"It is an agressive, unholy, and unjust war.... In the murder of Mexicans upon their own soil, or in robbing them of their own country, I can take no part either now or hereafter. The guilt of these crimes must rest upon others—I will not participate in them."

4. WALT WHITMAN (poet)—"Yes, Mexico must be thoroughly chastised! . . . Let our arms be carried with a spirit which shall teach the world that, while we are not forward for a quarrel, America knows how to crush, as well as how to expand."
5. ANONYMOUS WRITER TO THE *Cambridge Chronicle*—"Neither have I the least idea of 'joining' you, or in any way assisting the unjust war waged against Mexico. I have no wish to participate in such 'glorious' butcheries of women and children as were displayed in the capture of Monterey etc. . . . No sir-ee! As long as I can work, beg, or go to the poor house, I won't go to Mexico, to be lodged on the damp ground, half-starved, half-roasted, bitten by mosquitoes and centipedes, stung by scorpions and tarantulas—marched, drilled, and flogged, and then stuck up to be shot at, for eight dollars a month and putrid rations."
6. EDITOR TO THE *Illinois State Register*—"Shall this garden of beauty be suffered to lie dormant in its wild and useless luxuriance? . . . Myriads of enterprising Americans would flock to its rich and inviting prairies; the hum of Anglo-American industry would be heard in its valleys; cities would rise upon its plains and sea-coast, and the resources and wealth of the nation be increased in incalculable degree."
7. HISTORIAN OF THE NEW YORK VOLUNTEERS—". . . It is cruel to drag black men . . . white men from their homes under false inducements, and compelling them to leave their wives and children without leaving a cent or any protection, in the coldest season of the year, to die in a foreign and sickly climate! . . . Many enlisted for the sake of their families, having no employment, and having been offered "three months advance," and were promised that they could leave part of their pay for their families to draw in their absence . . . I boldly pronounce, that the whole Regiment was got up by fraud—a fraud on the soldier, a fraud on the City of New York, and a fraud on the Government of the United States. . . ."
8. MR GILES (Maryland representative to United States Congress)—"I take it for granted that we shall gain territory, and must gain territory, before we shut the gates of the Temple of Janus. . . . We must march from ocean to ocean. . . . We must march from Texas straight to the Pacific ocean and be bounded only by it's roaring wave. . . . It is the destiny of the white race, it is the destiny of the Anglo-Saxon race."
9. THEODORE PARKER (Unitarian minister from Boston)—"Let it be infamous for a New England man to enlist; for a New England merchant to loan his dollars, or let his ships in aid of this wicked war; let it be infamous for a manufacturer to make a cannon, a sword, or a kernel of powder to kill our brothers. . . ."
10. YOUNG NAVAL OFFICER—"Asia . . . will be brought to our very doors. Population will flow into the fertile regions of California. The resources of the entire country . . . will be developed. . . . The public lands lying along the route [of railroads] will be changed from deserts to gardens, and a large population will be settled."
11. HISTORIAN JOHN WEEMS—"Night blanketed weary men who fell asleep where they dropped on the trampled prairie grass, while around them other prostrate men from both armies screamed and groaned in agony from wounds. By the eerie light of torches the surgeon's saw was going the livelong night . . . those fields around Churubusco were now covered with thousands of human casualties and with mangled bodies of horses and mules that blocked the roads and filled the ditches."
12. INFANTRY LIEUTENANT—"General Lane . . . told us to avenge the death of the gallant Walker, to . . . take all we could lay our hands on." And well and fearfully was his mandate obeyed. Grog shops were broken open first, and then, maddened with liquor, every species of outrage was committed. Old women and girls were stripped of their clothing—and many suffered still greater outrages. . . . Men were shot by the dozens . . . their property, churches, stores and dwelling houses ransacked. . . . Dead horses and men lay about pretty thick, while drunken soldiers, yelling and screeching, were breaking open houses or chasing some poor Mexicans who had abandoned their houses and fled for life. Such a scene I never hope to see again. It gave me a lamentable view of human nature . . . and made me for the first time ashamed of my country."

13. SENATOR H.V. JOHNSON—"War has its evils. In all ages it has been the minister of wholesale death and appalling desolation; but however inscrutable to us, it has also been made, by the Allwise Dispenser of events, the instrumentality of accomplishing the great end of human elevation and human happiness. . . . It is in this view, that I subscribe to the doctrine of 'manifest destiny.'"
14. WILLIAM LLOYD GARRISON (abolitionist and writer)—"A war of aggression, of invasion, of conquest and of rapine—marked by ruffianism, perfidy, and every other feature of national depravity."
15. HENRY DAVID THOREAU (writer)—Thoreau refused to pay his Massachusetts poll tax because he did not want his taxes to be used to support the war effort. He was arrested and jailed for this action. His friend, Ralph Waldo Emerson, visited him in jail and asked him "What are you doing in there?" Thoreau answered, "What are you doing out there?"
16. JAMES RUSSEL LOWELL (abolitionist and poet)

    Ez fer war, I call it murder,
    There you hev it plain an' flat
    I don't want to go no furder
    Than my Testyment fer that. . . .
    They may talk o' Freedom's airy
    Tell they're purple in the face,—
    It's a grand gret cemetary
    Fer the barthrights of our race,
    They jest want our Californy
    So's to lug new slave-states in
    To abuse ye an' to scorn ye,
    An' to plunder ye like sin.

With the information you have gathered from the above quotes, what do you think were the main issues (things people argued about) concerning the Mexican War? Hypothesize in the space provided below.

The main issues of the Mexican War were:

HYPOTHESIS 1: ____

____

____

HYPOTHESIS 2: ____

____

____

HYPOTHESIS 3: ____

____

____

Check your hypotheses with your textbook, information from your school or local library, or with your teacher!

Name ______________________________ Date ______________

3–22

JUAN NEPOMUCENO CORTINA

A highly controversial historical figure in American history was a Mexican American named Juan Nepomuceno Cortina. This man was born on the land claimed by both Mexico and the United States (along the border of present-day Texas and Mexico), which led to the Mexican War of 1846–1848. Cortina was 16 years old when this war began and saw many atrocities committed during its course. When the United States won the war, approximately 80,000 Mexicans became Mexican Americans overnight. Cortina saw many Mexican Americans treated unfairly during their citizenship transition. The following are a few examples of this treatment: (1) Mexican Americans were required to register their land and pay property taxes; however, because most of them did not speak English, they neglected to do this and, therefore, lost much of their land. (2) Many European Americans who moved into the area newly possessed by the United States were extremely violent toward the Mexican Americans, who had little recourse in U.S. courts. When Cortina was 29 years old, he organized a small army of 100 Mexican Americans to raid European American settlements in Texas. He was chased out of Texas after one year by the United States Army and became a brigadier general and the governor of a Mexican state. He is referred to by some historians as a "bandit, mail robber, thief, murderer" and by other historians as "a champion, a hero, a noble avenger for his people."

DIRECTIONS: Imagine that you woke up today and read the following article in your local newspaper:

BORDER DISPUTE BETWEEN CANADA AND U.S.A.

The Canadian military moved into the strip of land 200 miles south of the current border between Canada and the U.S.A. to claim what they consider rightfully their own. All U.S. citizens who lived in this strip of land, which stretches from Washington state on the west to Minnesota on the east, were proclaimed, by the Canadian government, to be Canadians. This numbered approximately 80,000 former U.S. citizens. The U.S. military attempted to resist this attack, but were repulsed. They have decided to give up rights to this narrow strip of land.

One American has refused do give up. Don Cortina has begun organizing former U.S. citizens to attack Canadian military posts to force them to retreat. Though he is likely to be unsuccessful, he has received considerable backing from former U.S. citizens.

What would be your opinion of this man, "Don" Cortina? Write a letter to the editor of your local paper expressing your opinion of this man and his activities.

Dear Editor,

____

____

____

____

____

(Continue on the back.)

Name ________________________________ Date ____________

3–23

MEXICAN AMERICANS

The United States and Mexico went to war from 1846–1848 over disputed territory in what we today call Texas. The United States won the war and bought most of the land we now refer to as California, Arizona, New Mexico, Nevada, Utah, Colorado, Wyoming, and Texas (or one-third of the United States) from Mexico for $15 million. This land sale meant that 80,000 Mexicans became Mexican Americans (or Chicanos, as many Mexican Americans refer to themselves) overnight! This caused many problems. To get a sense of one of these problems, please read the following out loud (even if you do not know the language). Then, answer the questions.

Si el otorgador desea negar la transmisión de derechos reales sobre bienes inmuebles ajenos por la ejecución inadecuada de la escritura o por otras causas determinadas por exámenes objetivos y subjetivos de la corte, n.b., la reversión queda restricta por los estatutos de limitaciones aplicables para desalojar al posesor inmediatamente y a cualquiera que adversamente reclame al dueño y a quien le será subsecuentemente negado levantar una acción de desalojamiento. Bajo una reclamación de derecho, los requisitos estatutarios dan el derecho a reclamar la escritura la cual expresa, como antes mencionado, la adversidad necesaria.

1. What does the above paragraph describe? ________________________________

2. How did reading the above paragraph make you feel? ________________________________

Even if you speak fluent Spanish (the language in which the paragraph is written) you might have had a hard time reading it. It is written in very technical, legal language. (Ask your teacher for the translation in English!) Because most of the 80,000 Mexicans (who became Mexican Americans overnight in 1848) could not speak English, they did not realize they were required to register their property and pay property taxes to the American government. This handicap meant that many lost their small farms and businesses, their only means of livelihood. Imagine that, because your parents or guardians did not understand the above paragraph, they lost their jobs and homes. How would this situation make you feel? Answer this question in the space provided below.

____

____

(Continue on the back.)

Name ______________________________ Date ______________

3–24

THE CIVIL WAR—FOR WHOM WOULD YOU FIGHT?

CONFEDERATE FLAG
MAY 1863 - MARCH 1865

The Civil War shook the country from 1861 to 1865 and took the lives of over 600,000 Americans. Why did this destructive war occur? Historians differ on the answer to this question. Some historians believe that the main cause of the Civil War was the issue of slavery; they believe that the Northern soldiers fought to end slavery and the Southern soldiers fought to keep slavery. Other historians believe the main cause of the Civil War was the issue of States' rights; they believe that the Northern soldiers fought because they believed the Southern states did *not* have the right to leave the Union and the Southern soldiers fought because they believed they *did* have the right to leave the Union. Other historians believe the industrialization of America was the main cause; they believe that the Northern soldiers fought because they wanted free labor to expand to the South and provide more jobs and the Southern soldiers fought because they wanted to keep their agricultural, rural way of life. Put yourself in the shoes of the following Americans during the nineteenth century. Decide, in each case, if you would have supported the side of the Northerners (Union), the Southerners (Confederacy), or neither.

1. *NATIVE AMERICAN FEMALE FARMER*

   a. Native American Indians were not counted in the American census; they were not considered U.S. citizens, although many were living close to or among African Americans and European Americans.

   b. The United States Constitution did not give Native Americans or women the right to vote.

   c. The population of Native Americans decreased from 600,000 in 1800 to 250,000 in 1900 due to diseases brought by the Europeans, wars, starvation, and lack of land.

If I were a Native American female farmer in 1861, I would have supported the Northerners/the Southerners/neither side (circle one) because:

____

____

____

____

2. *LOW-INCOME EUROPEAN AMERICAN SOUTHERN MALE FARMER*
   a. Most farmers did not own any slaves; less than 15 percent of European Americans owned slaves in the United States
   b. Most southerners were supporters of "states rights"; they believed that if a state wanted to secede from the United States, it should have the right to do so.

If I were a low-income European American Southern male farmer in 1861, I would have supported the Northerners/the Southerners/neither side (circle one) because:

____

____

____

3. *FREE AFRICAN AMERICAN NORTHERN MALE ARTISAN*
   a. Many free African Americans had relatives living in slavery.
   b. Some free African Americans artisans lived comfortably; most free African Americans were relegated to low-paying jobs.
   c. Until 1862, the Northern army (Union) would not allow African American males to serve in the military; when they were finally allowed to serve, they were paid at a lower rate than European American soldiers.

If I were a free African American man living in 1861, I would have supported the Northerners/the Southerners/neither side (circle one) because:

____

____

____

4. *ENSLAVED AFRICAN AMERICAN WOMAN*
   a. The U.S. Constitution counted slaves as three-fifths of a person for the purposes of determining representation.
   b. Though President Lincoln had publicly admitted he did not like the institution of slavery, he still believed African Americans were inferior to European Americans and, at first, would not force the Southern states to outlaw slavery.
   c. Women in America were not allowed to vote or serve on juries.

If I were an enslaved African American woman in 1861, I would have supported the Northerners/the Southerners/neither side (circle one) because:

____

____

____

____

5. *WEALTHY EUROPEAN AMERICAN NORTHERN MALE FACTORY OWNER*
   a. Factory owners were in favor of heavy tariffs on foreign manufactured products imported to the United States (such as clothing or shoes) because they did not want competition with their own manufactured products; Abraham Lincoln supported this position.
   b. Southern farmers (especially large plantation owners) were *not* in favor of heavy tariffs on foreign manufactured products because they wanted to buy these products as cheaply as possible and trade them for their agricultural goods.
   c. Factory owners were interested in expanding their factories to areas in the South and West; they were opposed to slavery because this gave them a smaller number of eligible workers for their factories.

If I were a wealthy European American Northern male factory owner in 1861, I would have supported the Northerners/Southerners/neither side (circle one) because:

____

____

____

____

____

6. *WEALTHY EUROPEAN AMERICAN FEMALE SOUTHERN PLANTATION OWNER*
   a. Plantation owners needed slaves to provide the cheap labor to run their plantations.
   b. Plantation owners were interested in expanding their agricultural operations to the new territories and states in the western United States and therefore needed slavery in these areas; President Abraham Lincoln was opposed to allowing slavery to expand to the new areas.
   c. Plantation owners were opposed to high tariffs on foreign manufactured goods imported to the United States because they wanted to buy these products as cheaply as possible; President Lincoln supported heavy tariffs on imports.
   d. Women were not allowed to vote or serve on juries.

If I were a wealthy European American female Southern plantation owner in 1861, I would have supported the Northerners/Southerners/neither side (circle one) because:

____

____

____

____

____

7. *LOW-INCOME MEXICAN AMERICAN TEXAN FEMALE FARMER*
   a. After the Mexican War, the United States had taken over the lands in which many Mexican American families had farmed and ranched for many generations.

b. Mexican Americans were subjected to much racism and unfair treatment.

c. Slavery in Texas allowed large plantation owners to operate; this caused competition with smaller farms.

d. Women were not allowed to vote or serve on juries.

If I were a poor Mexican American Texan female farmer in 1861, I would have supported the Northerners/Southerners/neither side (circle one) because:

8. *CHINESE AMERICAN MALE RAILROAD WORKER*

a. Chinese immigrants were not allowed to become U.S. citizens; they could not vote or serve on juries.

b. President Abraham Lincoln's government (the Northerners) subsidized the construction of the transcontinental railroad; this was a major source of employment for many Chinese American immigrants.

c. Many Chinese Americans were imported to America in almost slavelike conditions.

d. Chinese Americans were subjected to much racism and unfair treatment.

If I were a Chinese American male railroad worker in 1861, I would have supported the Northerners/Southerners/neither side (circle one) because:

Name ______________________________ Date ______________

3–25

AFRICAN AMERICAN SOLDIERS

Approximately 180,000 African Americans (about 10 percent of the total army) served in the Union Army during the Civil War. This issue was extremely controversial. At the beginning of the war, African Americans were not allowed to serve. But as the war dragged on, President Lincoln finally gave his consent in 1862 because (1) the North was losing; (2) the North was having trouble recruiting European American soldiers; and (3) abolitionist forces were pressuring Lincoln to accept African American soldiers. By the end of the war, there were many all–African American army units. Read the description below of African American soldiers' experiences in the Civil War.

> "Under cover of darkness they stormed the fort, faced a stream of fire, faltered not till the ranks were broken by shot and shell; and in all these severe tests, which would have tried veteran troops, they fully met my expectations, for many were killed, wounded or captured on the walls of the forts."[(1)]

GENERAL STRONG, JULY 18, 1863

> "The enemy charged us so close that we fought with our bayonets, hand to hand. I have six broken bayonets to show how bravely my men fought. I was sick at heart when I saw how my brave soldiers had been slaughtered—one with six wounds, all the rest with two or three . . . two of my colored soldiers were killed; both brave, noble men, always prompt, vigilant . . . ready for the fray."[(2)]

CAPTAIN MATTHEW MILLER, JUNE 7, 1863

> "The sentiment of this army . . . to the employment of Negro troops has been revolutionized by the bravery of the blacks [in the] battle of Milliken's Bend. Prominent officers, who used to in private sneer at the idea, are now heartily in favor of it."[(3)]

ASSISTANT SECRETARY OF WAR CHARLES DANA, JUNE 10, 1863

> "I know . . . that some of the commanders . . . in the field . . . now believe that the emancipation policy and the use of colored troops constitute the heaviest blow yet dealt to the rebellion, and that at least one of the important successes could not have been achieved but for the aid of the black soldiers."[(4)]

PRESIDENT ABRAHAM LINCOLN, 1863

3-25 (continued)

Read the chart below (which uses the terminology of this historical period), showing the pay scale per month for European American (white) vs. African American (colored) servicemen as published by the *Chicago Tribune* in 1864.

	White	*Colored*
Sergeant Major	$ 21	$7
Quartermaster Sergeant	21	7
First Sergeant	20	7
Sergeant	17	7
Hospital Steward	30	7
Corporal	13	7
Private	13	7
Chaplain	100	7

DIRECTIONS: Imagine you are living in 1864. In the space provided below, write a letter to the editor of the *Chicago Tribune* expressing your opinion regarding this difference in pay scale.

July, 1864

Dear Editor,

Name ______________________________ *Date* ______________

3–26

ABRAHAM LINCOLN

Have you ever been "of two minds" about an issue? Abraham Lincoln was "of two minds" about the issue of slavery. Because of this, he is a controversial historical figure. Some historians view him as a progressive force in American history, a man who helped end slavery. Other historians view him as a conservative force in American history, a man who retarded the end of slavery. To understand such widely divergent views, read the following quotes of Abraham Lincoln.

July 1858—"Let us discard all this quibbling about this man and the other man, this race and that race and the other race being inferior, and therefore they must be placed in an inferior position. Let us discard all these things, and unite as one people throughout this land, until we shall once more stand up declaring that all men are created equal."

September 1858—"I will say then, that I am not, nor ever have been, in favor of bringing about in any way the social and political equality of the white and black races; that I am not, nor ever have been, in favor of making voters or jurors of Negroes, nor of qualifying them to hold office, nor to intermarry with white people. . . . And inasmuch as they cannot so live, while they do remain together there must be the position of superior and inferior, and I as much as any other man am in favor of having the superior position assigned to the white race."

1859—(in response to the Fugitive Slave Law)—"I confess I hate to see the poor creatures hunted down . . . but I bite my lips and keep quiet."

March 1861 (inaugural address) "I have no purpose, directly or indirectly, to interfere with the institution of slavery in the States where it exists. I believe I have no lawful right to do so, and I have no inclination to do so."

August 1862 (in response to a letter from Horace Greeley, editor of the *New York Tribune*)—"Dear Sir . . . I have not meant to leave any one in doubt. . . . My paramount objective in this struggle is to save the Union, and is not either to save or destroy Slavery. If I could save the Union without freeing any slave, I would do it; and if I could save it by freeing all the slaves, I would do it; and if I could do it by freeing some and leaving others alone, I would also do that. What I do about Slavery and the colored race, I do because it helps to save this Union; and what I forbear, I forbear because I do not believe it would help save the Union. . . . I have here stated my purpose according to my view of official duty, and I intend no modification of my oft-expressed personal wish that all men, everywhere, could be free. Yours, A. Lincoln."

September 1862 (Emancipation Proclamation)—"That on the first day of January, AD 1863, all persons held as slaves within any State or designated part of a State the people whereof shall then be in rebellion against the United States shall be then, henceforward and forever free. . . . "

3-26 (continued)

What was going on inside President Abraham Lincoln's head about the issue of slavery? Look at the drawing of President Lincoln below and note the two "thought bubbles" rising from his head. In these two bubbles, write phrases, single words or whole sentences to describe the "two sides" of the conflict going on inside this famous European American's mind.

In the space provided below, write your analysis of President Lincoln's thinking on the issue of slavery. Do you think it is understandable or do you think he should have taken a position—one way or the other?

____

____

____

____

____

____

____

(Continue on the back.)

Name ______________________________ *Date* ______________

3–27

ROBERT BROWN ELLIOT

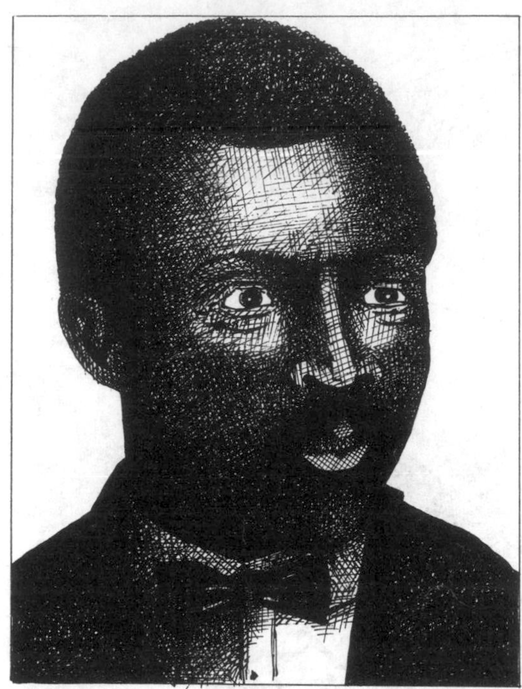

During Reconstruction (1867–1877), many African American men were elected to public positions. State senators, state congressmen, U.S. senators, U.S. congressmen, lieutenant governors, secretaries of state, state supreme court justices, state treasurers, were only some of the positions held by African Americans. One of the most famous African American public representatives of Reconstruction was Robert Brown Elliot, who was elected from South Carolina to the U.S. House of Representatives. He worked to get the first civil rights law passed in the United States. He met much opposition in the U.S. Congress, especially from formerly Confederate European Americans such as Alexander H. Stephens who was vice-president of the Confederacy during the Civil War. Elliot spoke in very complicated and eloquent language. Read excerpts of his speeches below, addressed to Alexander H. Stephens:

"It is a matter of regret to me that it is necessary at this day that I should rise in the presence of an American Congress to advocate a bill which simply asserts equal rights and equal public privileges for all classes of Americans. I regret sir, that the dark hue of my skin may lend a color to the imputation that I am controlled by motives personal to myself. . . . Sir, the motive that impels me is restricted by no such narrow boundary, but is as broad as your Constitution. I advocate it, sir, because it is right . . . the Constitution warrants it, the Supreme Court sanctions it, justice demands it. . . . The last vestiture only is needed—civil rights."

DIRECTIONS: Translate Elliot's speech into words to which a teenager today could relate. In other words, tell your reader what Elliot was saying!

Robert Brown Elliot was saying the following to Alexander H. Stephens:

____

____

(Continue on the back.)

Name ______________________ Date ____________

3–28
CLOSE QUARTERS

Study the picture below of a nineteenth-century female pioneer. In the space provided below, hypothesize what this woman is carrying in her wheelbarrow.

CLOSE QUARTERS: "ADA MCCOLL ON THE PRAIRIE NEAR LAKIM, KANSAS, GATHERING BUFFALO CHIPS" (1893) (KANSAS STATE HISTORICAL SOCIETY, TOPEKA KANSAS).

This pioneer woman is carrying the following in her wheelbarrow:

HYPOTHESIS 1 ______________________

____

HYPOTHESIS 2 ______________________

____

(Your teacher knows the correct answer!)

3-28 (continued)

Now, hypothesize what she will use the contents of her wheelbarrow for.

This pioneer woman will use the contents for:

HYPOTHESIS 1 ____

____

HYPOTHESIS 2 ____

____

(Ask your teacher for the correct answer!)

Imagine you are living in a small pioneer house in the Great Plains area of South Dakota. Your house is made of mud and sod. It is approximately 15 feet by 15 feet and has only one window. Food is cooked inside, but there is no chimney to exhaust the smoke and fumes. Your mother, father, five siblings, and you live in this dwelling—often without going outside for three months at a time while you are snowed in during the winter. Most activities, (eating, sleeping, bathing, personal hygiene) take place within this confined space. In the space provided below, describe a typical day in your pioneer house. Be sure to include all your activities, a description of the smells and sights of your house and the different emotions you felt during the day!

____

____

____

____

____

____

____

____

____

____

____

____

____

____

(Continue on the back.)

Name ______________________________ Date ______________

3–29

AFRICAN AMERICAN PIONEERS

Thousands of African Americans fled the poverty and violence of the post-Reconstruction South. Beginning in the early 1870s, many traveled up the Mississippi River to create African American towns. One of the leaders of this exodus movement was a man named Benjamin "Pap" Singleton. This remarkable man escaped from slavery, became a coffin maker in Tennessee, and was sickened by the many deaths of his fellow African Americans at the hands of racism and mob violence. He founded a town, Nicodemus, in Kansas. Read the poster advertising Nicodemus to African American settlers.

Study the picture on the following page that shows some of these African American pioneers waiting to catch a boat up the Mississippi River, to move to an African American town.

To the Colored Citizens of the United States.

NICODEMUS, GRAHAM CO., KAN., July 2d, 1877.

We, the Nicodemus Town Company of Graham County, Kan., are now in possession of our lands and the Town Site of Nicodemus, which is beautifully located on the N. W. quarter of Section 1, Town 8, Range 21, in Graham Co., Kansas, in the great Solomon Valley, 240 miles west of Topeka, and we are proud to say it is the finest country we ever saw. The soil is of a rich, black, sandy loam. The country is rather rolling, and looks most pleasing to the human eye. The south fork of the Solomon river flows through Graham County, nearly directly east and west and has an abundance of excellent water, while there are numerous springs of living water abounding throughout the Valley. There is an abundance of fine Magnesian stone for building purposes, which is much easier handled than the rough sand or hard stone. There is also some timber; plenty for fire use, while we have no fear but what we will find plenty of coal.

Now is your time to secure your home on Government Land in the Great Solomon Valley of Western Kansas.

Remember, we have secured the service of W. R. Hill, a man of energy and ability, to locate our Colony.

Not quite 90 days ago we secured our charter for locating the town site of Nicodemus. We then became an organized body, with only three dollars in the treasury and twelve members, but under the careful management of our officers, we have now nearly 300 good and reliable members, with several members permanently located on their claims—with plenty of provisions for the colony—while we are daily receiving letters from all parts of the country from parties desiring to locate in the great Solomon Valley of Western Kansas.

For Maps, Circulars, and Passenger rates, address our General Manager, W. R. HILL, North Topeka, Kansas, until August 1st, 1877, then at Hill City, Graham Co., via Trego.

The name of our post-office will be Nicodemus, and Mr. Z. T. Fletcher will be our "Nasby."

REV. S. P. ROUNDTREE, Sec'y.

NICODEMUS.

Nicodemus was a slave of African birth,
And was bought for a bag full of gold;
He was reckoned a part of the salt of the earth,
But he died years ago, very old.

Nicodemus was a prophet, at least he was as wise,
For he told of the battles to come:
How we trembled with fear, when he rolled up his eyes,
And we heeded the shake of his thumb.

CHORUS: Good time coming, good time coming,
Long, long time on the way;
Run and tell Elija to hurry up Pomp,
To meet us under the cottonwood tree,
In the Great Solomon Valley
At the first break of day.

3-29 (continued)

AFRICAN AMERICAN PIONEERS: "NEGRO REFUGEES WAITING ON LEVEE" (1897) (LIBRARY OF CONGRESS, #LC-US262-26365).

Choose one person in this picture and write what *you* believe is passing through this person's mind as he or she is waiting. I chose the ____ in this photograph. I imagine he or she is thinking and feeling the following (include fears, hopes, previous experiences, physical needs such as food and water):

____

____

____

____

____

(Continue on the back.)

Name ______________________________ Date ____________

3–30

COWBOY QUIZ

How much do you know about cowboys? Write a description in the space provided below of what you imagine cowboys looked like, dressed like, and ate.

____

____

____

Now, let's see if you can pass the following quiz! Circle the answer that you think is correct. Then check your answers with your teacher when you are finished.

1. American cowboys were:
   a. European American males
   b. African American and European American males
   c. Native American, Mexican American, African American, and European American males and females
2. The biggest danger to cowboys on the Chisholm Trail was:
   a. unfriendly Native Americans
   b. saloon shoot-outs
   c. stampedes
3. Most of the cowboy lingo (lasso, chaps, rodeo, ranch), was adapted from:
   a. Native Americans
   b. African Americans
   c. Mexican Americans
4. Most cowboys drove cattle from:
   a. Arkansas to Colorado
   b. Texas to railroads that shipped the cattle to Chicago
   c. Montana to New Mexico
5. The following person became a millionaire driving herds on the Chisholm Trail:
   a. Deadwood Dick
   b. Wild Bill Hickok
   c. Elizabeth E. Johnson
6. Longhorn cattle (which were the majority of cattle herded by American cowboys) were descendants of:
   a. cattle brought from Europe by the Spaniards
   b. cattle brought from Africa by the Nigerians
   c. cattle brought from China by the Chinese
7. Why did the cowgirl eat a box of bullets? (a real cowboy joke)
   a. so she could be tough as the men
   b. because they tasted good
   c. because she wanted to grow bangs

Name ______________________________ Date ______________

3–31

CHEYENNE NATIVE AMERICAN GAME

Americans played many sports and games during the nineteenth century. The following description is a game played by Cheyenne Native Americans as described by Carolyn Neithammer in her book *Daughters of the Earth: The Lives and Legends of Native American Women.*

"Many of the games involved the use of a ball, which was usually fashioned from hide stuffed with grass or animal hair. Cheyenne women played a kind of football in which they used about three hundred counter sticks and a ball about eight inches in diameter. They divided themselves equally into two teams. The first player went to the center and, balancing the ball on her instep, kicked it into the air, caught it on her foot, and kicked it again. She counted how many times she was able to kick the ball before she missed and took that number of counter sticks. Then a player from the other team had a turn. When all the counter sticks were claimed, the team with the most sticks won the game"[(1)]

HOW TO PLAY: Let's see if we can play a modern-day version of this Cheyenne game. You will need the following materials: a group (at least two!) of friends or classmates, an inflated balloon, three bowls, 300 stick pretzels (a large bag will do!), and the score card on the next page. Follow these steps:

1. Open the bag of pretzels and place 300 pretzels in one of the bowls.
2. Make an open space in the middle of the room (this may require you to push back desks and other furniture).
3. Divide your group of people into two teams. Each team must create a team name for itself and write the name of its team on the score card. Each team should also take one of the two remaining bowls.
4. Choose a kicking order for your team.
5. Flip a coin to see which team gets to kick first.
6. The team that kicks first must send its first kicker to the middle of the room. He or she must balance the balloon on his or her foot and kick it into the air. Then she or he must keep kicking the balloon as many times as possible to keep it from falling to the ground. After each turn, the player must record her or his score (how many times she or he kicked the ball) on the score card and place the same number of pretzels in the team's bowl.
7. The other team then sends a kicker to the middle of the room to take a turn.
8. The game continues until all 300 pretzels are won. Then the pretzels are counted, the score card is added up, and the team that has the most pretzels wins!

SCORE CARD

TEAM 1's NAME IS: ______________________	***TEAM 2's NAME IS:*** ______________________
PRETZEL POINTS	PRETZEL POINTS
TOTAL POINTS FOR TEAM 1:	TOTAL POINTS FOR TEAM 2:

Name ______________________ Date ____________

3–32

WHAT DO THEY HAVE IN COMMON?

Read the excerpts from nineteenth-century advertisements, books, quotes, ordinances, and signs. While you are reading them, think about what they have in common.

1. "WANTED—An English or American woman, that understands cooking, and to assist in the work generally if wished; also a girl to do chamber work. None need apply without a recommendation from their last place. IRISH PEOPLE need not apply. . . . Inquire at 359 Broadway.

   WANTED—To do general housework. . . . English, Scotch, Welsh, German, or any country or color except Irish"[1]
2. CALIFORNIA ALIEN LAND ACT—Chinese immigrants cannot own land in California nor begin their own farms.
3. "The first time Vanka threw mud at me, I ran home and complained to my mother, who brushed off my dress and said, quite resignedly, 'How can I help you, my poor child. Vanka is a Gentile. The Gentiles do as they like with the Jews.'"[2]
4. Signs for railroad cars in South Carolina:

   WHITE COLORED

   NEGROES AND FREIGHT
5. 1895 HELP WANTED! LABORERS FOR THE CROTON, NY, RESERVOIR!

   Common Labor, white $1.30 to $1.50

   Common Labor, colored $1.25 to $1.40

   Common Labor, Italian $1.15 to $1.25 (3)

WHAT DO THE ABOVE EXCERPTS HAVE IN COMMON? Using just one or two words, write your answer inside the circle provided below. Then outside the circle, write the words that express how you feel about the words inside the circle.

On a separate sheet of paper, write a short essay about this issue. Be sure to have an introduction, body, and conclusion—and include your opinions!

Name ______________________ *Date* ____________

3–33
IMMIGRATION

Over 15 million people immigrated to the United States during the nineteenth century. They came from all parts of the globe. Why would these millions of people leave their homelands to travel thousands of miles and risk everything to build a new life on a new continent? In the space provided below, hypothesize as to the reason why millions of immigrants moved to the United States.

Evidence that **supports** *this hypothesis:*	***Millions of immigrants came to the United States during the nineteenth century because:***	*Evidence that* **refutes** *this hypothesis:*
	Hypothesis 1: ______ ______ ______ ______	
	Hypothesis 2: ______ ______ ______ ______	
	Hypothesis 3: ______ ______ ______ ______	
	Hypothesis 4: ______ ______ ______ ______	

Below you will find facts about immigration to the United States during the nineteenth century. These facts will help you determine if your hypotheses are correct or incorrect. Read each fact and decide if it *supports* or *refutes* your hypotheses. Write the number (1, 2, 3) under the SUPPORT or REFUTE columns next to your hypothesis. You can do additional research in your local or school library to explore your hypotheses further.

FACT 1: "That was the first time that I heard of America, and my childhood imagination took possession of a land covered partly with majestic trees, partly with flowery prairies, immeasurable to the eye, and intersected with large rivers and broad lakes—a land where everybody could do what he thought best, and where nobody need be poor, because everybody was free."

GERMAN IMMIGRANT KARL SCHURZ

FACT 2: Due to potato rot which began in 1845, the potato crop in Ireland began to fail. From 1845 to 1850 there were famine conditions in Ireland. More than one million people died of starvation. One-fourth of the Irish population moved to the United States.

FACT 3: Because of improved farming methods such as crop rotation—and therefore greater abundance of food—the population of Europe doubled between 1750 and 1850.

FACT 4: A Chinese worker could earn one dollar a day in the United States. This was double or triple the wage that the same person could have earned in China at that time. If a Chinese man could save $500, he could return to China and be prosperous. If he could saved $1000, he went home very rich.

FACT 5: At the beginning of the nineteenth century, there was no railroad in America. By the end of the nineteenth century, railroads connected every major city in the nation.

FACT 6: Improvements in European farming technology reduced the need for farm workers. Many peasants were forced off land that they had lived on for generations.

FACT 7: A severe drought struck parts of western Europe in the 1870s and 1880s.

FACT 8: The Russian government began to carry out pogroms (organized attacks) against the Jews of eastern Europe. Russian soldiers massacred hundreds of Jews living in this area.

FACT 9: The rulers of Austria-Hungary, Russia, Turkey, and Japan had not permitted their people to emigrate because they feared that migration would reduce the supply of workers, soldiers, and taxpayers. Because of the increase in populations by the end of the nineteenth century the rulers of these countries were no longer opposed to their people's leaving.

FACT 10: The passage to the United States in sailing vessels took three months, on the average, at the beginning of the 1800s. The passage in steamships (which began to be used in the mid-nineteenth century) took ten days.

FACT 11: The U.S. Congress passed the Contract Labor Law in 1864, which permitted employers to recruit foreign workers. Employers could make contracts with workers in other countries and many employers lent money to foreign workers to pay for their transportation to the United States. After the workers arrived, they were required to pay the money back out of their wages.

FACT 12: "We eat here every day."

LETTER FROM A POLISH IMMIGRANT TO HIS FAMILY IN POLAND

3-33 (continued)

You have read the facts and decided if they *support* or *refute* your hypotheses. Can you think of some new hypotheses? Perhaps you learned something from the above information that you did not know beforehand. Write your new hypotheses below:

Evidence that **supports** *this hypothesis:*	*Millions of immigrants came to the United States during the nineteenth century because:*	*Evidence that* **refutes** *this hypothesis:*
	Hypothesis 5: ____________	
	Hypothesis 6: ____________	
	Hypothesis 7: ____________	

Name ______________________ *Date* ____________

3–34

WORDS WE USE EVERY DAY

Millions of people immigrated to the United States between 1860 and 1900. Look at the statistics below and create a bar graph to illustrate these numbers:

1861–1870 2.5 million

1871–1880 2.9 million

1881–1890 5.3 million

1891–1900 3.8 million

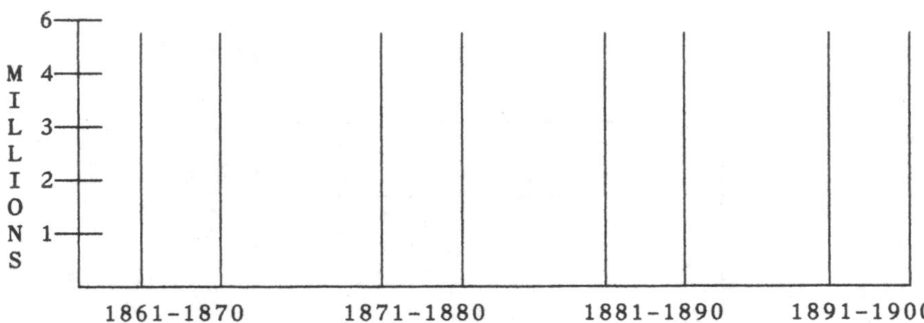

We still feel the impact of these immigrants from all over the world, even as we speak our everyday language! Look at the list of countries in List A. They represent some of the countries from which these immigrants came. Then look at the words in List B. These are words that originated in these countries. Draw a line from each word in List B to the country in List A from which you think that word came! Check your educated guesses with your teacher. The next time you use these words, you will know you are actually speaking French, Italian, German, Chinese, and so on!

LIST A	*LIST B*
hamburger	Germany
troll	Ireland
spaghetti	Holland
Yankee	France
bagel	Mexico
paddywagon	China
Santa Claus	Yiddish (German Jews)
frankfurter	Italy
seltzer	Sweden
dessert	
rodeo	
ranch	
ketchup	

Name ______________________ Date __________

3–35

GERMAN AMERICANS

More than 5 million Germans immigrated to the United States in the nineteenth century. They were the largest European immigrant ethnic group during that century. The German culture (foods, customs, traditions) they brought to this country are still practiced today by many people, even those of us who are not of German ancestry! Below are listed some of these cultural contributions made by Germans. Next to each word, write what you associate with it (experiences with, advertisements for).

1. CHRISTMAS TREE

2. HAMBURGER

3. FRANKFURTER (HOT DOG)

4. BEER

5. SELTZER

6. "GESUNDHEIT"

7. OATMEAL

8. KINDERGARTEN

9. PRETZELS

10. GYMNASIUM

On the next page, you will read a short history of each of the above words.

3-35 (continued)

1. *Christmas Tree*—Germans began the custom of cutting down pine trees and decorating them. This tradition dates back to the 1400s.
2. *Hamburger*—The American hamburger gets its name from the city of Hamburg in Germany. This food was originally a patty made of any ground meat and cooked over an open fire.
3. *Frankfurter*—The American frankfurter, or hot dog as it is more commonly called, was an Americanization of the German wiener—a pork sausage. It gets it name from the city of Frankfurt in Germany.
4. *Beer*—This English word originates from the German word "bier." Germans specialized in making many delicious varieties of this beverage. They established beer breweries in Milwaukee, Wisconsin, which produced beers such as Miller, Schlitz, and Pabst.
5. *Seltzer*—This beverage gets its name from the town of Nieder Selters in Germany, which has many natural springs that produce naturally effervescent water.
6. *"Gesundheit"*—This phrase, often used in our everyday conversations, means "Good Health" in German. It is said after someone sneezes—to ward off further illness.
7. *Oatmeal*—This dish was originated by a German American during the nineteenth century. It is a cousin to the many hot "mush" grain meals eaten in Germany during that time.
8. *Kindergarten*—This word, often used in our everyday conversations, means "children's garden" in English. The Germans were strong promoters of public education and saw the need for a stimulating education—even for young children.
9. *Pretzel*—This food originated in Germany as a large, bent piece of dough cooked until it was hard and covered with salt.
10. *Gymnasium*—The Germans promoted exercise as a means to a long and healthy life. They carried this custom to the United States when they immigrated.

Create a short story incorporating all of the above words. You will have created a German American story!

TITLE ______________________________

____

____

____

____

____

____

____

____

____

(Continue on the back.)

Name ______________________________ *Date* ____________

3–36
JEWISH AMERICANS

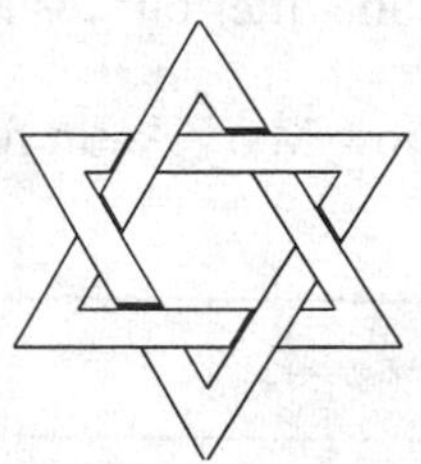

Have you ever been limited or confined to one space for a long period of time? Perhaps you have taken a long exam (such as the SAT), or have been "grounded" by your parents, or cramped in a car for a long trip. In the space provided below, describe your "limited" experience; how did it feel to be confined? how did it feel once you were "set free"?

____

____

____

____

____

____

____

____

____

____

From 1791 through the 1800s, many eastern European Jews were limited to a confined area. The Russian government, which had just acquired much of this area, required them to remain in what was called the Jewish Pale of Settlement. Few Jews were permitted to move "beyond the Pale." A Russian Jew, Mary Antin, lived this existence for much of her childhood. She later immigrated to America (along with more than 500,000 other Jews) and wrote an autobiography entitled *The Promised Land.* Read the excerpts from this book, which describe how she felt living in "the Pale" and how she felt when she arrived in America.

1. "The first time Vanka threw mud at me, I ran home and complained to my mother, who brushed off my dress and said, quite resignedly, 'How can I help you poor child? Vanka is a Gentile. The Gentiles do as they like with us Jews.' The next time Vanka abused me, I did not cry, but ran for shelter, saying to myself, 'Vanka is a Gentile.' But the third time, when Vanka spat on me, I wiped my face and thought nothing at all. . . . The world was made a certain way and I had to live with it."(1)

2. "So many lamps [in Boston}, and they burned until morning, my father said, and so people did not need to carry lanterns. In America then, everything was free, as we had heard in Russia. Light was free; the streets were as bright as a synagogue on a holy day. Music was free . . . we had been serenaded, to our gaping delight, by a brass band of many pieces, soon after our installation on Union Place."(2)

What words would you use to describe how Mary Antin felt living in the Jewish Pale of Settlement?

____

____

What words would you use to describe how Mary Antin first felt living in America?

____

____

Now you are going to do an exercise that will give you the experience of being "limited" and then "set free." For this exercise you will need a chair and a clock or a watch. In a quiet space, set up your chair and clock. Record the time you begin this exercise in the space below.

I began this exercise at __________ AM/PM (circle one).

Now, sit in the chair and do not move (except for breathing, blinking your eyes, and swallowing!). Do not watch TV. Do not talk to anyone. Do not cross or uncross your arms or legs. How long can you sit there motionless? Record the time you stop sitting still in the space below.

I ended this exercise at __________ AM/PM (circle one).

What words would you use to describe how you felt while you were sitting motionless on the chair?

____

____

____

What words would you use to describe how you felt when you were "set free"?

____

____

____

____

Do you think any of the feelings you had, either being "limited" to one space or being "set free" were feelings that Jewish Americans who emigrated from the Pale of Settlement in eastern Europe to America had? (Circle the feelings, in your answer above, that you think they would have had.)

Name ______________________ *Date* ____________

3–37

LITTLE BAGS OF IRISH EARTH

During the nineteenth century, over 4 million Irish immigrated to America. They settled primarily in the Northeast—Massachusetts, Pennsylvania, New York—and also in Illinois. Today people of Irish ancestry live all over the United States and constitute the second largest ancestral group in America. Look in your local phone book and see how many names you find that begin with "0" (O'Neill, O'Reilly, etc.), as does a typical Irish name.

I found __________ names in the phone book that begin with "O."

Why did so many Irish risk their lives to emigrate across the dangerous Atlantic Ocean? Read the following facts about Ireland and Irish immigrants to America. As you read, think about how you could use these facts to create a story about one Irish immigrant.

Fact 1: The "Emerald Island" is the nickname given by many people to the country of Ireland. Rich, green fields, lovely blue lakes, and beautiful ocean views are only part of its charming beauty. Many artists, poets, and songwriters have found inspiration in Ireland. It was a place where people loved their land.

Fact 2: During the 1800s, most of the Irish population were landless farmers. Landed Irish aristocracy owned most of the good farm land. The landless farmers were forced to worked for the aristocracy. They had no rights to the soil and rented the use of enough land. They were known as "tenant farmers" and when the tenant was unable to pay rent, the landlord often evicted the whole family.

Fact 3: The life of these tenant farmers was very difficult. They lived in small cottages that were built of wood and sod with a dirt floor. The family bedded on straw and their diet consisted mainly of potatoes, milk, and herring. A small garden was cultivated near the house to provide occasional green vegetables for the family's food. A pig, surviving on potato peelings, usually wandered the yard. A hen or two would provide them with eggs.

Fact 4: One-fourth of the farm land in Ireland was used for growing potatoes, which were the mainstay of the Irish diet. In 1845 a potato blight reached Ireland and destroyed much of the crop until 1850. This resulted in a famine. A million Irish people died of starvation or starvation-related diseases. Many chose to emigrate. Approximately one-fourth of the Irish population immigrated to America.

Fact 5: The voyage to America was long and frightening. Many people did not survive. Those who did would often empty little bags of Irish earth, which they had carried with them, on the ground upon arrival in America. This symbolized the wedding of Ireland and America.

Fact 6: Irish farmers were not familiar with American farming tools and techniques. They were not accustomed to the solitary life found on the American frontier. Many of the Irish immigrants chose or were recruited to work on building the canals, roads, and railroads being constructed during the mid-nineteenth century. This work was grueling and dangerous. Canal workers often worked in knee-deep water and were in danger of contracting many diseases such as cholera, dysentery, and malaria. Railroad workers were in constant danger from cave-ins or dynamite blasts.

Fact 7: The family and the Catholic Church played a large role in most Irish immigrants' lives. They banded together in the face of much persecution and prejudice from the people of America.

Using the above information about Irish immigrants, create a short "faction" (a combination of fiction and fact) story about one Irish immigrant in the space provided below. Your main character can be a man, woman, teenager, or child. Be sure to give your reader an idea of what this person left behind and what he or she endured in the new life in America. On balance, was the decision to leave Ireland viewed as positive or negative?

TITLE ____

(Continue on the back.)

Name ______________________________ Date ____________

3–38

THE GROWTH OF THE CITIES

American cities grew at an incredible rate during the nineteenth century. Look at the sentences below that give you information about why this growth occurred. Using four diffently colored pencils, markers, or crayons, create four pie graphs to illustrate what each sentence is stating.

1. In 1820, approximately 70 percent of American workers were agricultural workers and 30 percent were nonagricultural workers. In 1900, approximately 40 percent of American workers were agricultural workers and 60 percent were nonagricultural workers.

AMERICAN AGRICULTURAL AND NONAGRICULTURAL WORKERS

IN 1820

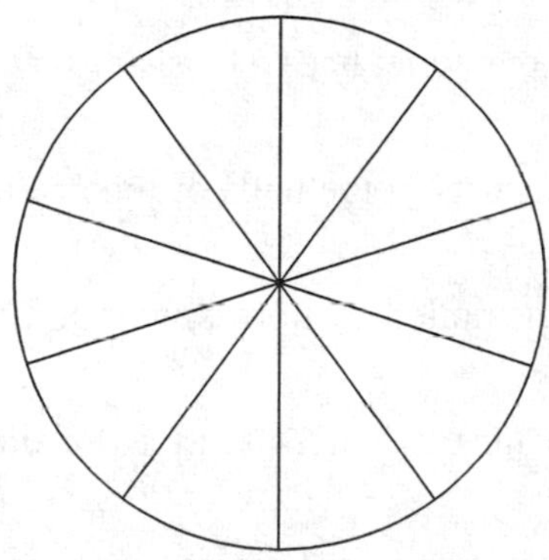

IN 1900

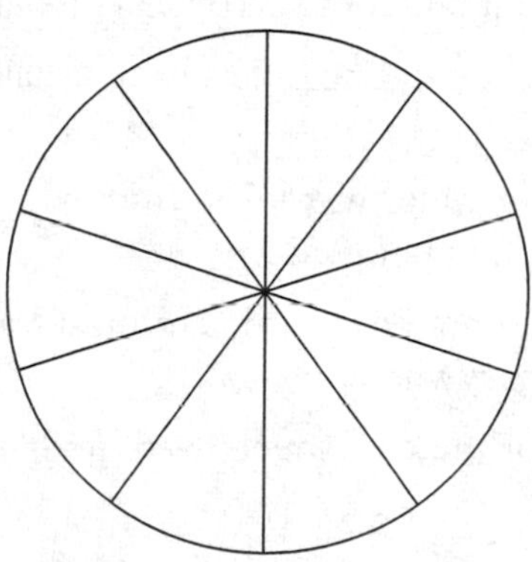

2. In 1860, approximately 80 percent of Americans lived in rural areas and 20 percent of Americans lived in urban areas. In 1900, approximately 65 percent of Americans lived in rural areas and 35 percent of Americans lived in urban areas.

RURAL AND URBAN AMERICANS

IN 1860

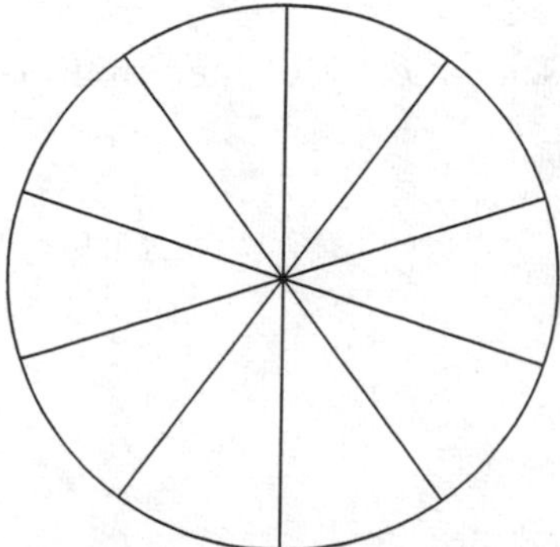

IN 1900

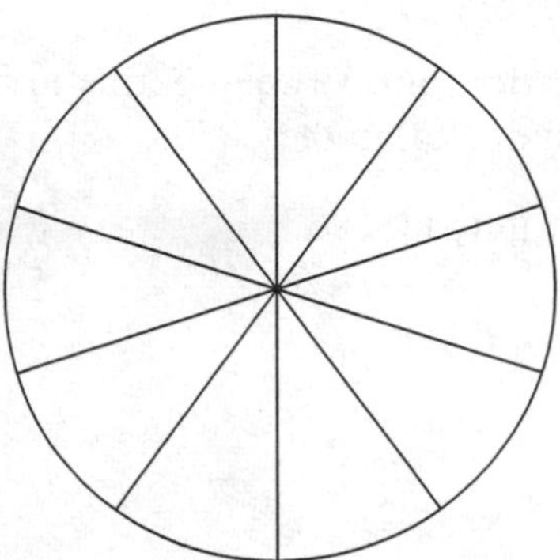

Especially for the poor, life in American cities during the nineteenth century was very difficult. A European American man, Jacob Riis, a newspaper reporter and photographer, wanted these difficulties to be exposed. He wrote a book entitled *How the Other Half Lives*, which described city life for the poor. Read the following short excerpt from his book that describes a New York City Tenement building.

"Be a little careful, please! The hall is dark and you might stumble. . . . Here where the hall turns and dives into utter darkness is . . . a flight of stairs. You can feel your way, if you cannot see it. The sinks are in the hallway, so that all the tenants may have access—and all be poisoned alike by their summer stenches. . . . Here is a door. Listen! That short, hacking cough, that tiny, helpless wail—what do they mean? . . . A child is dying of measles."[1]

DIRECTIONS: Imagine you are a city newspaper reporter during the nineteenth century. Read the following information regarding living conditions in American cities and tenement buildings. Then, create five headlines for "exposé" articles you have written about these conditions.

1. By 1900, more than one million poor New Yorkers were living in tenement buildings where the apartments were small, dark, and airless.
2. Tenement building apartments often housed 10 to 12 people in a room.
3. Tenement building toilets were usually located in the hall and one toilet had to be shared by 20 or more people.
4. Drinking water was taken from pumps on the street or from faucets in the halls of tenement buildings; it was often polluted.
5. Cars had not been invented; most transportation in the city was pulled by horses, who left their excrement everywhere.
6. Many of the city streets were nothing more than dirt lanes; Chicago had 1400 miles of dirt streets in 1890.
7. Traffic jams would clog the streets because they were filled with wagons, horses, carriages, handcarts, and pedestrians. Many street vendors would sell their goods from wagons set up on the sides of the street.
8. Epidemics of cholera, measles, and typhoid swept through Chicago and Philadelphia during the late 1880s.
9. There was no public sewage system; most sewage ran through open gutters in the street. The Chicago River became one big sewage canal by 1890, due to the amount of waste dumped into it.
10. In the poorest sections of New York City, there were only an estimated 300 bathtubs for 250,000 people.
11. By the end of the nineteenth century, there were over 700 people per acre living on the Lower East Side of New York City.
12. The relationship between germs in filth and disease became scientifically verified by Robert Koch, a German doctor, in the 1870s.

HEADLINE 1:

HEADLINE 2:

HEADLINE 3:

HEADLINE 4:

HEADLINE 5:

EXTRA CREDIT! Choose one of your headlines and create a newspaper story to describe these conditions.

TITLE ______________________________

____

____

____

____

____

____

____

____

____

(Continue on the back.)

Name ______________________________ Date ____________

3–39

QUEEN LILIUOKALANI

The last queen of the Hawaiian islands was Queen Liliuokalani. She inherited the throne in 1891. She was forced to make some important decisions regarding the future of Hawaii during her reign. Read the following facts about Hawaiian history, and then put on Queen Liliuokalani's crown for a day and decide *you* would have done if you were placed in the same situation.

1. Polynesians began immigrating to the Hawaiian islands as early as 600 A.D., traveling in large canoes and bringing with them prepared foods, domestic animals, and plant cuttings for agriculture. They developed a unique culture that was cut off from the international world for centuries.
2. In 1778, a European explorer, Captain James Cook, made contact with the island peoples. During the early nineteenth century, European whaling expeditions began to make regular stops at the islands, and an exchange of cultures began.
3. During the American Civil War (1860s) the demand for sugar skyrocketed and made the Hawaiian sugar cane industry boom. Workers were imported from Korea, China, Japan, and the Philippines to work in the sugar cane fields. Many European plantation owners became very rich.

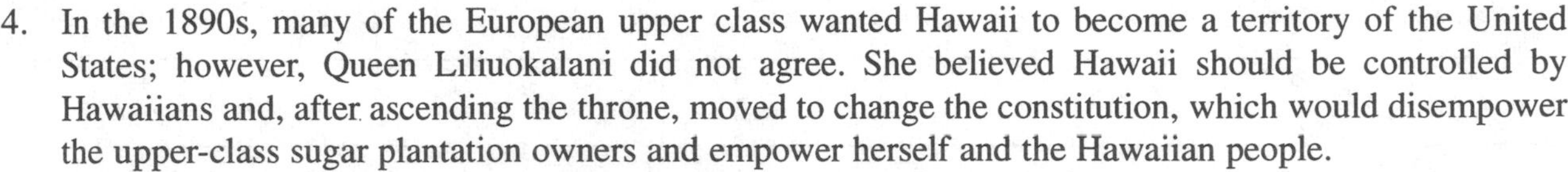

4. In the 1890s, many of the European upper class wanted Hawaii to become a territory of the United States; however, Queen Liliuokalani did not agree. She believed Hawaii should be controlled by Hawaiians and, after ascending the throne, moved to change the constitution, which would disempower the upper-class sugar plantation owners and empower herself and the Hawaiian people.
5. The annexationists formed a Committee of Safety and created a provisional government and militia. They took over government buildings and offices. They wanted the Queen to step down from her throne so Hawaii could become a territory of the United States.
6. Queen Liliuokalani knew that if she declared martial law and arrested the annexationists, civil war could break out and blood would be spilled. She knew if she did not fight this insurrection, Hawaii would be taken over by the United States and no longer controlled by the Hawaiians.

What would you do if you were Queen Liliuokalani? Would you fight the insurrection or surrender? In the space provided below, write an ending to this story based on what *you* would have decided to do. Be sure to explain what factors contributed to your decision.

(Continue on the back.)

Name ______________________________ Date ______________

3–40

PEOPLE TO REMEMBER

In the blanks provided, write the letter of the description that matches each name on the column on the left.

______ 1. FREDERICK DOUGLASS	A. Chinese American man who brought the case regarding racism against Chinese laundry owners to the Supreme Court and won
_____ 2. TECUMSEH	B. African American woman who was a leader of the abolitionist movement in Philadelphia
_____ 3. LEE YICK	C. publisher of the *North Star* newspaper and African American leader of the abolitionist movement
_____ 4. JUAN NEPOMUCENO CORTINA	D. Native American woman who helped Lewis and Clark during their expeditions in the early 1800s
_____ 5. ABRAHAM LINCOLN	E. African American representative for South Carolina during Reconstruction
_____ 6. SUSAN B. ANTHONY	F. Mexican American man who attempted to stop the expansion of the United States into the Southwest
_____ 7. QUEEN LILIUOKALANI	G. Native American man who attempted to unite all the Eastern tribes and stop expansion of the United States
_____ 8. ROBERT BROWN ELLIOT	H. Deaf European American man who invented the electric light bulb
_____ 9. THOMAS EDISON	I. African American female lecturer for the abolitionist and women's rights movements whose name meant "Traveler of Truth"
_____ 10. SOJOURNER TRUTH	J. European American president during the Civil War; wrote the Emancipation Proclamation
_____ 11. SARAH FORTEN	K. Last Hawaiian monarch, who attempted to stop the United States takeover of the islands
_____ 12. SACAGAWEA	L. European American woman who built the women's rights movement into a national organization

SECTION *Four*

THE 1900S

Teachers' Guide to Activities for the 1900s

4–1 DRAW!

How has technology changed our lives? This map exercise encourages our students to think about this question in a new and personal way.

4–2 HOW MUCH DO WE KNOW?

Before students launch into studying a subject area anew, it is important to review their *prior knowledge*. It is also important to see the biases and misconceptions we may bring to the subject area. This survey will help your students ponder what we do and do not know about the 1900s and hypothesize as to why we may have these misconceptions. ANSWERS: (1) 1920 (2) 1938 (3) 2/week (4) over 25% (5) True (6) 13 months (7) 1924 (8) Chinese (9) Mexican (10) German

4–3 CHILD LABOR

What would life be like if you were a child laborer in the early twentieth century? This exercise helps students to think about this question and be creative in solutions to remedy it!

4–4 SHOVEL AND PICK

Much is written in most U.S. history textbooks about immigrants' coming to America. Often, little is written about their frequent desire or decision to go back to their home country. This exercise about Italian immigrants gives students an idea of the difficulty of life for early twentieth-century immigrants and the decisions they were forced to make.

4–5 IDA B. WELLS FIGHTS MOB VIOLENCE

It is difficult for our students to fathom the kind of violence endured by many ethnic groups. This exercise puts them into the shoes of a courageous woman, Ida B. Wells, who fought back against mob violence.

4–6 W.E.B. DU BOIS AND BOOKER T. WASHINGTON

Being able to contrast and compare the thinking of two important African American leaders in the early twentieth century enables our students to think critically about ideas espoused by our political leaders today.

4–7 FIRST WOMAN IN CONGRESS

What was it like to be the first woman elected to Congress (*before* the Nineteenth Amendment was passed!) and to take an unpopular stand on a controversial issue the first day on the job? Your students will get a taste of this experience by doing this exercise!

4–8 WORLD WAR I

During World War I, many Americans had close relatives still living in Europe. How did these family relations complicate the support the U.S. government received for entering the war? This exercise helps our students understand this complex issue.

4–9 THE SUFFRAGE MOVEMENT

The struggle to obtain the vote for women was a long journey. This exercise will help your students understand the uncomfortable and often dangerous situations women had to endure to win this right!

4–10 "ROARING TWENTIES" BINGO

Let's have fun and learn something too! Using their prior knowledge and new knowledge obtained by playing this bingo game, your students will have a good overview of the "Roaring Twenties."

4–11 THE GREAT DEPRESSION

With their prior knowledge of the 1930s and their creative thinking skills, students will be able to review the information they already have obtained about this time period and create new hypotheses about its character.

4–12 WOMEN AND WORLD WAR II

Meet Rosie the Riveter and help decide her fate! Should she remain in the factory or should she return to her home? Watch out! This can create a great discussion in your classroom!

4–13 INTERNMENT CAMPS FOR JAPANESE AMERICANS

Most of our students have studied about Hitler's concentration camps but few know about the ordeal Japanese Americans faced *in America* during World War II. The photograph in this exercise can engender a good class discussion.

4–14 THE CIVIL RIGHTS MOVEMENT

Most of our students have learned bits and pieces about the Civil Rights movement throughout their elementary education. This exercise helps to pull together students' prior knowledge and challenge them to learn more about this important period of American history.

4–15 WHERE WOULD YOU STAND?

What was it like to integrate Central High School in Little Rock, Arkansas? This exercise is best done *in class*!

4–16 THE 1960S

What a decade it was! Categorizing the many elements of the dynamic 1960s will help our students realize the varying events and influences of the times.

4–17 ORAL HISTORY INTERVIEW—THE 1960s

How can our students learn from their parents and friends about important historical periods? By doing this exercise your students will realize that textbooks are not their only resource for learning important historical information!

4–18 ORAL HISTORY INTERVIEW—THE VIETNAM WAR

Because this war was so controversial, it is important to approach this exercise with much preparation. Students should be made aware that this subject, especially with Vietnam War veterans, should be handled with great sensitivity.

4–19 THE VIETNAM WAR—PRO OR CON?

Why was the Vietnam War so controversial? This exercise aids your students in analyzing the many different opinions about this war.

4–20 GENDER STEREOTYPES

Do stereotypes about men and women still exist in our society? Use this exercise as a homework assignment to prepare your students for a great discussion in class the following day!

4–21 WORKING OUTSIDE THE HOME

Why have so many women begun working outside the home? Use this exercise to explore the forces that have led and encouraged women to take jobs outside their homes.

4–22 ELEANOR ROOSEVELT AND HILLARY RODHAM CLINTON

What are the similarities and differences between these two dynamic women of the twentieth century? This exercise can be a springboard for further research.

4–23 PUERTO RICO—COMMONWEALTH, STATE, OR INDEPENDENCE?

Understanding the history of the relationship between Puerto Rico and the United States is an important basis for critical analysis of U.S. foreign policy. Results of the 11/14/93 plebiscite-referendum: 46.2 percent of the voters chose statehood; 4.4 percent of the voters chose independence; 48.4 percent of the voters chose to continue as a commonwealth of the United States.

4–24 TRYING TO FIT IN

How do peer pressure and multiculturalism intersect in American society? Many of your students have felt the same pressure this talented Puerto Rican writer describes.

4–25 IMMIGRATION BY SEA

How have times changed or *not* changed? Immigration by sea, whether in the seventeenth century or the twentieth century can be a life-threatening experience! (Excerpt 1—Vietnamese, Excerpt 2—German, Excerpt 3—Haitian)

4–26 SWEATSHOPS

This exercise explores the similarities and differences of two cultural groups and their experience enduring difficult working conditions.

4–27 THE FARMWORKERS AND NONVIOLENCE

Why was the farmworkers' movement of the 1960s such an important chapter in United States history? This exercise will help your students understand the philosophy of *nonviolence*, and how it can be used to make important changes.

4–28 SEPARATION OR ASSIMILATION?

This exercise explores a dilemma that many American students of color face.

4–29 A BASKETBALL STAR

This exercise is for the sports lovers in your class. It also gives an insight into the life of a talented Native American young woman.

4–30 SMILES A LOT

Your students have probably seen the movie *Dances with Wolves*. After reading this interview and doing the accompanying writing exercise, they will probably want to see it again!

4–31 ARAB AMERICANS

This exercise will sensitize your students to the uncomfortable situation many Arab Americans faced during the Persian Gulf Conflict of 1991.

4–32 BRINGING IN THE NEW YEAR

There are many celebrations around the turn of the year. By comparing and contrasting two—Kwanzaa and the Japanese New Year—our students will gain a new appreciation for these celebrations' similarities and differences.

4–33 TYPECASTING

This exercise strikes close to home for many students. By thinking through this exercise, your students will begin to look at movies and TV shows in a new light.

4–34 AMERICAN AS APPLE PIE?

What do yogurt, golf, and pizza have in common? They all originated in a different part of the world! This exercise is fun and helps your students realize the ethnic origins of many important American people and everyday objects. ANSWERS:

ITALIAN AMERICAN—Mario Cuomo (former governor of New York 1983–1994), pizza, Mother Cabrini (1850–1917—opened schools, orphanages, hospitals for the poor in New York and Chicago), Geraldine Ferraro (first woman to run for vice-president), Amerigo Vespucci (1454–1512—mapmaker for whom America is named), Joe DiMaggio (baseball star), Madonna (singer)

EAST INDIAN AMERICAN—yogurt, chess, cloves, cumin, yoga, Dalip Singh Saund (one of first Asians to serve in House of Representatives), Santha Rama Rau (writer), badminton, parcheesi, Behari Lal (Pulitzer Prize winner in science in 1937).

JAPANESE AMERICAN—tempura, Seiji Ozawa (musician and conductor), Hideyo Noguchi (1876–1928—scientist noted for research in yellow fever and syphilis), Isamu Noguchi (sculptor), karaoke, sukiyaki, kimono

FRENCH AMERICAN—Jack Kerouac (novelist), fondue, reservoir, Thomas Hopkins Gallaudet (founded first free American school for the deaf in 1817), soup du jour, John James Audubon (1785–1851—artist and naturalist), Kate Chopin (1851–1904—writer), mustard, omelette, French fries, hors d'ouevres

DUTCH AMERICAN—Theodore Roosevelt (president of United States 1901–1909), Franklin D. Roosevelt (U.S. President 1933–1945), Martin Van Buren (U.S. President 1837–1841), golf, ice skating, Santa Claus

POLISH AMERICAN—Casimir Funk (scientist who invented vitamins), city public playgrounds, vitamins, Dr. Marie Elizabeth Zakrzewska (1829–1890—founded New England Hospital for Women and Children)

4–35 NAMES

Your students will never look at the phone book in the same way after doing this exercise! ANSWERS:

HISPANIC AMERICAN—Cesar Chavez (leader of the farmworkers), Henry Gonzalez (congressman from Texas), Joan Baez (singer), Henry Cisneros (Secretary of Housing in Clinton Administration), Vilma Martinez (president of Mexican American Legal Defense and Education Fund 1973–1981)

ITALIAN AMERICAN—Arturo Toscanini (1867–1957—orchestral conductor), Geraldine Ferraro (first woman to run for vice-president), Mario Cuomo (governor of New York 1983–1994), Frank Stella (painter), Lawrence Ferlinghetti (writer)

GREEK AMERICAN—Michael Dukakis (former governor of Massachusetts), George Papanicolaou (scientist who invented the "pap" smear for women), Olympia Dukakis (actress)

VIETNAMESE AMERICAN—Nghi Huynh (editor of *Asian Business and Community News*), Jean Nguyen (first Vietnamese American graduate of West Point), Eugene Trinh (astronaut), Dr. Nguyen Anh Nga (counselor for Vietnamese refugees)

ARAB AMERICAN—Ralph Nader (consumer rights activist), Philip Habib (negotiator for the Paris Peace Talks), Mary Rose Oakar (journalist)

CZECH AND SLOVAK AMERICAN—Jarmila Novotna (opera singer), Alois F. Kavorik (physicist), Antonin Dvořák (composer)

CHINESE AMERICAN—Jade Snow Wong (writer), Chien-shuing Wu, Ieoh Ming Pei (architect), Connie Chung (journalist), Hiram L. Fong (former senator from Hawaii), Maya Lin (sculptor)

HUNGARIAN AMERICAN—Adolph Zukor (film maker for Paramount Pictures), Joseph Pulitzer (journalist), Zsa Zsa Gabor (actress)

POLISH AMERICAN—Zbigniew Brzezinski (served in Johnson Administration), Korczak Ziolkowski (sculptor of monument of Indian Chief Crazy Horse), Wanda Landowska (musician), Edmund Muskie (U.S. senator from Maine)

4–36 MAJORITY-MINORITY

Because European American culture has dominated U.S. society for so many centuries, it is difficult to fathom American life when European Americans become a minority (as is predicted in the twenty-first century!) This exercise will surprise many of your students and prepare them for the future.

4–37 ANCESTRIES

What are the ten most mentioned ancestries when Americans are asked the question, "Where did your ancestors originate?" This little publicized data from the U.S. census is fun to explore!

4–38 ASIAN AND PACIFIC ISLANDER AMERICANS

What are the origins of Asian and Pacific Islander Americans? This exercise combines math and social studies skills.

4–39 HISPANIC AMERICANS

What are the origins of Hispanic Americans? This exercise combines math and social studies skills.

4–40 PEOPLE TO REMEMBER

Women, men, Native Americans, African Americans, European Americans, Asian Americans, and Hispanic Americans are all on this list! Divide your class into small groups and encourage them to use your classroom or library resources (encyclopedias or other references) to see who can finish this list first! ANSWERS: (1)F (2)D (3)E (4)I (5)H (6)B (7)K (8)J (9)G (10)A (11)L (12)C

Name ______________________________ Date ______________

4–1
DRAW!

The 1900s was a century of great technological change for the United States. Look at the map below, which shows the railroads that had been built by thc year 1900. Then, take a large piece of paper (legal size or larger construction paper), and a pencil and redraw this map. Do not trace or use an overhead projector to enlarge the image! You can do it! Using brightly colored pencils, draw the railroads that linked the states together.

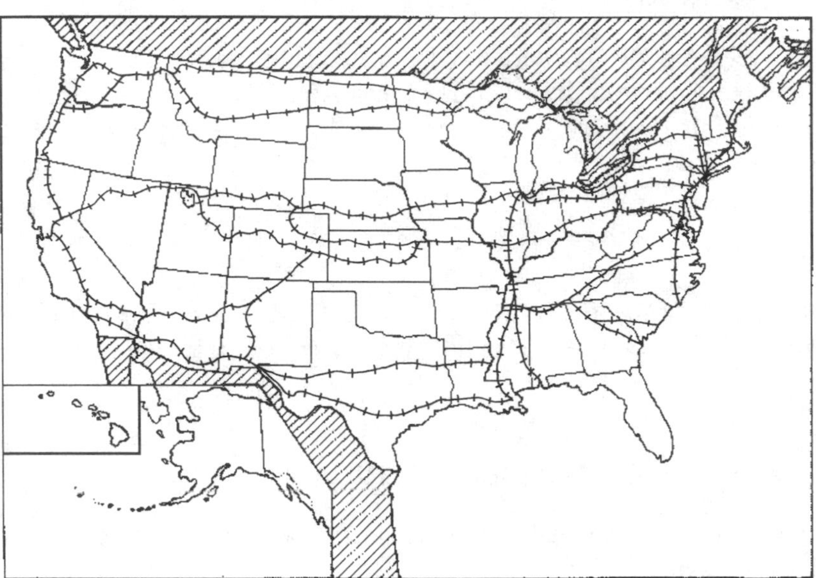

Imagine you were born on January 1, 1900, in New York, New York, and you had a cousin born that same day in San Francisco, California. You and your cousin have both lived long and healthy lives and are about to celebrate your 100th birthdays in the year 2000! Make ten entries into a diary describing how you communicated with this cousin throughout the twentieth century. Perhaps you took a trip on the railroad to visit him or her when you were 10 years old (1910). Perhaps you talked to her or him on the telephone when you were 20 years old (1920). Perhaps you took a car trip to visit him or her when you were 30 years old (1930). Perhaps you flew in an airplane to visit her or him when you were 50 years old (1950). Use your knowledge of the history of technology (TV, telephones, buses, videos, fax machines) to create your imaginary diary. Use the space provided below to make your first diary entry. Then use additional sheets of paper to make the other nine entries.

1910

Dear Diary,

____

____

____

(Continue on the back.)

Name ______________________ Date ____________

4–2

HOW MUCH DO WE KNOW?

How much do we Americans know about the history of our country? Many times there are myths and misconceptions that people have accepted as truths. Put your name in the first box of this survey and answer the questions to the best of your knowledge. Then, review the correct answers with your teacher. Finally, choose five people (neighbors, relatives, friends, other teachers, anyone!) and ask them the questions, recording their answers on the chart.

NAMES							
1. Women won the right to vote in every election: local, state, and national, in the year: a. 1900 b. 1920 c. 1950							# correct ____ # incorrect ____
2. Child labor was outlawed in the United States in the year: a. 1910 b. 1938 c. 1955							# correct ____ # incorrect ____
3. The number of African Americans who were lynched in the early twentieth century was estimated to be: a. 2/week b. 2/month c. 2/year							# correct ____ # incorrect ____
4. Unemployment during the Great Depression was estimated to be: a. 10%–12% b. 15%–20% c. over 25%							# correct ____ # incorrect ____

NAMES							
5. During World War II, the U.S government imprisoned 110,000 Japanese Americans for over three years in internment camps: a. True b. False							# correct _____ # incorrect ____
6. To change the Montgomery, Alabama, segregated bus policy, African Americans refused to ride the buses for: a. 3 days b. 1 month c. 13 months							# correct _____ # incorrect ____
7. Native Americans became citizens of the United States in: a. 1885 b. 1924 c. 1945							# correct _____ # incorrect ____
8. The largest Asian American ethnic group is: a. Chinese b. Japanese c. Korean							# correct _____ # incorrect ____
9. The largest Hispanic American ethnic group is: a. Puerto Rican b. Mexican c. Cuban							# correct _____ # incorrect ____
10. The largest European American ethnic group is: a. English b. Irish c. German							# correct _____ # incorrect ____

4-2 (continued)

Now, let's do some math. Answer the following questions below:

1. How many responses did you receive? (Add up the total number of people who took the quiz and multiply by 10.)

____

2. How many responses were correct? What percentage of the total responses was this number?

____

3. How many responses were incorrect? What percentage of the total responses was this number?

____

Why do you think people do not know all the answers to these questions? Write two hypotheses below. Many people have misconceptions about the history of our country because:

Hypothesis 1 ___________________________________

____

____

____

____

____

____

Hypothesis 2 ___________________________________

____

____

____

____

____

____

Name ____ *Date* _______________

4–3

CHILD LABOR

What memories do you have of your childhood? Think back to the time when you were 5 to 12 years old. Answer the following questions:

1. What are your favorite memories of your childhood? For example, what was your favorite game? Your favorite playground? Your favorite food? Your favorite toy? Who was your favorite teacher? Your favorite friend?

____

____

____

____

____

During the early twentieth century, many children did not go to school, play, or go to the movies. Over 250,000 children between the ages of 10 and 15 worked in mines, mills, and factories at the opening of the century. They labored 10–12 hours a day, 6–7 days a week under working conditions that were dangerous and exhausting. Read the excerpts that describe their working conditions.

"All the year in New York and in other cities you may watch children radiating to and from such pitiful homes [in which sweatshops were located]. Nearly any hour on the East Side of New York City you can see them—pallid boy or spindling girl—their faces dulled, their backs bent under a heavy load of garments piled on head and shoulders, the muscles of the whole frame in a long strain. . . ."

"In these disease-breeding holes [factories] we, the youngsters together with the women and men toiled seventy and eighty hours a week! Saturdays and Sundays included! . . . A sign would go up on Saturday afternoon: 'If you don't come in on Sunday, you need not come in on Monday' . . . children's dreams of a day off shattered. We wept, for after all, we were only children. . . ."

"A considerable number of the boys and girls die within the first two or three years after beginning work . . . 36 out of every 100 of all the men and women who work in the mill die before or by the time they are 25 years of age. . . ."

"Every day little children came into Union Headquarters, some with their hands off, some with the thumb missing, some with their fingers off at the knuckle. They were stooped little things, round shouldered and skinny. . . ."

DIRECTIONS: Having read the excerpts, think about your own life. How would your childhood have been different if you were one of the 250,000 children who were forced to work in a mill, mine, or factory during the early twentieth century? Write a short description of how your life would have been different in the space provided below.

If I had been a child laborer, my life would have been different in the following ways:

____

____

____

____

____

____

____

____

____

____

Child labor was finally outlawed in the United States in 1938; however, it took much action on the part of workers to attain this result. One famous labor organizer in the early twentieth century was a woman named

Mother Jones. She organized a Children's March in 1903 from New York to Washington, D.C., to publicize the terrible working situation for these child laborers. She described this march as follows:

"I asked some of the parents if they would let me have their little boys and girls for a week or ten days, promising to bring them back safe and sound. . . . The children carried knapsacks on their backs in which there was a knife and fork, a tin cup and plate. . . . One little fellow had a drum and another had a fife. . . . We carried banners that said: . . . 'We want time to play,' 'We want to Go to School,' and '55 hours or nothing!'"

Imagine you are one of the children who went on the Children's March to Washington, D.C., in 1903. It is your assignment to make more banners and posters to carry in the march. What do you think these banners should say? What would your demands be? Create five banners in the space provided below.

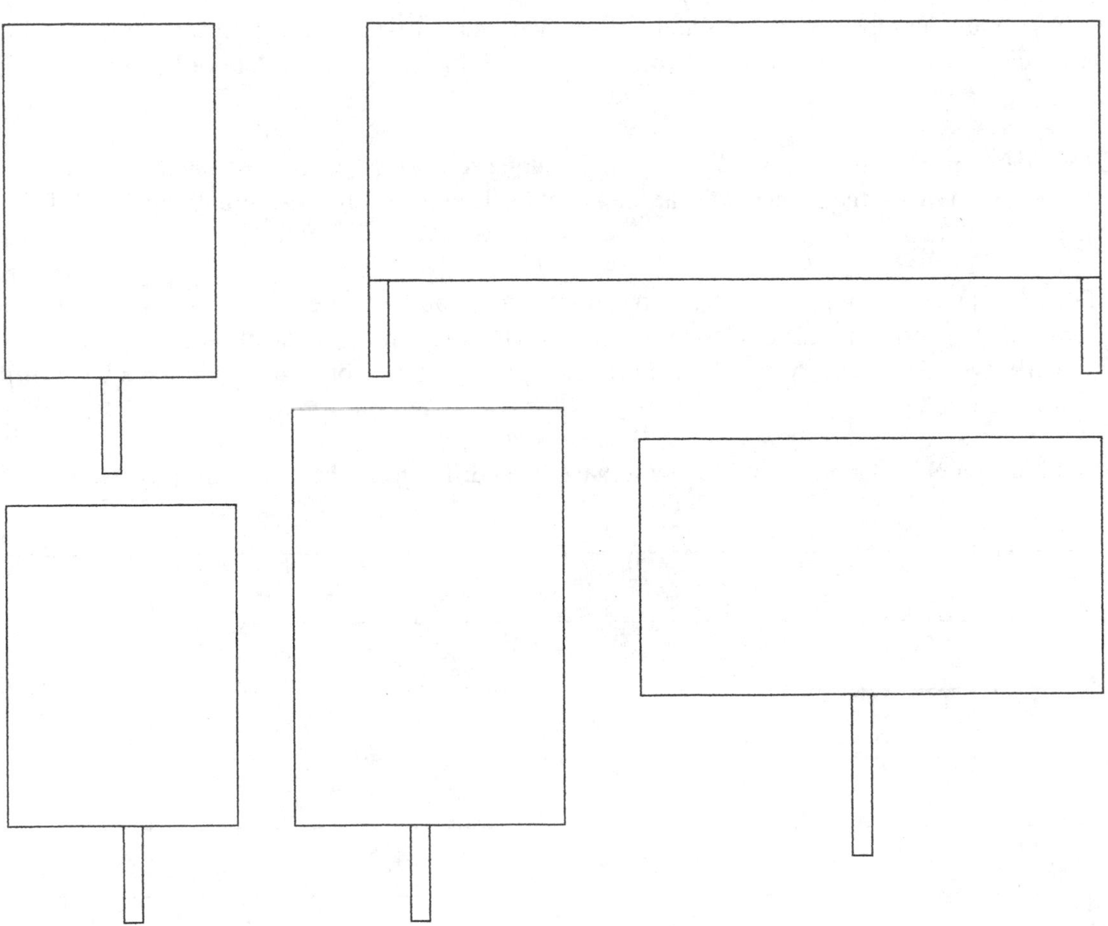

Name ______________________ Date ____________

4–4

SHOVEL AND PICK

Americans who are partially or fully of Italian descent represent the fifth largest ancestral group in America. A few Italian glassmakers came to America with the English Jamestown colonists in 1607. Then another 200 persecuted Protestant Italians founded New Castle, Delaware, in 1657. By 1850, there were still only approximately three thousand Italians living in America. Because of difficult political and economic conditions, and some natural disasters (volcano eruptions, earthquakes, etc.) in Italy between 1850 and 1930, millions of Italians began immigrating to America. The excerpts from Italian immigrants' writings give you an idea of why they came, how they came, what they did for work in America, and what their living conditions were. Step into their shoes as you read these excerpts.

LIFE IN ITALY

"We had to live the best we could. I remember my mother, sometimes she used to go to the city—we lived in a small [Italian] village—she'd go to the city and buy macaroni and then she'd cook. We used to say, 'Come on, Mom, eat.' 'No, I want to see that you get enough. You have enough, and then I'll get some,' she said. We used to fight for survival."(1)

(CLARENCE SILVA, IMMIGRANT TO THE UNITED STATES IN 1920)

THE TRIP TO AMERICA

". . . The ventilation [on board the ships] is almost always inadequate, and the air soon becomes foul. The unattended vomit of the seasick, the odors of not too clean bodies, the reek of food and the awful stench of nearby toilet rooms make the atmosphere of the steerage such that it is a marvel that human flesh can endure it. . . . Most immigrants lie in their berths for most of the voyage, in a stupor caused by the foul air. The food often repels them .. . . It is almost impossible to keep personally clean. All of these conditions are naturally aggravated by the crowding."(2)

(THE DILLINGHAM COMMISSION REPORT, 1911)

GETTING WORK IN AMERICA

"We began to make inquiries about jobs and were promptly informed that there was plenty of work at 'pick and shovel.' We were also given to understand by our fellow boarders that 'pick and shovel' was practically the only work available to Italians. Now these were the first two English words I had heard and they possessed great charm. Moreover, if I were to earn money and return home and this was the only work available to Italians, they were very weighty words for me, and I must master them as soon as possible and then set out to find their hidden meaning. I practiced for a day or two until I could say 'peek' and 'shuvle' to their perfection. Then I asked a fellow boarder to take me to see what the work was like. He did. He led me to Washington Street, not far from the colony, where some excavation work was going on, and there I did see, with my own eyes, what the 'peek' and 'shuvle' were all about. My heart sank within me, for I had thought it some form of office work; but I was game and since this was the only work available to Italians, and since I must have money to return home, I would take it up."(3)

(CONSTANTINE PANUNZIO, 1902 IMMIGRANT)

Most Italians faced very difficult working conditions in America; many were forced to work in almost slavelike conditions in factories, in mines or on railroad crews. Faced with this difficult existence, Italians had three choices: they could settle for these difficult working conditions, they could organize unions and fight for better working conditions, or they could return to Italy. Read the pros and cons below of each possible decision. Then decide, if you were an Italian immigrant living in early twentieth-century America, which choice you would make and why!

ACCEPTING DIFFICULT WORKING CONDITIONS

Pros:

1. You could hope to be one of the lucky few (such as Amedeo Obici who started Planters Peanuts; Marco J. Fontana and Antonio Ceruti who started Del Monte Products; or Amadeo Pietro Giannini, who started the Bank of America) and strike it rich.

Cons:

1. You would live a poor life with miserable working and living conditions.

FIGHTING FOR BETTER WORKING CONDITIONS BY ORGANIZING A UNION

Pros:

1. You could join such a labor movement of the early twentieth century, as the IWW (International Workers of the World) and help lead strikes like the 1912 Textile Strike in Lawrence, Massachusetts. These strikes were effective in slowly increasing wages and improving working conditions.

Cons:

1. You could be one of the many union organizers who were brutally repressed by the factory, mine, and railroad owners and the U.S. government.

RETURNING TO ITALY

Pros:

1. You would be back home among family and friends on familiar terrain.

Cons:

1. You would be faced with all the economic, political, and natural disasters of Italy during the early twentieth century.

If I were an Italian American living in the early twentieth century, I would have chosen to: (Complete this sentence and write at least one paragraph explaining why you would make this choice!)

____

____

____

____

____

Name ______________________ Date ____________

4–5
IDA B. WELLS FIGHTS MOB VIOLENCE

Mob violence reached an unprecedented peak at the turn of the twentieth century. Most of this violence was directed at African Americans; between 1878 and 1917 more than 11,100 lynchings had occurred—mostly of African American citizens. (It was not unusual for a lynching to be advertised in the local newspapers and for crowds to come from afar on chartered trains.) Other cultural groups, however, were also victims of these attacks. Read the accounts that describe several of these incidents.

1. "An inflammatory Anti-Chinese meeting was held last evening on Kearny Street. . . . The speaker read a long series of resolutions condemning the importation of coolies [racist reference to Chinese immigrants]. . . . 'We must take this insidious monster by the throat,' shouted the speaker, 'and throttle it until its heart ceases to beat, and then hurl it into the sea!' At the conclusion of this speech . . . a car passed along in which a Chinaman was riding. Yells of 'Pull him off! Lynch him! Kill the greasy slave!' etc. rent the air. . . ."(1)

   San Francisco newspaper, April 1876

2. ". . . The leading citizens of New Orleans led a mob of six thousand to eight thousand and stormed the jail. Ten Italians [prisoners] were shot to death and it was decided to take a man [another Italian prisoner] named Polize, who was only wounded, outside to be executed. The mob wanted a public hanging. Polize . . . in order to satisfy the people on the outside, who were crazy to know what was going on within, was dragged down the stairs and through the doorway by which the crowd had entered. A rope was provided and tied around his neck and the people pulled him up on the crossbars. Not satisfied that he was dead, a score of men took aim and poured a volley of shot into him, and for several hours the body was left dangling in the air."(2)

3. "Anti-Filipino riots erupted; the worst was in Watsonville, California, in 1930. There, an angry mob, infuriated at seeing Filipinos dancing with white women in their local dance hall, went on a rampage. One Filipino was killed and over fifty injured."(3)

4. "In August of 1904, the state of Georgia was rocked by occurrences in the small town of Statesboro . . . a mob that had formed surged upstairs and forced itself into the courtroom, after overpowering a company of Savannah militia whose rifles were not loaded 'in tender consideration for the feelings of the mob.' The Negroes were dragged out and burned alive. This was the signal for wholesale terrorism against the black man. One Negro was severely whipped for riding a bicycle on the sidewalk, while another was lashed 'on general principles.' The Negro mother of a three-day-old infant was beaten and kicked, and her husband was killed. Houses were wrecked, and countless terrified Negroes left the county. Although there was talk of punishing the leaders of the mob, nothing was ever done."(4)

5. (1909) "SOUTH OMAHA RIOTS ON GREEKS—Fearing another outbreak of mob spirit the Greeks began leaving South Omaha this morning. Few signs of life are seen in the Greek colony. Those who are there kept indoors. Not a Greek was at work in the packing houses this morning."

VICTIMS OF THE RIOT

Chris Monk, Greek, scalp wounds, beaten about the head
Dionisio Catopodia, Greek, shot in the leg
George Demontphulia, Greek, nose broken, face beaten and scalp wounds"[5]

One African American woman named Ida B. Wells began to fight back against these injustices. Ms. Wells published the first statistical account of lynching entitled *Red Record* in 1895. She waged an unrelenting struggle against mob violence and lynching through writing articles and editorials, traveling on lecture tours throughout the United States and Europe, and holding protests at the White House.

Imagine you are Ida B. Wells, living at the turn of the twentieth century. Choose one of the accounts above and write an editorial (a short opinion piece) about the incident to publish in your local newspaper. Begin your editorial in the space provided below.

(Continue on the back.)

Name ______________________________ Date ______________

4–6

W.E.B. DU BOIS AND BOOKER T. WASHINGTON

Two of America's most notable twentieth-century African American leaders were Du Bois and Washington. These two men held very different beliefs regarding the best path for the advancement of African Americans in U.S. society. Read excerpts of writings and speeches below and think about what their major agreements and disagreements were regarding this issue.

W.E.B. DUBOIS: "I believe that all men, black and brown and white, are brothers, varying through Time and Opportunity, in form and gift and feature, but differing in no essential particular, and alike in soul and in the possibility of infinite development. . . . I believe in the pride of race and lineage itself; in pride of self so deep as to scorn injustice to other selves; in the pride of lineage so great as to despise no man's father. . . . I believe in the Liberty of all men; the space to stretch their arms and their souls; the right to breathe and the right to vote; the freedom to choose friends, enjoy the sunshine, and ride on railroads, uncursed by color; thinking, dreaming, working as they will. . . ."

"So it is with all great movements. They must be preceded by agitation. In the present status of the Negro it is particularly necessary that we today make the world realize what his position is—make them realize that he is not merely insisting on ornamental rights and neglecting our plain duties, but that the rights we want are the rights that are necessary, inevitable before we can rightly do our duties."

BOOKER T. WASHINGTON: "In all things that are purely social we [whites and blacks] can be as separate as the fingers, yet [he balled his fingers into a fist] one as the hand in all things essential to mutual progress. . . . The wisest among my race understand that the agitation of questions of social equality is the extremest of folly, and that progress in the enjoyment of all the privileges that will come to us must be the result of severe and constant struggle rather than artificial forcing."

"Brains, property and character for the Negro will settle the question of civil rights. The best course to pursue in regard to the civil rights bill in the South is to let it alone; let it alone and it will settle itself. Good schoolteachers and plenty of money to pay them will be more potent in settling the race question than many civil rights bills and investigating committees."

With which of these men do you *disagree*? Write him a letter and explain why you believe his opinion of the best path for advancement of African Americans is *wrong*!

Dear ,

____

(Continue on the back.)

Name ______________________________ Date ______________

4–7

FIRST WOMAN IN CONGRESS

Jeannette Rankin was one of America's most remarkable European American women of the twentieth century. Born in Montana, she was the first woman to be elected to the U.S. House of Representatives (1916). This occurred *before* the Nineteenth Amendment to the U.S. Constitution resolved that women had the right to vote in every state of our nation. This was not the only distinction of Ms. Rankin, however; during her first day in the House, she was one of the few (50 representatives) who voted against U.S. involvement in World War I. Again in 1941, during her second term in Congress, she voted against U.S. involvement in World War II, this time being the *only* representative to do so. Why did Ms. Rankin take such an adamant stand? Read her statements below.

1. When the roll call was taken for the vote on World War I, Ms. Rankin responded, "I want to stand by my country, but I cannot vote for a war. I vote no."
2. When the roll call was taken for the vote on World War II, Ms. Rankin responded, "As a woman, I can't go to war and I refuse to send anyone else."
3. Reflecting on these votes many years later she said, "I believe that the first vote I cast was the most significant vote and a most significant act on the part of women, because women are going to have to stop war. I felt at that time that the first woman [in Congress] should take the first stand, that the first time the first woman had a chance to say no to war she should say it. That was what held me up with all the pressures being brought to get me to vote for war."[1]

DIRECTIONS: Jeannette Rankin considered herself a "pacifist." What words do you associate with this term? Around the circle below, write words that come to your mind when you hear the word *pacifism.* Then look this word up in the dictionary and write its definition inside the circle.

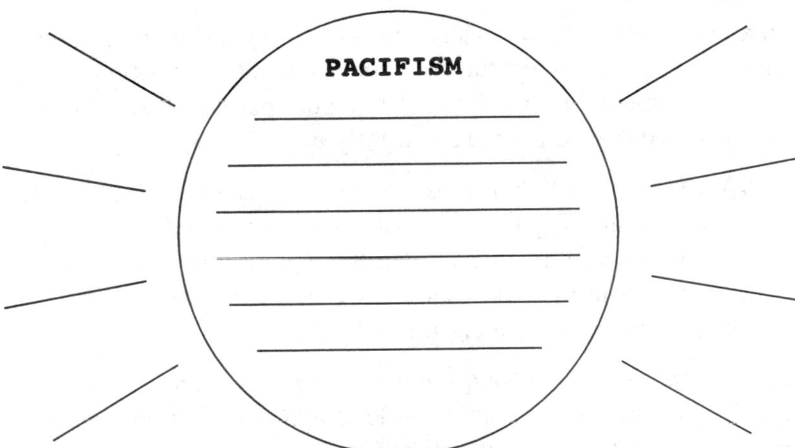

What is your opinion of Ms. Rankin's votes in Congress on war and her pacifist stand? Would you have voted with her or against her if you had been in Congress in 1917 and 1941? Write your answer to this question in the space provided below.

____

(*Continue on the back.*)

Name ______________________________ Date ____________

4–8

WORLD WAR I

When war started in Europe between the Axis Powers (Germany, Austria-Hungary, and Italy) and the Allied Powers (France, England, and Russia) in 1914, most people in the United States did not want to get involved. Isolationism (a national policy of remaining aloof from political entanglements with other countries) was at its height. By 1917, however, President Woodrow Wilson had decided to commit American troops to the Allied cause and, though the vote was 374 for and 50 against, the majority of Congress supported his decision. Three million young American men were drafted to serve in World War 1; over 112,000 died and 230,000 were wounded by the end of the war. Throughout the war, sentiments—pro and con—ran strong. Many Americans had close relatives still living in Europe, which influenced these sentiments. Put yourself in the shoes of the following Americans in the year 1917. Decide, in each case, if you would have: (1) supported ; (2) *not* supported; or (3) remained neutral toward U.S. involvement in World War I.

1. *GERMAN AMERICAN MALE MIDWESTERN FARMER*

a. Eight million Americans were of German or Austrian descent.

b. Many German Americans had close relatives living in Europe.

c. The U.S.A. was fighting *against* Germany.

d. The U.S. army bought much produce from Midwestern farmers to feed the troops.

If I were a German American male Midwestern farmer in 1917, I would have supported/not supported/remained neutral toward (circle one) U.S. involvement in World War I because:

____

____

____

2. *IRISH AMERICAN FEMALE HOUSE SERVANT (New York City)*

a. Four and a half million Americans were of Irish descent.

b. Many Irish Americans had close relatives living in Europe.

c. Many Irish Americans hated England because of its treatment of Ireland.

d. The United States was fighting on the side of England (Allied Powers).

If I were an Irish American female house servant in New York City, I would have supported/not supported/remained neutral toward (circle one) U.S. involvement in World War I because:

____

____

____

3. *AFRICAN AMERICAN MALE FIELD LABORER*

a. Four hundred thousand African Americans served in the U.S. army.

b. Most African American soldiers were relegated to the segregated labor battalions; only a very few were allowed to engage in combat, also in segregated units.

c. Racism was at a height. An average of two lynchings a week was occurring in the United States due to activities of groups like the Ku Klux Klan.

d. Most African Americans could not vote or sit on juries due to Jim Crow laws.

e. Many African Americans viewed service in the military as a means to elevating their economic and social status.

If I were an African American male field laborer in 1917, I would have supported/not supported/remained neutral toward (circle one) U.S. involvement in World War I because:

____

____

4. *ENGLISH AMERICAN MALE ARMS MANUFACTURER*

a. The U.S. army needed many military supplies to carry on the war effort.

b. Because over three million European American men were drafted to serve in the U.S. army, many women and African American men took their places in factories; these workers were generally paid lower wages.

c. Many English Americans had relatives still living in England.

If I were an English American male arms manufacturer in 1917, I would have supported/not supported/remained neutral toward (circle one) U.S. involvement in World War I because:

____

____

5. *HUNGARIAN AMERICAN FEMALE FACTORY WORKER*

a. Women were paid, on the average, much lower wages than men were paid to do the same factory work.

b. Many women's husbands were drafted into the U.S. army.

c. Many factories began hiring more women during World War I.

d. Many Hungarian Americans still had relatives living in Hungary.

e. The U.S. was fighting against Austria-Hungary.

If I were a Hungarian American female factory worker in 1917, I would have supported/not supported/remained neutral toward (circle one) U.S. involvement in World War I because:

____

____

Name ______________________________ Date ______________

4–9

THE SUFFRAGE MOVEMENT

American women worked for 72 years to win the right to vote. Beginning in 1848 with the first Women's Rights National Convention, women suffragists educated the public and pressured politicians to accept their demands. They used every tactic available to make their issue visible, from petitions and lectures to demonstrations and civil disobedience. Finally, in 1920, the Nineteenth Amendment to the Constitution was passed—giving women the right to vote in every election—local, state, and national. Why was it so difficult to change the minds of many American men and some American women? Read the following quotes from two presidents at the beginning of the century.

President Grover Cleveland: "Sensible and responsible women do not want the vote. The relative positions to be assumed by man and woman in the working out of our civilization were assigned long ago by a higher intelligence than ours."(1)

President Theodore Roosevelt: "The President of the United States does not absent himself from the country during the term of his Presidency, it is his domain. So it will be with woman: she is the queen of her empire and that empire is the home."(2)

If you were a woman living in the early twentieth century, what would your response to this kind of attitude be? Would you agree with these two presidents? Would you not care either way? Or would you protest against this kind of attitude? Write your response below.

____

____

____

____

Women employed many creative tactics to bring attention to the suffrage issue. One example of this was the 1913 "surprise" demonstration that upstaged the inaugural parade of President-elect Woodrow Wilson—over 8000 women arrived quietly in Washington, D.C. (including the daughter of former president Theodore Roosevelt, Alice Roosevelt Longworth) and, with bands blaring, marched down Pennsylvania Avenue, which was all decorated for the inaugural occasion. Another time, members of the National College Women's Suffrage League rode bicycles (at that time considered very "unladylike") with yellow and blue ribbons woven into the spokes and VOTES FOR WOMEN placards tied to their handlebars. They were nicknamed "The Militants" and marched in their demonstrations to homemade songs such as the following:

UNCLE SAM'S WEDDING (Tune: Yankee Doodle)

Of all the songs that have been sung
Within the States and Nation,
There's none that comes so near the heart
As Uncle Sam's relation.
When Uncle Sam set up his house,
He welcomed ev'ry brother,
But in his haste of his new life,
He quite forgot his mother.
Now his house is up in arms,
A keeper he must find him
To sweep and dust and set to rights
The tangles all about him.
Uncle Sam is long in years,
And he is growing wiser;
He now can see 'twas a mistake
To have no Miss-advisor

Some women rights activists felt so strongly about the suffrage issue that they engaged in *civil disobedience* to let their views be known. Led by Alice Paul, these women stood outside the White House for hours each day, every day of the month. They were attacked by hostile men, and the police did not protect them. Finally, President Wilson was so embarrassed by their presence, he had them arrested. But they returned to their vigil, day after day.

If you had lived in early twentieth-century America, would you have joined in any kind of suffrage movement action? (sign petitions, ride bicycles and sing songs, demonstrate, engage in civil disobedience?) To answer this question, gather together a group of classmates (at least two) and divide yourself into two groups—Group A and Group B. Then follow these directions:

1. Find a space approximately 10 feet by 5 feet. With masking tape, divide the space into three rectangles as shown below:

YES	MAYBE	NO

2. Write "YES," "NO," and "MAYBE" on three separate sheets of paper, and put one sheet in each rectangle.
3. Have Group A sit as the audience and Group B encircle the space marked off by the masking tape.
4. Have one person in Group A read out loud the questions on the following page. After each question is read, everyone in Group B must stand in a "YES," "NO," or "MAYBE" rectangle.
5. After Group B completes reactions to the questions, then Group B should sit down and be the audience while Group A responds to each question by standing in the "YES," "NO," or "MAYBE" rectangle.

QUESTION 1: If you were living in 1913, would you have signed a petition demanding the vote for women?

4-9 (continued)

QUESTION 2: If you were living in 1913, would you have participated in a demonstration demanding the vote for women?

QUESTION 3: If you were living in 1913, would you have engaged in civil disobedience in front of the White House, holding posters that demanded the vote for women, enduring physical abuse from hostile men, and risking being arrested by the police?

After both groups have an opportunity to answer the questions by standing in the "YES," "NO," or "MAYBE" rectangles, everyone should sit down and answer the following questions:

1. I chose to stand in the YES/NO/MAYBE (circle one) box for Question 1 because:

____

____

2. I had the following feelings when choosing my answer for Question 1:

____

____

3. I chose to stand in the YES/NO/MAYBE (circle one) box for Question 2 because:

____

____

4. I had the following feelings when choosing my answer for Question 2:

____

____

5. I chose to stand in the YES/NO/MAYBE (circle one) box for Question 3 because:

____

____

6. I had the following feelings when choosing my answer for Question 3:

____

____

Name ______________________________ Date ______________

4–10
"ROARING TWENTIES" BINGO

How much do you know about the 1920s—the decade known as the "Roaring Twenties"? Test and improve your knowledge by playing "Roaring Twenties" Bingo. For this game you will need the following:

1. at least two other classmates
2. 51 small white cards or pieces of paper (2" x 5")
3. 25 coins (pennies, nickels, dimes) per person
4. an encyclopedia, a dictionary, and a U.S. history book.

Look at the list of terms and names associated with this historical period. Those that you do not know, look up in your dictionary, text book, or encyclopedia. Then turn to the next page to play "Roaring Twenties" Bingo:

LIST A	*LIST B*	*LIST C*
bootlegging	Margaret Sanger	Scopes Trial
speakeasy	radios	Ku Klux Klan
flapper	washing machines	speculation
boom	high employment	business cycle
Marcus Garvey	Claude McKay	Louis Armstrong
talkies	Jim Crow laws	automobiles
Cotton Club	Stock Market Crash	run on the bank
stocks	buying on margin	capitalism
refrigerators	supply and demand	Charleston
millionaires	suffrage for women	Herbert Hoover
Model T Fords	Charles Lindbergh	Calvin Coolidge
overproduction	Teapot Dome Scandal	Will Rogers
Langston Hughes	Sacco & Vanzetti Trial	Amelia Earhart
gangsters	Harlem Renaissance	Zora Neal Hurston
William Faulkner	F. Scott Fitzgerald	Ernest Hemingway
jazz	Jean Toomer	Bessie Smith
electric irons	birth control movement	bankruptcy

4-10 (continued)

ROARING TWENTIES BINGO

1. Three people must take one list each of the terms and, on 17 small white cards or pieces of paper (2" x 5"), write the term or name on one side and a definition or description on the other.
2. Combine the white cards into one pile and place them inside a hat (or box). One person is the leader and holds the "hat" of cards.
3. The other two people, the players, must fill up the bingo card below with any twenty-five of the terms or names. Write them in pencil or pen in the small squares of the bingo card.
4. The leader draws the cards, one by one, out of the hat and reads *only* the definition or description. (The drawn cards are placed in a separate pile.) Each player places a penny over the term on his or her bingo card that he or she believes matches the term or name.
5. When one of the players fills up an *entire* bingo card, he or she calls out, "BINGO." The leader must check the terms and definitions to see if the player matched them correctly. If the player has matched all the terms or names and definitions or descriptions, she or he wins the "Roaring Twenties" Bingo game!

Name ______________________________ Date ______________

4–11

THE GREAT DEPRESSION

What do you associate with the word "depression"? Around this encircled word below, write any word that comes to your mind when you hear the term "depression."

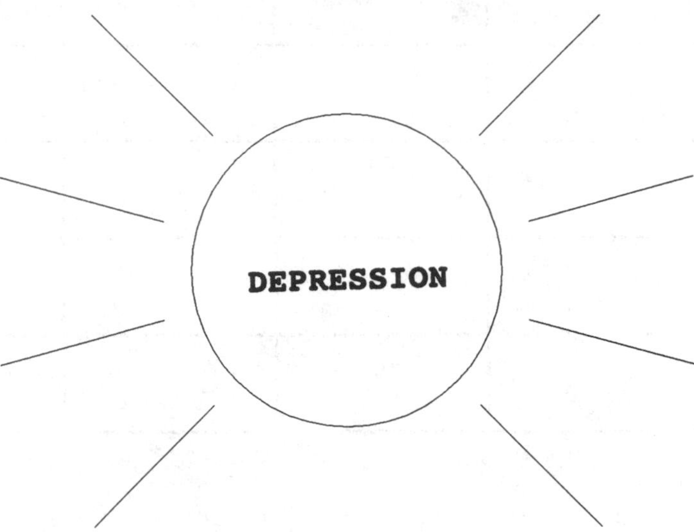

Look up the word depression in your dictionary and write its definition *(that has to do with the economy)*, in the space provided below.

DEPRESSION:

The "Great Depression" of the U.S.A. occurred during the decade of the 1930s. Let's imagine for a moment that you discovered a time capsule filled with photographs from this era while you were digging in a sandbox with your younger brother or sister in your local park. What would you expect to see in these pictures? Write your answers in the box provided below.

Also in the time capsule were scraps of paper with words describing the 1930s written on them. It was as if the person who made the time capsule was trying to create a puzzle that the person in the future who found the time capsule (you!) would have to solve. On the next page are the words. Read these words and think about which words fit together in a group in your mind.

WORDS FROM THE GREAT DEPRESSION 1929–1940

dust storms	labor strikes	Okies
social security	evictions	bread lines
Stock Market Crash	demonstrations	sharecropper
farm auction	overproduction	soup kitchens
25% unemployment	Franklin Roosevelt	dumped milk
Woody Guthrie	rent strikes	starvation
business cycles	minimum wage	Herbert Hoover
"run on a bank"	homeless people	Roaring Twenties
John L. Lewis	social security	bankruptcy
tenant farmers	capitalism	sit-down strikes
Southern Tenant Farmers Union	Congress of Industrial Organizations	collective bargaining
Works Progress Administration	maximum working hours	supply and demand
Communist Party	Eleanor Roosevelt	Paul Robeson
Civilian Conservation Corps	The New Deal	Federal Theater Project
Scottsboro Case	Mary McLeod Bethune	NAACP

Group the above words into categories. In other words, decide which words have something in common and fit together in a group. You can decide to have three, four, five, or more categories. Then write these words in the category boxes on the next page.

4-11 (continued)

CATEGORY BOXES

4-11 (continued)

Look at each of your categories and decide what the words in each box have in common. Select *one word* or a *label* that best describes each grouping and write it at the top of each box. Based on this grouping, what hypotheses can you make about life during the Great Depression? Write three of your hypotheses in the space provided below.

HYPOTHESIS 1: ____

____

____

____

____

____

____

HYPOTHESIS 2: ____

____

____

____

____

____

____

HYPOTHESIS 3: ____

____

____

____

____

____

____

Name ______________________ Date ____________

4–12

WOMEN AND WORLD WAR II

More than any other event in the 20th century, World War II overturned attitudes about women in the work place and altered women's place in the labor force. Symbolized by the figure, "Rosie the Riveter," women were recruited to replace men who had been sent to fight overseas. Women worked in factories where they operated giant overhead cranes, cleaned blast furnaces, drove tanks off the production line, handled gun powder, riveted, welded, cut lathes, and loaded shells. They also worked in offices and in the service industry as bus drivers, truck drivers, lumberjacks, train conductors, barbers, firefighters, gas pump operators, and secretaries. Six million women took paying jobs during World War II; the proportion of women in the work force rose from 25 to 36 percent. Former housewives, beauticians, saleswomen, waitresses, and others showed that a woman could do any job a man could do.

At the end of World War II, most soldiers wanted to return to civilian life and civilian jobs. There was a large controversy over what should be done with all the women workers. Should they be allowed to keep their jobs? Should they be forced to leave their jobs and make way for the returning male soldiers? Read the quotes below that reflect the different attitudes toward these questions. As you read them, think about what *your* views are.

1. "Women would do well to recapture those functions in which they have demonstrated superior capacity. Those are, in general, the nurturing functions around the home. Fields belonging to the male area of exploit or authority—law, mathematics, physics, business, industry, and technology—government and socially minded organizations should . . . make it clear that such pursuits are not generally desirable for women."[1]
2. We think that it is a right that belongs to the individual, man or woman, to decide whether or not he or she wants to work. Industry, business, or government should not make that decision. If there is a job to be done, the worker should be accepted according to training and ability."[2]
3. "Women are needed to restore order to our insecure world. . . . What ails these women who consciously or unconsciously reject their children? . . . The poor child whose mother has to work has some inner

security because he knows in his little heart that his mother is sacrificing herself for his well-being. But the neglected child from a well-to-do home, who realizes instinctively that his mother prefers her job to him, often hates her with a passionate intensity."[3]

4. "There were those whose husbands would not return from the war, or who would return injured; of those who would never marry because the war had decimated the ranks of men. There were those who *wanted* to work: those who found happiness in a job, who found the child-rearing role unduly restrictive or who, having experienced the relative independence and responsibility of wage-earning, would simply refuse to retreat to the home."[4]

With which of the above opinions do you agree? Write your answer to this question in the space provided below. Be sure to explain *why* you agree with this opinion!

___

___

___

___

(Continue on the back.)

Many women were laid off from their war-time employment. In just heavy industry alone, two million women had been fired by 1946. At the beginning of World War II, 95 percent of the women who took outside jobs intended to quit when the men came home; by the end of World War II, 80 percent of the working women wanted to stay in their jobs.

Imagine you are a woman living in 1946 with two children. You took a factory job during the war and were laid off in 1946. What reaction would you have had to this situation? Would you have been relieved? Would you have been angry? Write an entry in your diary below.

1946

Dear Diary,

___

___

___

___

___

___

___

___

Name ______________________ Date ______________

4–13

INTERNMENT CAMPS FOR JAPANESE AMERICANS

During World War II, over 110,000 Japanese Americans were rounded up and imprisoned in internment camps for over three years. The U.S. Army was given the power to arrest every Japanese American on the West Coast (without warrants, indictments, or hearings) and forcibly remove them from their homes to be "relocated" for the "security of the country." Read the following quotes that reflect the action of the U.S. government:

"I'm for catching every Japanese in America, Alaska, and Hawaii now and putting them in concentration camps. . . . Damn them! Let's get rid of them now!"(1)

CONGRESSMAN JOHN RANKIN
CONGRESSIONAL RECORD, 12/15/1941

"ALL PERSONS OF JAPANESE ANCESTRY, BOTH ALIEN AND NONALIEN, WILL BE EVACUATED FROM THE ABOVE DESIGNATED AREA BY 12 O'CLOCK NOON"(2)

U.S. GOVERNMENT POSTER
EXECUTIVE ORDER 9066

Japanese Americans lost their homes, businesses, and jobs because of this action by the U.S. government. Read the following quotes, which describe the ordeal most Japanese Americans experienced.

"The government did not tell us whether we would be able to come back or not. They did not promise us anything. So I told my wife that perhaps the best thing would be to sell our furniture and buy food and medicines and things like that. Our younger daughter was only four months old, and the older one was four years old, and we didn't know if there would be doctors or hospitals in the camp. So we took in as much medicine and baby food as possible."(3)

ROY YANO

"To pack and evacuate in forty-eight hours was an impossibility. I saw mothers completely bewildered with children crying from want and peddlers taking advantage and offering prices next to robbery. . . ."(4)

JOE KURIHARA, WORLD WAR I VETERAN

"Colonel Bendetsen [in charge of the relocation] showed himself to be a little Hitler. I mentioned that we had an orphanage with children of Japanese ancestry and that some of these children were half Japanese, others one-fourth or less. I asked which children should we send. . . . Bendetsen said: 'I am determined that if they have one drop of Japanese blood in them, they must go to camp.'"(5)

FATHER HUGH T. LAVERY
CATHOLIC MARYKNOLL CENTER, LOS ANGELES

"I was rather disappointed at the barracks which we evacuees were to live in. I thought at least each individual family would be assigned to a separate apartment. Instead, two or three families were crowded into a six beam apartment, offering no privacy."(6)

HEART MOUNTAIN REPORTS DIVISION, MAY 1943

INTERNMENT CAMPS FOR JAPANESE AMERICANS: "CHILDREN AWAITING EVACUATION" (5/8/1942) BY DOROTHEA LANGE (NATIONAL ARCHIVES #210-G-2C-155).

"Evacuees ate communally, showered communally, defecated communally. Again with an eye toward economy, no partitions had been built between toilets. . . . In interior California camps, the hot summer sun beating down on paper-thin roofs turned living quarters into sizzling ovens causing the floors [made of asphalt] to melt."(7)

JAPANESE EVACUEE

"The barbed wire stockade surrounding the 18,000 people there was like that of the prison camps of the Germans. There were the same turrets for the soldiers and the same machine guns for those who might attempt to climb the high wiring. . . . The buildings were covered with tarred paper over green and shrinking shiplap—this for the low winter temperatures of the high elevation of Tule Lake. . . . .No federal penitentiary so treats its adult prisoners. Here were the children and babies as well."(8)

CHIEF JUDGE WILLIAM DENMAN
NINTH CIRCUIT COURT OF APPEALS, 8/26/49

Look at the picture above of two Japanese American children and an elderly woman who are being deported to an internment camp in 1942. Answer the following questions:

1. How old do you think these two children were at the time of this picture? ____________________

____

4-13 (continued)

2. How old would these two children be if they are still living today? ______________________________

____

Imagine you are one of the children in this picture, who has lived to be 65+ years old. Imagine that you have had several children and many grandchildren and you are showing them this picture of yourself and your sister. What stories would you tell your grandchildren about your experience during World War II in the internment camp and what lessons would you want to teach them regarding this experience? Write your conversation with a grandchild below.

Grandparent:

Grandchild:

Grandparent:

Grandchild:

Grandparent:

Grandchild:

Grandparent:

Grandchild:

Grandparent:

Name ________________________________ *Date* ______________

4–14
THE CIVIL RIGHTS MOVEMENT

What do you associate with the words "civil" and "rights"? Around the encircled words below, write any word that comes to your mind when you hear the terms "civil" and "rights."

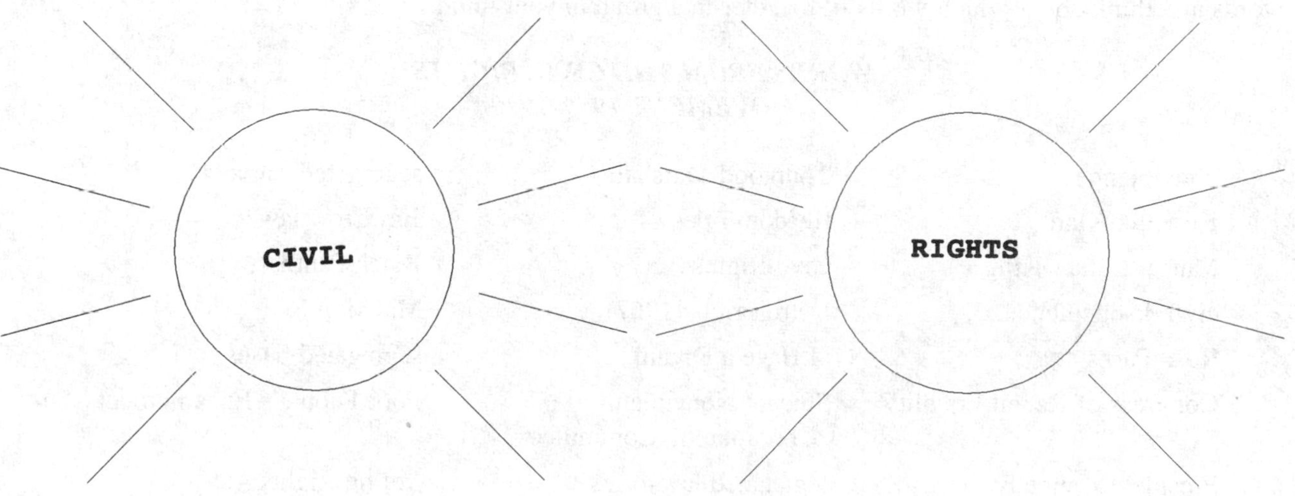

Look up these terms in your dictionary and write their definitions in the space provided below.

CIVIL:

RIGHTS:

Equality and justice are two goals that Americans have been struggling to achieve since the birth of this country. What is usually referred to as the "Civil Rights Movement" of the United States was the time period approximately between 1950 and 1970 when African Americans led an intensified struggle to make American society more equal and just. Let's imagine, for a moment that you discovered a time capsule filled with photographs from this era while you were digging in a sandbox with your younger brother or sister in your local park. What would you expect to see in these pictures? Write your answers in the box provided below:

Also in the time capsule, were scraps of paper with words written on them describing the Civil Rights Movement. It was as if the person who made the time capsule was trying to create a puzzle that the person in the future who found the time capsule (you!) would have to solve. On the next page are the words. Read these words and think about which words fit together in a group in your mind.

WORDS FROM THE CIVIL RIGHTS MOVEMENT 1950–1970

nonviolence	Thurgood Marshall	segregated schools
Ku Klux Klan	freedom rides	Jim Crow laws
Martin Luther King	Civil Rights Act	Black Panthers
civil disobedience	Detroit riots (1967)	Malcolm X
Rosa Parks	"I Have a Dream"	segregated buses
Congress of Racial Equality	Student Nonviolent Coordinating Committee	Poor People's Encampment
President Kennedy	segregated lavatories	Voting Rights Act
lynching	FBI Cointelpro	Urban League
"We Shall Overcome"	Brown vs. Board of Education	Coretta Scott King
segregated neighborhoods	segregated lunch counters	Schwerner, Chaney, and Goodman
NAACP	desegregation	fire hoses
attack dogs	Bull Connors	church bombings
Angela Davis	sit-ins	demonstrations
Montgomery, Alabama	Little Rock, Arkansas	Lyndon B. Johnson
George Wallace	"Bloody Sunday"	Mahatma Ghandi

Group the above words into categories. In other words, decide which words have something in common and fit together in a group. You can decide to have three, four, five, or more categories. Then write these words in the category boxes on the next page.

CATEGORY BOXES

CATEGORY BOXES

4-14 (continued)

Now, look at each of your categories and decide what the words in each box have in common. Select *one word* or a label that best describes the grouping and write it at the top of each box. Based on this grouping, what hypotheses can you make about life during the Civil Rights Movement? Write three of your hypotheses in the space provided below.

HYPOTHESIS 1: ____

____

____

____

____

____

____

HYPOTHESIS 2: ____

____

____

____

____

____

____

HYPOTHESIS 3: ____

____

____

____

____

____

____

Name ______________________ *Date* ______________

4–15

WHERE WOULD YOU STAND?

The Civil Rights Movement involved people of all ages—young through old. Many teenagers were thrust into situations where they had to make decisions and take leadership in very tense and potentially violent situations. Elizabeth Eckford, Melba Patillo Beals, and Ernest Greene were examples of these teenagers. In 1957, they were among the nine African American students who first integrated the previously segregated Central High School in Little Rock, Arkansas. Read the following descriptions of this experience and imagine yourself in their shoes.

> "... I walked across the street [toward Central High School] conscious of the crowd that stood there, but they moved away from me. . . . [Then] the crowd began to follow me, calling me names. I still wasn't afraid—just a little nervous. Then my knees began to shake all of a sudden and I wondered whether I could make it to the center entrance a block away. It was the longest block I ever walked in my whole life . . . somebody started yelling 'Lynch her! Lynch her!' I tried to see a friendly face somewhere in the mob . . . I looked into the face of an old woman, and it seemed a kind face, but when I looked at her again, she spat at me. . . ."
>
> ELIZABETH ECKFORD

> "... The white hand of a uniformed officer reached out toward the car, opening the door and pulling me toward him as his urgent voice ordered us to hurry. The roar coming from the front of the building, made me glance to my right. Only a half block away, I saw hundreds of white people, their bodies in motion, their mouths open wide as they shouted their anger. 'The niggers. Keep the niggers out!' . . . Hustled along, we walked up the few concrete stairs, through the heavy double doors that led inside the school. . . . 'Here are your class schedules and homeroom assignments. Wait for your guides,' Mrs. Huckabuy [vice-principal] said. . . . Three thirty-nine, that was the number of the homeroom on my card. . . . We quickly compared notes. Each of us was assigned to a different homeroom. 'Why can't any of us be in the same homeroom or take classes together?' I asked. From behind the long desk, a man spoke in an unkind booming voice. 'You wanted integration . . . you got integration.' I turned to see the hallway swallow up my friends. . . . Suddenly I felt it—the sting of a hand slapping the side of my cheek, and then warm slimy saliva on my face, dropping to the collar of my blouse. . . . As I entered the classroom, a hush fell over the students. The guide pointed me to an empty seat, and I walked toward it. Students sitting nearby quickly gathered their books and moved away . . . 'Are you gonna let that nigger coon sit in our class?' a boy shouted as he glared at me. . . . 'We can kick the crap out of this nigger,' the heckler continued. 'Look, it's twenty of us and one of her. They ain't nothing but animals.'"(1)
>
> MELBA PATILLO BEALS

"One of the youngsters, Minniejean Brown [a new African American student], happily recounted that she had been invited by her white classmates to join the glee club. Some of the students had asked the black kids to eat lunch with them. . . . The president of the student council told reporter Mike Wallace that if only the white parents would stay away from school, there would be no violence. Another student commented, 'I think it [the opposition to integration] is downright un-American. . . . I always thought all men were created equal.'"[(2)]

"Ernest Greene became the first black student to graduate from Central High [in May, 1958]. Police officers and federal troops stood guard as Greene and his 601 white classmates received their diplomas. . . . 'I knew I was walking for the other eight students who were there,' Greene said years later. 'I figured I was making a statement and helping black people's existence. . . .' The mostly white audience applauded enthusiastically as one by one the students came to receive their diplomas. Then came Ernest Greene's moment. 'When they called my name, there was nothing. Just the name and then there was eerie silence. Nobody clapped. But I figured they didn't have to . . . because after I got that diploma, that was it. I had accomplished what I had come for.'"[(3)]

ERNEST GREENE

What would *you* have done if you were put in a situation such as this? To answer this question, gather together a group of friends (at least two) and divide yourself into two groups—Group A and Group B. Then follow these directions:

1. Find a space approximately 10 feet by 5 feet. With masking tape, divide the space into three rectangles as shown below:

YES	MAYBE	NO

2. Write, "YES," "NO," and "MAYBE" on three separate sheets of paper and put one sheet in each rectangle.
3. Have Group A sit as the audience and Group B encircle the space marked off by the masking tape.
4. Have one person in Group A read out loud the following questions. After each question is read, everyone in group B must stand in the "YES," "NO," or "MAYBE" box.
5. After Group B completes reactions to the questions, they should sit down. Group A should stand up and encircle the space marked off by the masking tape. Then Group B will ask the questions and members of Group A must answer each question by standing in the "YES," "NO," or "MAYBE" box.

QUESTION 1: If you were an African American high school student in Little Rock, Arkansas, in 1957, would you have joined the nine students who integrated Central High School?

QUESTION 2: If you were a European American high school student in Little Rock, Arkansas, in 1957, would you have welcomed the nine new African American students into Central High School?

After both groups have an opportunity to answer the above questions by standing in the "YES," "NO," AND "MAYBE" boxes, everyone should sit down and answer the following questions:

4-15 (continued)

1. I chose to stand in the YES/NO/MAYBE (circle one) box for Question 1 because:

____

____

____

____

____

____

2. I had the following feelings when choosing my answer for Question 1:

____

____

____

____

____

____

3. I chose to stand in the YES/NO/MAYBE (circle one) box for Question 2 because:

____

____

____

____

____

4. I had the following feelings when choosing my answer for Question 2:

____

____

____

____

____

Name ______________________________ Date ______________

4–16

THE 1960s

What do you associate with the decade of the 1960s? Around the encircled decade below, write any word that comes to your mind when you hear the term "1960s."

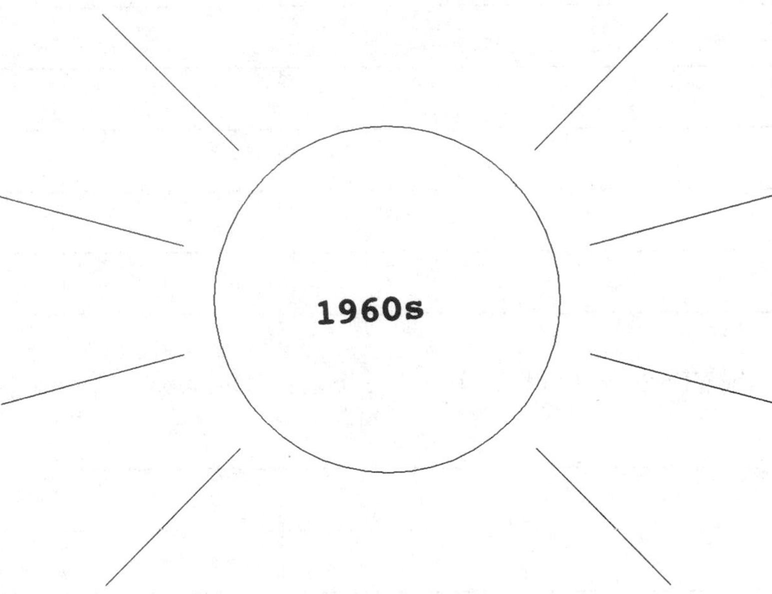

The 1960s was a decade of turmoil and change in the United States. Let's imagine for a moment that you discovered a time capsule filled with photographs from this era while you were digging in a sandbox with your younger brother or sister in your local park. What would you expect to see in these pictures? Write your answers in the box provided below.

Also in the time capsule were scraps of paper with words describing the 1960s written on them. It was as if the person who made the time capsule was trying to create a puzzle that the person in the future who found the time capsule (you!) would have to solve. On the next page are the words. Read these words and think about which words fit together in a group in your mind.

WORDS FROM THE 1960s

nonviolence
hippies
Martin Luther King
civil disobedience
napalm
The Beatles
draft dodgers
My Lai Massacre
the draft
NAACP
attack dogs
hunger strikes
marijuana
the Young Lords
Pentagon Papers
love beads
Moon Landing
Cuban Missile Crisis
Caesar Chavez
the Supremes
Betty Friedan

Vietnam War
"Love Ins"
Civil Rights Act (1968)
Detroit riots (1967)
birth control pills
President Johnson
conscientious objectors
FBI Cointelpro
President Kennedy
desegregation
fragmentation bombs
Pete Seeger
Cambodia
the Temptations
body counts
flower children
Black Power
United States invasion of the Dominican Republic
Mahatma Ghandi
the Cold War
La Raza

bell-bottom jeans
Jim Crow laws
Black Panthers
Malcolm X
"I Have a Dream"
Woodstock
Voting Rights Act
miniskirts
Medicare
fire hoses
police horses
long hair
President Nixon
grape boycott
Vietnamese refugees
heroin
War on Poverty
Bay of Pigs
farm workers
Afros
The Feminine Mystique

Group the above words into categories. In other words, decide which words have something in common and fit together in a group. You can decide to have three, four, five, or more categories. Then write these words in the category boxes on the next page.

4-16 (continued)

CATEGORY BOXES

Look at each of your categories and decide what the words in this box have in common. Select *one word* or a *label* that best describes each grouping and write it at the top of each box. Based on this grouping, what hypotheses can you make about life during the 1960s? Write three of your hypotheses in the space provided below.

HYPOTHESIS 1: __________

HYPOTHESIS 2: __________

HYPOTHESIS 3: __________

Name ______________________________ Date ______________

4–17

ORAL HISTORY INTERVIEW—THE 1960s

One of the best ways to get historical information on a historical period is to talk to someone who has lived through it! Find someone (a relative, neighbor, friend) who is at least 40 years old and lived in the U.S.A. from 1960 to 1970. Tell this person that you are studying the 1960s and would like to ask a few questions about what he or she experienced then. If you have a tape recorder handy, use it to tape the conversation. Then summarize the person's answers to the following questions in the space provided below. (Add additional questions if you would like!) If you do not have a tape recorder, take notes on a separate sheet of paper and then summarize the answers.

1. How old were you in the 1960s and where were you living? Describe your farm, town or city.

____

____

____

2. What were you doing during the years 1960–1970? (student?, working?)

____

____

____

3. What pictures come to your mind when you hear the words "1960s"?.

____

____

____

4. Do you have memories of music groups (the Supremes, the Beatles, the Beachboys, the Temptations, the Rolling Stones) and if so, what are they?

____

____

____

5. What kinds of clothes did you and other people wear during the 1960s? (Please describe in detail.)

6. What kinds of news reports (on the radio, on TV, or in the newspaper) do you remember?

7. What memories do you have of social disruptions in the cities (e.g., Watts, Washington, D.C., Newark, Detroit)?

8. Were you aware of the Civil Rights movement during the 1960s and, if so, what memories do you have of it?

9. Were you aware of the Vietnam War during the 1960s, and if so, what memories do you have of it?

10. Did you know someone who fought in the Vietnam War and, if so, what stories did you hear of their experience?

11. Were you aware of the Mexican American and Filipino American farm workers' movement led by Caesar Chavez and Larry Itliong? If so, what memories do you have of it?

12. What memories do you have of President Kennedy, President Johnson, and President Nixon and what opinions did you have of these three leaders?

13. In general, what other pictures or stories come to your mind when you think of the years 1960–1970?

14. What lessons did you learn, having lived through the 1960s?

Name ______________________________ Date ______________

4–18

ORAL HISTORY INTERVIEW—THE VIETNAM WAR

One of the best ways to get historical information on a particular historical period is to talk to someone who has lived through it! Find someone (a relative, neighbor, friend) who is at least 45 years old and lived in the U.S.A. during the period 1960 to 1975. Tell this person that you are studying the Vietnam War and would like to ask a few questions about what he or she experienced then. Use a tape recorder to record the conversation, then summarize the answers the person gave to the following questions in the space provided below. (Add additional questions if you would like!) If you do not have a tape recorder, take notes on a separate sheet of paper and then summarize.

1. How old were you between the years 1960 and 1975 and where were you living? Describe your farm, town or city.

____

____

____

2. What were you doing during the years 1960–1975? (student? working?)

____

____

____

3. What pictures come to your mind when you hear the words "the Vietnam War"?

____

____

____

4-18 (continued)

4. Were you aware of the military draft during this time and were you, or anyone you knew, drafted to fight in Vietnam? If so, what memories do you have of the draft?

____

____

____

5. Did you fight in the Vietnam War or did you know anyone who fought in the Vietnam War? If so, what memories and stories did you experience or hear about?

____

____

____

____

____

____

6. What opinions did you have about men who refused to fight in the Vietnam War?

____

____

____

7. What pictures come to your mind when you think about demonstrations against the Vietnam War? What opinions did you have about these demonstrations?

____

____

____

8. What memories do you have of President Johnson and President Nixon, and what opinions did you have about the leadership of these two men during the Vietnam War?

____

____

____

4-18 (continued)

9. In general, what other pictures or stories come to your mind when you think of the Vietnam War?

10. What lessons did you learn, having lived through the Vietnam War?

Name ______________________________ Date ______________

4–19
THE VIETNAM WAR—PRO OR CON?

The Vietnam War (1955–1975) was highly controversial; some Americans were extremely supportive of the war effort (PRO) and other Americans were extremely opposed (CON). Read the following quotations of Americans who fought in Vietnam or lived during this war and decide if they were PRO or CON regarding U.S. involvement in this war. Place the number of this American in the chart below. After you have finished reading all of the quotes, hypothesize, in the space provided at the end of this exercise, as to what you think the main issues of this war were.

Pro	*Con*

1. "Dear Mom and Dad,

   Today we went on a mission and I am not very proud of myself, my friends, or my country. We burned every hut in sight!

   It was a small rural network of villages and the people were incredibly poor. My unit burned and plundered their meager possessions. Let me try to explain the situation to you. The huts here are thatched palm leaves. Each one has a dried mud bunker inside. These bunkers are to protect the families, kind of like air raid shelters. My unit commanders, however, chose to think that these bunkers are offensive. So every hut we find that has a bunker we are ordered to burn to the ground. When the ten helicopters landed this morning, in the midst of these huts, and six men jumped out of each "chopper," we were firing the moment we hit the ground. We fired into all the huts we could. . . .

It is then that we burned these huts. . . . Everyone is crying, begging, and praying that we don't separate them and take their husbands and fathers, sons and grandfathers. The women wail and moan.

Then they watch in terror as we burn their homes, personal possessions, and food. Yes, we burn all rice and shoot all livestock."

U.S. SOLDIER IN VIETNAM

2. "Communist control of all of Southeast Asia would render the U.S. position in the Pacific offshore island chain precarious and would seriously jeopardize fundamental security interests in the Far East. . . . Southeast Asia, especially Malaya and Indonesia, is the principal world source of natural rubber and tin, and a producer of petroleum and other strategically important commodities. . . ."

MEMBER OF THE U.S. NATIONAL SECURITY COUNCIL

3. "What is the attraction that Southeast Asia has exerted for centuries on the great powers flanking it on all sides? Why is it desirable, and why is it so important? First, it provides a lush climate, fertile soil, rich natural resources, a relatively sparse population in most areas, and room to expand. The countries of Southeast Asia produce rich exportable surpluses such as rice, rubber, teak, corn, tin, spices, oil and many others. . . ."

U. ALEXIS JOHNSON,
UNDERSECRETARY OF STATE
FOR THE KENNEDY ADMINISTRATION, 1963

4. "Somehow this madness must cease. We must stop now. I speak as a child of God and brother to the suffering poor of Vietnam. I speak for those whose land is being laid to waste, whose homes are being destroyed, whose culture is being subverted. I speak for the poor of America who are paying the double price of smashed hopes at home and death and corruption in Vietnam. I speak as a citizen of the world, for the world stands aghast at the path we have taken. I speak as an American to the leaders of my own nation. The great initiative in this war is ours. The initiative to stop it must be ours."

DR. MARTIN LUTHER KING, JR., 1967

5. "Lieutenant Calley and a weeping rifleman named Paul D. Meadlo—the same soldier who fed candy to the children before shooting them—pushed the prisoners into the ditch. . . . There was an order to shoot by Lt. Calley, I can't remember the exact words—it was something like 'Start firing.' Meadlo turned to me and said 'Shoot, why don't you shoot?' He was crying. I said, 'I can't, I won't.' Then Lt. Calley and Meadlo pointed their rifles into the ditch and fired. People were diving on top of each other; mothers were trying to protect their children."

JAMES DURSI,
U.S. RIFLEMAN IN VIETNAM TESTIFYING
AT THE MY LAI MASSACRE TRIAL OF LIEUTENANT CALLEY

6. "When Army investigators reached the barren area in November, 1969, in connection with the My Lai probe in the United States, they found mass graves at three sites, as well as a ditch full of bodies. It was estimated that between 450 and 500 people—most of them women, children and old men—had been slain and buried there."[(1)]

JOURNALIST SEYMOUR HERSH

7. "I am determined to stop the spread of communism into South Vietnam."[2]

JOHN FOSTER DULLES, SECRETARY OF STATE UNDER PRESIDENT EISENHOWER

8. "The loss of Indochina [to Communism] will cause the fall of Southeast Asia like a set of dominoes . . . we are not going to run out and leave it for the Communists to take over . . . I am not going to be the President who saw Southeast Asia go the way of China."

PRESIDENT EISENHOWER

With the information you have gathered from the quotes, what do you think were the main issues (things people argued about) concerning the Vietnam War? Hypothesize in the space provided below:

The main issues of the Vietnam War were:

HYPOTHESIS 1: ____________________

____

____

____

____

HYPOTHESIS 2: ____________________

____

____

____

____

HYPOTHESIS 3: ____________________

____

____

____

____

Name ______________________ *Date* __________

4–20
GENDER STEREOTYPES

What do you associate with the word "stereotype"? Around the encircled word below, write whatever words comes to mind when you hear the term "stereotype."

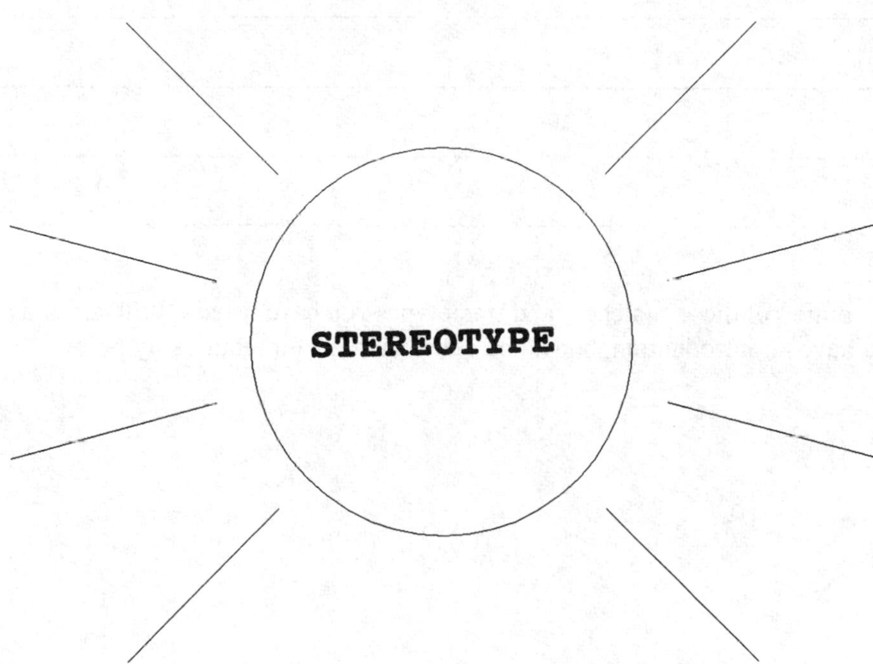

Look up the definitions of the words "stereotype" and "gender" in the dictionary and write them in the space provided below.

GENDER:

STEREOTYPE:

4-20 (continued)

Write at least five sentences that start with "All women . . ." and five sentences that start with "All men . . . ." They should represent some of the gender stereotypes of our society.

1. All women ______________________________.
2. All women ______________________________.
3. All women ______________________________.
4. All women ______________________________.
5. All women ______________________________.

1. All men ______________________________.
2. All men ______________________________.
3. All men ______________________________.
4. All men ______________________________.
5. All men ______________________________.

What is your opinion of these sentences and stereotypes you have listed? Write an essay expressing your opinion. Be sure to have an introduction, body, and conclusion! Begin your essay below.

Name ______________________ Date ____________

4–21
WORKING OUTSIDE THE HOME

During the 1970s and 1980s, women began to take jobs outside the home in unprecedented numbers. Look at the statistics below and create a graph in the space provided to illustrate this increase.

Year	*Percentage of Women in the Civilian Labor Force*[1]
1970	49.0%
1980	59.5%
1985	64.7%
1990	69.1%

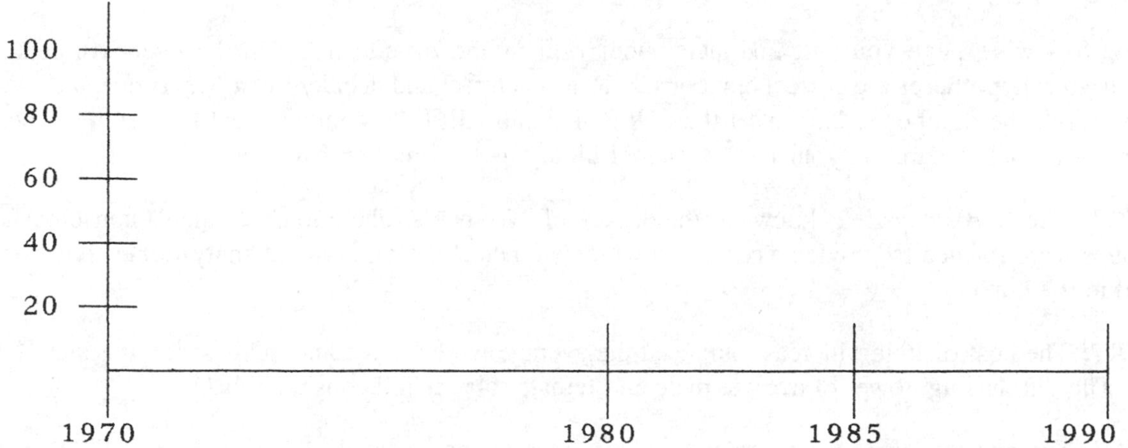

Why did so many more women join the civilian labor force during the 1970s and 1980s? Hypothesize the answer to this question in the space provided on the next page.

Evidence that **supports** *this hypothesis:*	*Women began joining the civilian labor force in record numbers during the 1970s and 1980s because:*	*Evidence that* **refutes** *this hypothesis:*
	HYPOTHESIS 1: ___________ ______________________ ______________________ ______________________	
	HYPOTHESIS 2: ___________ ______________________ ______________________ ______________________	
	HYPOTHESIS 3: ___________ ______________________ ______________________ ______________________	

On the following page you will find facts about women and American life in the twentieth century. Determine if your hypotheses are correct or incorrect. Read each fact and decide if it *supports* or *refutes* your hypotheses. Write the number (1,2,3) under the SUPPORT and REFUTE columns next to each hypothesis. You can do additional research in your local or school library to explore your hypotheses.

FACT 1: The 1970s decade is known as the decade of "Women's Liberation." Women's consciousness raising groups were formed to provide a context in which women could discuss and analyze their position in society and in the home.

FACT 2: The cost of living increase outpaced the average worker's income increases in the late 1970s and 1980s. The purchasing power of average male and female salaries fell considerably.[(2)]

FACT 3: The purchasing power of the national minimum wage declined 31 percent from 1979 to 1989. By 1995, it fell to its lowest point in forty years. [(3)]

FACT 4: The birth control pill became available in the 1960s. This was the first method of birth control made widely available to all American women that proved to be extremely successful in preventing pregnancies.

FACT 5: Medical costs increased twice the rate of inflation during the 1980s. Many families felt they could no longer get by without health insurance. Many employers could no longer afford to offer health insurance to their workers.[4]

FACT 6: Many women felt unfulfilled remaining at home to be full-time mothers and housekeepers. Many women preferred working full-time or part-time in a job outside the home.

FACT 7: Abortion became legalized in all states in 1971.

FACT 8: The number of day care centers increased threefold from 1976 to 1990.[5]

FACT 9: The divorce rate rose to an all-time high during the 1970s and 1980s. By 1992, one out of every two marriages (50 percent) ended in divorce.[6]

You have read the facts and decided if they *support* or *refute* your hypothesis; can you think of some new hypotheses? Perhaps you learned something from the above information that you did not know beforehand. Write your new hypotheses below.

Evidence that supports *this hypothesis:*	*Women began joining the civilian labor force in record numbers in the 1970s and 1980s because:*	*Evidence that* refutes *this hypothesis:*
	HYPOTHESIS 4: ________ ________________ ________________ ________________ ________________ ________________ HYPOTHESIS 5: ________ ________________ ________________ ________________ ________________ ________________	

Name ______________________________ Date ____________

4–22

ELEANOR ROOSEVELT AND HILLARY RODHAM CLINTON

Two well-known twentieth-century women were the wives of two twentieth-century presidents—Franklin D. Roosevelt and Bill Clinton. They have many similarities and differences. Read the facts below that highlight aspects of their lives. In the Venn diagram on the next page, visually display how these two women are similar and how they are different.

ELEANOR ROOSEVELT('S)

1. saw herself as a social activist.
2. was among the first First Ladies who took active roles in their husbands' administrations and greatly influenced public policy.
3. political convictions were more liberal than her husband's political convictions.
4. did much work to respond to the needs of many overlooked American groups such as women, unskilled workers, and ethnic minorities, and she prodded her husband to provide programs for the poor and unemployed.
5. helped women become 50 percent of the Democratic Party platform committee in 1936.
6. wrote books and a syndicated newspaper column, maintaining a career of her own while in the White House.
7. advised women to leave their "womanly personalities at home" and "disabuse their male competitors of the old idea that women are only 'ladies in business.'"
8. husband was struck with polio and spent most of their married life as a physically handicapped person.
9. believed women have a humanizing and moralizing effect on government.
10. during her stay in the White House, traveled throughout the United States, lecturing frequently, making radio broadcasts, and visiting slums, coal mines, prisons, factories, and schools.

HILLARY CLINTON('S)

1. kept her maiden name but, as First Lady preferred to be called Hillary Rodham Clinton.
2. was appointed chair of the Clinton administration's health care task force (the first time a First Lady has chaired a task force of such high profile).
3. banned smoking in the White House.
4. worked closely with Marian Wright Edelman and the Children's Defense Fund, an advocacy group for children's needs.
5. was outspoken on the need to address poverty and reform of the welfare system.
6. supported affirmative action and her husband's attempts to appoint a cabinet that was diverse both in terms of ethnicity and gender.
7. maintained her own career as a lawyer during her marriage.
8. traveled extensively throughout the United States, lecturing on topics ranging from health care needs to women's rights.
9. participated in many high-level Clinton administration decisions.

DIFFERENCES AND SIMILARITIES OF ROOSEVELT AND RODHAM CLINTON

ROOSEVELT

____

____

____

____

____

SIMILARITIES

____

____

____

____

____

____

____

____

____

CLINTON

Name ______________________________ Date ______________

4–23

PUERTO RICO—COMMONWEALTH, STATE, OR INDEPENDENCE?

PUERTO RICO

As compensation for winning the Spanish-American War, the United States took control of Puerto Rico, Cuba, the Philippines, and Guam from Spain in 1898. Puerto Rico became a territory of the United States, and the Foraker Act of 1900 institutionalized U.S. military and political control over the island and its inhabitants. The Jones Act of 1913 imposed U.S. citizenship on all Puerto Ricans. This act allowed a limited amount of self-government to Puerto Ricans but did not allow Puerto Ricans to participate in national U.S. elections. (It also made Puerto Rican men eligible for the military draft!) In 1952 Puerto Rico was granted commonwealth status by the U.S. government. This gave Puerto Ricans a larger amount of self-government, but left most Puerto Rican affairs under control of the U.S. government. Some Puerto Ricans believe that Puerto Rico should be an independent country. Other Puerto Ricans believe that Puerto Rico should become a state of the United States. Still other Puerto Ricans believe that the island should remain a commonwealth of the United States. Read the three opinions below. Decide which person believes Puerto Rico should: (1) become independent; (2) become a state; or (3) remain a commonwealth. While you are reading these three opinions, decide with whom you agree!

JOSE:

There are many reasons why Puerto Rico should break away from the United States. First of all, since 1898 when the United States invaded our island, it has used our land as a military base. It has used these bases as departure points for military invasions into Caribbean and Central American countries such as Grenada, Nicaragua, and Cuba. By force, it has taken over nearby islands, such as Vieques, and used them for bombing target practices. Second, the United States has made Puerto Ricans dependent on the U.S. economy. Ninety percent of the companies operating in Puerto Rico are U.S. owned and 75 percent of the consumer goods are imported from the United States. Because of the uneven economic development, we have a consistently high unemployment rate and 65 percent of Puerto Ricans are dependent on food stamps. This has created a welfare dependency that is not good for our people. Third, U.S. pharmaceutical companies and oil companies have been allowed to operate *without* paying any taxes to the island. They have also been allowed to dump many toxic chemicals on the island; a U.S. Geological Survey of 1982, which tested 18 wells on the island, found all but one to be contaminated so seriously that they had to be shut down. Puerto Rico needs to be free!

This person believes that Puerto Rico should: become a state/become independent/remain a commonwealth (circle one).

MARIE:

Puerto Ricans are being shortchanged by not officially being recognized as equal to other U.S. citizens. Puerto Rican men can be drafted to fight in the U.S. military but Puerto Ricans are not allowed to vote for the U.S. President nor in any other national elections. Puerto Ricans are represented by only one nonvoting representative in Washington, D.C. Poor Puerto Ricans receive fewer government benefits than poor people living in the United States; welfare benefits would jump by billions of dollars if Puerto Rico became a state of the United States. Also, companies running factories and businesses on the island should be required to pay taxes to the Puerto Rican government to support the needs of the people, something from which they are exempt right now. This is a moral issue, one that revolves around democracy, equality, justice, and fundamental human rights. If we do not make this change, Puerto Ricans are doomed to being second-rate U.S. citizens!

This person believes that Puerto Rico should: become a state/become independent/remain as a commonwealth (circle one).

GLORIA:

Language, culture, and economic security are what Puerto Ricans care most about. If we become any more entangled with the United States, we could lose all three of these. If Puerto Rico becomes a state, the U.S. government could dictate that English be the first language of the island. What other state in the United States speaks another language? With the loss of Spanish would come a loss of our culture. The many traditions and holidays we celebrate are directly related to our unique Spanish, African, and Native American heritage. If Puerto Rico becomes a state, Puerto Ricans would begin paying federal income taxes, this in the midst of over 30 percent unemployment! If Puerto Rico becomes independent, we would lose the $6 billion of Federal Aid we receive per year in the form of food stamps. If we become a state or become independent, U.S. companies would not be allowed to operate tax-free on the island and might move elsewhere. This would cost us more of the precious few jobs on the island. It is better for Puerto Rico to remain as it is today. Change has too many dangerous possibilities!

This person believes that Puerto Rico should: become a state/become independent/remain a commonwealth (circle one).

In 1993, Puerto Ricans voted to decide whether Puerto Rico should become a state, become independent, or remain as a commonwealth of the United States. If you were a Puerto Rican voting in this plebiscite, how would you vote? Write the answer to this question in the space provided below. Be sure to give reasons why you would vote in this way.

____

____

____

(Continue on the back.)

In class tomorrow, tally up the vote in your classroom. In other words, find out what percentage of your class voted for Puerto Rico to: (1) become a state; (2)become independent; (3) remain as a commonwealth. Compare these results with the actual results received in Puerto Rico in 1993. (Your teacher has that info!)

Name ______________________ Date ____________

4–24
TRYING TO FIT IN

What words do you associate with the phrase "peer pressure"? Write those words around the circle below.

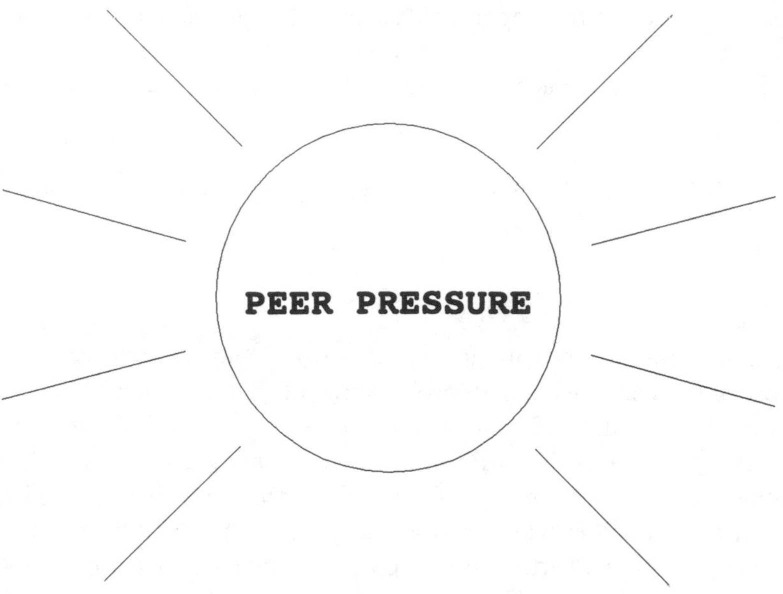

Do you observe examples of "peer pressure" in your everyday life?
If so, write a few examples in the space provided below.

____

____

____

____

____

____

____

____

A well-known writer, Piri Thomas, writes often about his process of trying to fit in, due to peer pressure, during his adolescent years as a Puerto Rican (whose culture stems from a blend of Native American, African, and European heritages). Read two of his autobiographical excerpts below. As you read the first one from *Stories from el Barrio*, think about the pressures the author felt.

"When I was a kid, many folks spent a lot of time, effort and money trying to pass for white. Very few homes did not have some kind of skin-bleaching creme. If poverty prevented its purchase, raw lemon juice would suffice. Cream or juice was liberally applied to the skin with the hope of turning it yellow, which was light if not white.

Parents were constantly pinching the noses of their children so that flat, wide nostrils could be unnaturally forced into sculptured images of white folks' noses.

Running neck and neck were hair-straightening and coloring effects. The very poor made up batches of Vaseline, lye and harsh brown octagon soap for their hair-straightening. For those who could afford it, there were jars of heavy white cream with 'You too can have beautiful hair' advertised on the label."(1)

What peer pressure was Piri feeling as a child? How did he and other Puerto Rican Americans try to fit in? What is your opinion of these efforts to fit in? Have you ever felt this way? Write your response to these questions in the space provided below.

____

____

____

____

(Continue on the back.)

Now read the second excerpt from Piri Thomas's autobiography *Down These Mean Streets*. The excerpt begins in the middle of an argument Piri is having with his parents:

"I looked at Poppa. 'Cause Poppa,' I said, 'him [Piri's brother], you and James [Piri's other brother] think you're white, and I'm the only one that's found out I'm not. I tried hard not to find out. But I did, and I'm almost out from under that kick you all are copping out to.' I got up from my knees. 'Poppa.' I added, 'what's wrong with not being white? What's so wrong with being tregeno [dark complected]? Momma must think it's great , she got married to you, eh? We gotta have pride and dignity, Poppa; we gotta walk big and bad. I'm me and I dig myself in the mirror . . . I'm black and it don't make no difference whether I say good-bye or adios—it means the same.'

Nobody said anything; everyone just stood there. I said, 'I'm proud to be Puerto Rican, but Puerto Rican don't make the color.' "(2)

What is Piri trying to explain to his parents? To what peer pressure was he accusing his parents of succumbing? Do you agree with Piri's attitude toward being Puerto Rican? Write your response to these questions in the space provided below.

____

____

____

____

____

(Continue on the back.)

Name ______________________________ Date ______________

4–25

IMMIGRATION BY SEA

Except for those of us who are of Native American descent, we are a nation of immigrants. Some have come on foot, others have flown, and others have traveled by boat to arrive in the United States. Read the accounts below that describe the experiences of three different people who have traveled by boat to the United States: one is a German who came in the 1700s; one is a Vietnamese who came in the 1970s; and one is a Haitian who came in the 1990s.

1. "[He] was only six years old when he and his family left. . . . When his father told him they were going on a long trip, [he] was excited at first . . . [he] still has nightmares about the horrible events of his family's escape . . . the boat they sailed on was attacked by pirates. The boat's captain was shot, and the pirates took all the food and water and several of the young girls from the refugee boat, including his sister. Two days later a second pirate ship stopped the boat and took the people's clothes. Suffering from hunger, thirst, cold and fear, the refugees tried to find land. Because of the rough seas, the boat people finally had to abandon ship and swim ashore. . . . [he] and his parents have never heard from his sister."(1)

   This immigrant was coming from (1) Germany, (2) Vietnam, (3) Haiti (circle one).

2. "During the journey the ship is full of pitiful signs of distress—smells, fumes, horrors, vomiting, various kinds of sea sickness, fever, dysentery, headaches, heat, constipation, boils, scurvy, cancer, mouth-rot, and similar afflictions, all of them caused by the age and the high salted state of the food, especially the meat, as well as the very bad and filthy water. . . . Add to all that shortage of food, hunger, thirst, frost, heat, dampness, fear, misery, vexation, and lamentation as well as other troubles. . . . On board our ship, on a day on which we had a great storm, a woman about to give birth and unable to deliver under the circumstances, was pushed through one of the portholes into the sea. . . ."(2)

   These immigrants were coming from (1) Germany, (2) Vietnam, (3) Haiti (circle one).

3. "Straw seat mats were laid over the ribs of the boat, a 50-gallon water barrel was secured over the keel, and provisions were hastily tossed in. . . . There were 10 passengers under age 15, the youngest barely a year old. As the sun grew hotter, plastic jugs of tepid water were passed around and the euphoria of a successful getaway faded. . . . As five-foot swells rocked the boat, gourds were passed to the seasick, then emptied over the side. One man fainted and his friends fought for space so that he could breathe fresh air. Others helped a seasick woman to drink water. Because of the crowded conditions, muscles stiffened and arguments erupted. People nodded uncomfortably, heads on their chests, or leaned against

one another to doze. Minor movements, like eating caused discomfort to one's neighbors; major physical efforts, like standing up, caused pain. After a day and a half under these conditions, most of the food was gone and a grim realization set in: Surviving the two weeks . . . might be impossible."[(3)]

These immigrants were coming from (1) Germany, (2) Vietnam, (3) Haiti (circle one).

In the Venn diagram below, identify the similarities and differences experienced by these immigrants during their journeys.

	German Immigrant	
Vietnamese Immigrant	*Similarities to Experiences of All Three People*	*Haitian Immigrant*

4-25 (continued)

Imagine you are a U.S. Immigration official. On what basis might you permit each immigrant group's entry to the United States? On what basis might you deny their entry? Write your answers below.

Name ______________________________ Date ______________

4–26
SWEATSHOPS

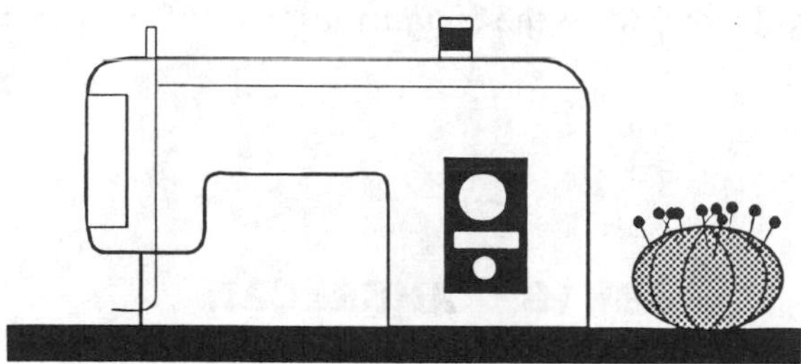

American immigrants have been forced to work long hours for low wages at what are called "sweatshops"—small, illegal factories. By 1900, over 200,000 Jewish Americans worked in sweatshops. In 1995, Central Americans, Asian Americans, and others still labor in substandard and now illegal conditions—with low wages, dangerous working conditions, and long hours. Read the accounts below, which describe the experiences of Jewish Americans in the early twentieth century and Central Americans in 1993. As you read, think about the similarities and differences in their experience.

"Around 1900, for a sixty hour week [in a sweatshop] pressers would make $500 a year, skilled men $600 and $700. . . . Women got less. . . . In a study of New York living standards at that time, the Russell Sage Foundation concluded $800 a year was the minimum for a decent life, which meant families had to take in boarders or put wife and children to work to make ends meet. . . . One day young Harry [Roskolenko] visited the [sweatshop] factory to bring a letter from Russia and an apple. Years later, Harry recalled what he saw:

'It was just an ordinary shop, I discovered, with nothing special about the men, the work, the heat, the dirt, the pay, the boss, the production. It was a factory with a hundred workers stripped down to their pants. All sorts of tailoring, cutting and pressing machines were whirling, whirring and steaming away. I was fascinated for a few minutes—then I saw my father. I lost the magic of a new place at once. The inventions were gone, and there was a man of fifty, pressing a cloak with a ten-pound steam iron. . . . It was summer sweat, winter sweat, all sorts of sweat: bitter, sour, stinking, moldy—through all the seasons of the year. Not one fan to blow up some wind. The fans were blowing in the boss's office. . . . Instead of fans there were foremen walking about, fuming and blowing, their voices like dogs barking at other dogs. The workers seldom paused, no matter what they were at. . . . How long to urinate, how long to move your bowels? Nothing in nature took very long over piecework . . . or the need to produce downtown what was needed uptown at the end of the day. . . . With this system of sweating, every worker gave up his lunchtime—the minutes saved, to earn a bit more. . . . The day began in the dark, too early for the sun's rising, and it ended in the dark, too late for the sun's setting. It was 12 hours, 14 hours, 16, depending on what the worker needed at home. . . . It was a death-ridden loft making a young man middle-aged and the middle-aged ancient.' "(1)

"From their fifth floor room in a gloomy tenement reeking of urine and cheap perfume, Maria Chun and Thomas Krische have a bird's eye view of the sewing factory where they work. The couple trim threads there and press clothes. The hours are 7 A.M. to 7 P.M., and Maria and Thomas put in six days a week. Their take-home pay is $111. That's combined. For Maria, 32, and Thomas, 38, America is the promised land. They traded their lives in war-torn Guatemala, temporarily leaving their children for Los Angeles and a chance at prosperity. In their tiny room across from their employer, however, prosperity has so far eluded the couple. For the room they must pay $400 a month. To help cover the rent, they share their cramped quarters with a boarder, another man. Like most garment workers, Maria and Thomas are paid by the piece. . . . Maria earned

9 cents a piece one week not long ago. It didn't add up to $4.25 an hour. . . . Working the long hours she does makes Maria Chan's back ache and her legs numb. Her stomach is constantly upset. . . . Is Maria Chun glad she came to America? She ponders the question and shakes her head side to side. Then she starts to cry."[2]

Using the Venn diagram below, write the *similarities* and *differences* of these two cultural groups' experiences in sweatshops.

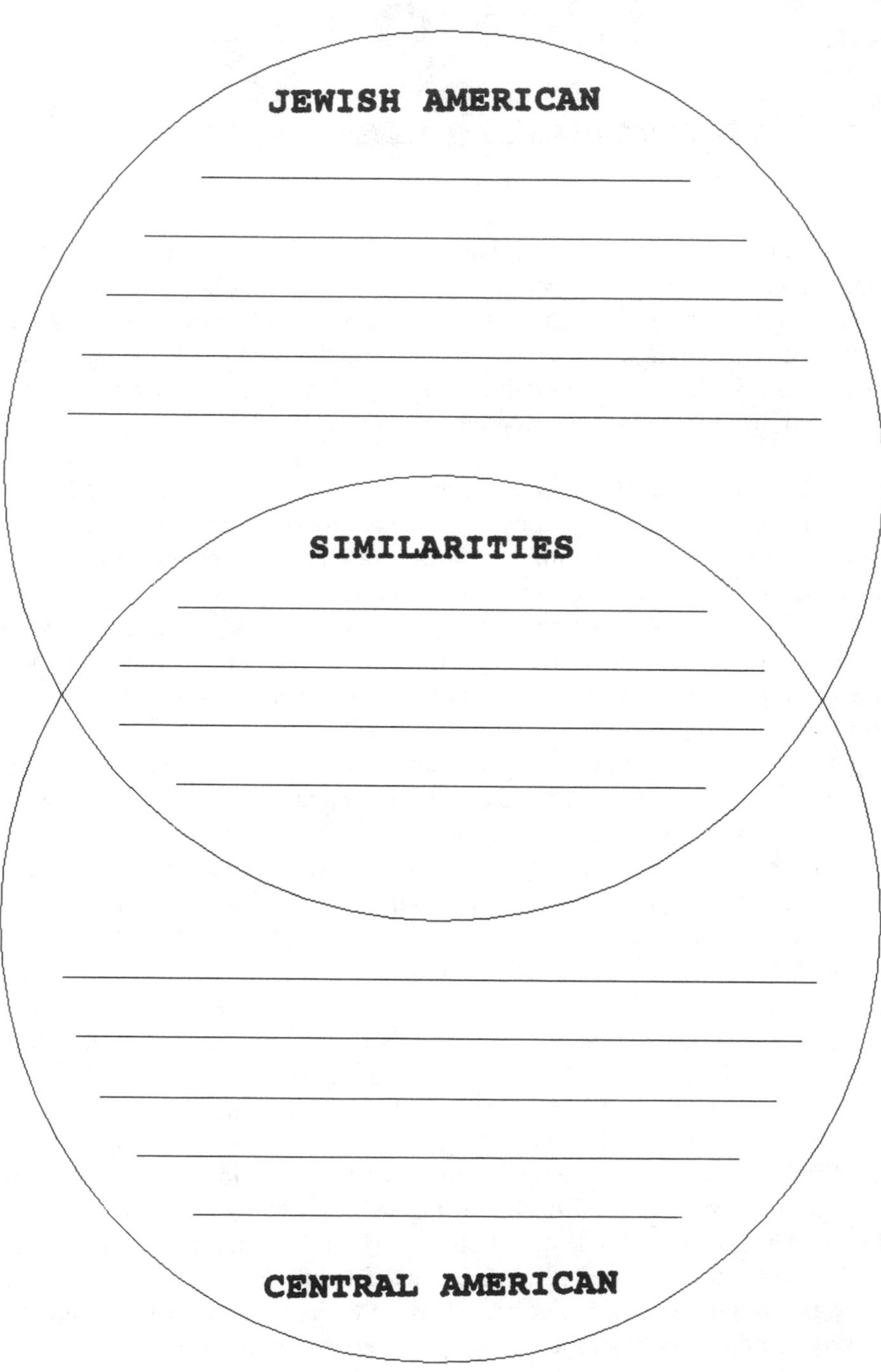

Name ______________________________ *Date* ____________

4–27

THE FARMWORKERS AND NONVIOLENCE

Mexican American and Filipino American farm workers came together from 1965 to 1970 to improve their working conditions and wages. Under the leadership of Mexican American Cesar Chavez and Filipino American Larry Itliong, the famous Delano Grape Strike brought national attention to the desperate situation of many farm workers. Read the excerpts describing the life of farm workers. Then decide if *you* agree with the tactics and philosophy of *non-violence*, which they used to bring about change.

"Most farmworkers live, at best, in sterile, prisonlike compounds and, at worst, in crumbling shanties in rural slums and have little voice in community affairs. Nor do they have much to say on the job, where they may work 10 or 12 hours a day, six and seven days a week, often lacking such simple amenities as toilets and clean drinking water."[1]

". . . Vineyard workers share the plight of farm workers generally—working and living conditions that, in the words of the United States Senate Subcommittee on Migratory Labor, 'must be recognized for what they are—a national disgrace' "[2]

"Yet the vineyard workers also average far less on a yearly basis than the $3000 poverty level figure (somewhere between $2000 and $2300, according to union figures), are lucky to find more than six months of work in any one year, and are rare indeed if they can afford to keep their children from joining them in the vineyards. Overtime pay, sick leave, paid holidays, vacations, pensions, and unemployment benefits generally are denied them, and those laws that are suppose to provide them some rudimentary protections are but laxly enforced."[3]

"I'd never seen them [farmworkers] picking for wine before. It was awful. They picked into buckets and pans and dumped them into gondolas that pulled down the row by tractor. The workers were covered with juice and grime, and the gnats and flies were everywhere. It was really awful work."[4]

Cesar Chavez, in particular, was devoted to *nonviolence*, a philosophy developed by India's leader Mahatma Ghandi to bring about social, economic, and political change in India. Read the following quotations, which describe Chavez's commitment to nonviolence:

"We advocate militant nonviolence as our means for social revolution and to achieve justice for our people. . . . We hate the agribusiness system that seeks to keep us enslaved, and we shall overcome and change it not by retaliation and bloodshed, but by a determined nonviolent struggle carried on by those masses of farmworkers who intend to be free and human."[5]

What does it mean to carry on a nonviolent strike? Read the following descriptions of some situations in which farmworkers involved in the Delano Grape Strike were placed. Then decide if *you* could have reacted to these situations nonviolently.

"The pickets [farmworkers] carried handmade signs . . . with a single word or two: HUELGA! (STRIKE!). . . . The farmer [who employed the farmworkers] and his foreman drove their pickup trucks furiously up and down farm roads, boiling dust up on the picket lines, nearly running pickets down if they stood their ground. Frequently the farmer would drive up, skid to a stop, jump out of the pickup, and then slowly, menacingly, confront the strikers. . . . Some of the foremen were verbally insulting."[6]

"When the strike began, there were over 100 arrests [of farmworkers engaged in civil disobedience]. Twenty-five of our pickets were severely beaten by growers and the police. . . . When the growers beat us, we did not fight back. Finally, they began to respect us for this."[7]

". . . Suddenly a caravan of cars pulled up and a group of growers spilled across the street, where they began jabbing the pickets with their elbows, stepping on their feet and trying to trip them. One of the smallest pickets was finally knocked down. . . . Chavez called to the pickets to remember their oath of nonviolence."[8]

"Growers were accused of running pickets off the road with their trucks, assaulting others, and running rigs along the edges of the fields to spray the strikers with poisonous chemicals. . . . On the morning of October 15, a large number of pickets had assembled outside the Mosesian packing shed on Glenwood Ave. Infuriated when some of the truck drivers appeared reluctant to cross the picket lines, a company salesman by the name of Schy climbed into a truck and attempted to drive through the lines himself. Manuel Rivera, who had been befriended by Chavez back in 1962, was knocked to the ground and critically injured as one of the heavy wheels passed over his body. While some of the pickets rushed forward to kneel beside the unconscious Rivera, the others surrounded the truck trying to get at Schy. . . . Fighting his way through the crowd, Chavez crawled under the truck and rose abruptly beside the door by the driver's seat. There were angry yells from some of the farm workers for him to get out of the way, but Chavez stood his ground. 'If you want to kill someone, then you'll have to kill me first,' he told them. When the voices had quieted and all had moved back to stand sullenly on the picket lines again, Chavez personally escorted Schy to safety inside the packing shed. In time Rivera recovered, but he had suffered disabling injuries. Chavez found a permanent job for him on the Schenley ranch so that he could support his family."[9]

What would have been your response if you had been a striking farm worker harassed in the above manner? What feelings would you have had? Would you have retaliated with violence or would you have remained nonviolent? Write your response in the space provided below.

The growers and the farm workers finally came to an agreement in 1970. The final wage package agreed upon was $1.80 an hour (increased from $1.10 an hour), plus 20 cents per box during the harvest season. Do you think this pay was enough of an increase? Do you think that the nonviolent tactics pursued by the farm workers lengthened or shortened their five year strike? Write your answer below.

(Continue on the back.)

Name ______________________________ Date ______________

4–28

SEPARATION OR ASSIMILATION?

Many Americans feel strongly about the traditions and values found in their specific cultural heritage (e.g., African Americans, Korean Americans, Mexican Americans). They may experience a conflict between how much they want to *separate* themselves from the mainstream of U.S. society to maintain their cultural identity and how much they want to *assimilate* themselves into U.S. society. Read the three accounts below of young Mexican Americans who represent three views on this conflict. As you read, identify who among these three teenagers wants to separate, who wants to assimilate, and who wants to find a middle road.

1. *PAUL:* "I don't want to be known as a Mexican American, but only as an American. I was born in this country and raised among Americans. I think like an Anglo, I talk like one, and I dress like one. It's true that I don't look like an Anglo and sometimes I am rejected by them, but it would be worse if I spoke Spanish or said that I was of Mexican descent. . . . I wish those people who are always making noise about being Mexican Americans would be quiet. We would be better off if they would accept things as they are. . . ."[(1)]
2. *ROBERTO:* "I am proud of being a Mexican American. We have a rich heritage. Mexico is a great country that is progressing fast. It has a wonderful history and culture . . . I don't want to be like the 'Paddys' [Anglos]. . . . They don't like anyone who is different. . . . Most people, even some Mexican Americans, look down on us because we are Mexicans. . . . It is unhealthy and unnatural to want to be something you are not."[(2)]
3. *ROSA:* "I am happy to be an American of Mexican descent. Because I am Mexican, I learned to be close to my family, and they have been a source of strength and support for me. . . . My Spanish also helped me a lot in my education and will open a lot of doors for me when I look for a job. As an American I am happy to live in a great progressive country where we have the freedom to achieve anything we want. . . . I feel very rich and fortunate because I have two cultures rather than just one."[(3)]

Complete the following sentences:

PAUL/ROBERTO/ROSA (circle one) wants to *assimilate* into American society.

PAUL/ROBERTO/ROSA (circle one) wants to *separate* from American society.

PAUL/ROBERTO/ROSA (circle one) wants neither to assimilate nor to separate from American society but rather to take a *middle road.*

Choose *one* of these three teenagers and write a letter to this person. Tell her or him what your opinion is of her or his thinking about separation or assimilation. What do you disagree with? What do you agree with? Can you relate to this teenager? Why or why not?

Dear ______________________,

I have the following response to your thoughts about separation from/assimilation into (circle one) American society.

____

____

(Continue on the back.)

Name ______________________________ Date ______________

4–29

A BASKETBALL STAR

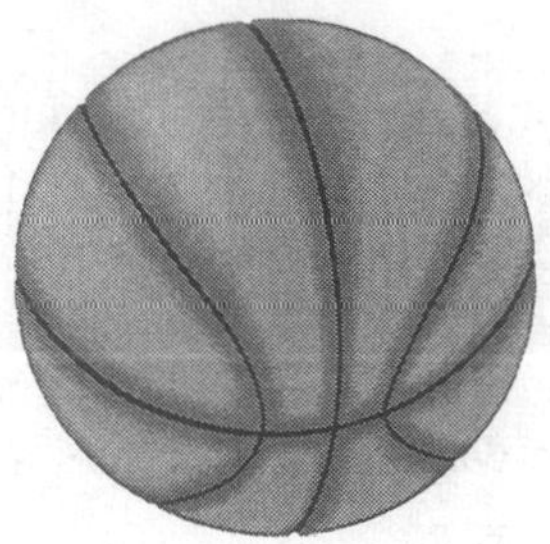

Who is your favorite sports star? Write the person's name and describe why you admire this person in the space provided below.

____

____

____

____

Ryneldi Becenti is a female Native American of the Navajo (or "Dine" which means "The People" as they refer to themselves) tribal group, she is a basketball star on the Arizona State University team. The Dine are the largest Native American tribal group in the United States, numbering over 200,000. Most members of the Dine live on their reservation in the northeastern corner of Arizona, in an area that is the size of Connecticut, Rhode Island, Massachusetts, and Vermont combined. Ryneldi is much admired by other members of her tribe, who drive for hours to watch her play basketball at Arizona State. An article written about Ryneldi in *Sports Illustrated* magazine describes a conflict this basketball star is having. Read the following excerpt from the article which describes this conflict:

"So many voices filled Sis's (Ryneldi's nickname) head as she walked across campus to the arena for that evening's game. There were the words of Peterson Zah, the tribal president, who had designated her a youth ambassador to speak at alcohol and drug clinics, schools, and youth conferences across the reservation the past two summers: 'She is perhaps the first role model we have every had. She is a pioneer. When she speaks, all the children are quiet and listen intently. She is helping to teach us the competitive attitude, which is what we have lacked. We haven't taught our children how to go out into the cold world—we need her to come back here and to be seen physically, to explain to them how she did it. She has the qualities to be president of our tribe'. . . . 'You're coming back after graduation,' he (her father) said. 'You've had enough fun. If you don't come back then, you'll never come back.'

Then she would hear the voice of Margaret McKeon, the young Arizona State assistant coach from New York City who had taken Sis under her wing, urging her to explore the possibility of professional ball in Europe, or to accept that request to speak in front of 350 whites and blacks at Arizona State, or to see what her hair looked like long or to try on a pretty blouse and a pair of designer jeans at the mall. . . . Who could not wish to be as confident and loose as Margaret, as full of life and laughter? Sis could be all silliness and giggles too, but she usually had to be in a place with lines around it, a basketball court or a reservation in northeastern Arizona."[1]

In your own words, briefly summarize the conflict Ryneldi is having in the space provided below.

In your opinion, to whose voices should Ryneldi listen? To the tribal president and her father? To Margaret McKeon, the assistant basketball coach? Write the pros and cons of each possible decision.

DECISION:	*PROS*	*CONS*
1. To play professional basketball in Europe after graduation.		
2. To return to the Navajo reservation after graduation.		

In the space below, express *your* opinion as to whom Ryneldi should listen to. Be sure to explain your reasons why she should make this decision.

(Continue on the back.)

Name ______________________________ Date ______________

4–30

SMILES A LOT

Have you seen the movie *Dances with Wolves*? What was your opinion of it? How much do you know about the Sioux Native Americans who were featured in the film? What are three facts you know about Native American ways of life? Write your answers in the space provided below.

____

____

____

____

____

____

____

____

____

Read the interview below of the teenager who played the part of Smiles a Lot in the film *Dances with Wolves*.

"My Indian name is Brown Eagle. . . . My legal name is Nathan Lee Chasing His Horse. . . . My movie name is Smiles a Lot.

. . . The way we were portrayed in *Dances [with Wolves]* is real. It's the opposite of the old Hollywood stereotype of showing Indians as ignorant or savages (like the old John Wayne movies when he'd single-handedly defeat a bunch of Indians, or when he they'd use non-Indians to play Indian roles). That was unreal. The Lakota, one of the three divisions of the Sioux, were a family of people with great respect for one another and nature. Very strong, humble, and wise, they fought and died courageously to defend their freedom and the sacred Black Hills— mountains on the South Dakota prairie. . . .

The experience of working on the movie made me even more proud to be what and who I am. I'm sixteen years old and a member of the Rosebud Sioux Tribe of the Great Sioux Nation, born in April on the twenty-eighth on the Rosebud Indian Reservation. I live with my parents, two sisters and one brother. I am a descendent of the great Sioux chief Crazy Horse and many other great leaders of the Sioux. I am a sophomore at White River High School in South Dakota. My favorite sport is basketball. . . .

I took part in the Reconciliation Ceremony they had at Crazy Horse Monument between whites and Indians of South Dakota. The governor of the state of South Dakota proclaimed 1990 as the Year of Reconciliation between Indians and whites. Both groups planned workshops and gatherings in order to better understand one another's culture and to counter racism. I led the singing of the Sacred Songs. . . . The Tree-Song sings of the tree of life and how all races are a part of the creation or nature. . . . I was taught to learn who you were, who you are, and who you're going to be. For me, I'm learning my culture, and I believe in it. . . ."[(1)]

4-30 (continued)

Imagine you had helped organize the Reconciliation Ceremony of 1990. What workshops would you have planned for the different ethnic groups to better understand one another's culture and to counter racism? What questions might you have asked Smiles a Lot at his workshop? Answer these questions in the space provided below.

Write a letter to Nathan Lee Chasing His Horse (alias Smiles a Lot). Perhaps you would like to ask him some questions such as "What was it like to make the movie *Dances with Wolves*?" or "What is it like to be a teenage movie star?" What questions do you have about the Sioux Native American culture?

Date:

Dear Nathan Lee Chasing His Horse (Smiles a Lot),

(Continue on the back.)

Name ______________________________ Date ______________

4–31

ARAB AMERICANS

Have you ever heard of Casey Kasem (host of "America's Top 40"), Ralph Nader (consumer rights activist), Philip Habib (U.S. negotiator for the Paris Peace Talks that ended the Vietnam War), or Donna Shalala (Secretary of Health and Human Services in the Clinton administration)? These are all Arab Americans who have contributed a great deal to the United States. Arab Americans (primarily Christian Syrians) began immigrating to this country in the late nineteenth century. Many settled in the newly developing industrial centers in Ohio, Indiana, and Michigan. In 1916 a small community of Muslim Syrians moved to Dearborn, Michigan (suburb of Detroit). With the large influx of Muslim Palestinian, Yemenis, and Lebanese immigrants after World War II, this community has grown to be the largest Muslim Arab American community in the United States today.

Unfortunately, many U.S. citizens do not understand the culture or history of Arab Americans. An example of this occurred during the Persian Gulf Conflict, between the United States and Iraq, in 1991. Read the excerpt from *Sports Illustrated* below.

They're Americans Too

"One of the early casualties of the Gulf War has been a sense of fairness and tolerance here at home. Some Arab Americans, through no fault of their own, have already been victims of bias and ignorance.

The problem is of special concern in Dearborn, Michigan, which has one of the largest Arab American communities in the country. Eleven of the 13 players on the basketball team at Dearborn's Fordson High are Arab Americans. All season long, the team has been a target of nasty taunts. Says junior point guard Haisam Abadi, 'In one game someone said, "Go back to Saudi Arabia. You're not wanted here." Every game something like that is said.'

Never mind that Saudi Arabia is an ally of the U.S.—or for that matter, that most of the Fordson players are of Lebanese descent. Bigotry hasn't time for such fine distinctions. Fordson athletic director John Spain told Mick McCabe of the *Detroit Free Press* of a phone call he got recently from a parent complaining that a Fordson wrestler had 'HUSSEIN' written on his warmup. 'She didn't think it was appropriate,' Spain told McCabe. 'Well, that's the kid's name.'"[1]

Imagine you were Fordson athletic director John Spain during the Persian Gulf War. You are being interviewed by the local TV station on your reaction to the bigotry being displayed toward students on your basketball and wrestling teams. How would you respond to the following questions?

Interviewer: Good evening Mr. Spain. We are here to record your reaction to the recent displays of hostility toward Arab Americans at Fordson High School athletic events.

Mr. Spain:

Interviewer: How would you describe the atmosphere at the basketball games and wrestling matches this season? Specifically, what kinds of comments have been made to your players and what has been their response?

Mr Spain:

Interviewer: Would you say the people who have exhibited this bigotry have a clear understanding of your Arab American basketball and wrestling team members? Why or why not?

Mr. Spain:

Interviewer: We understand that a parent complained about "HUSSEIN" being on the back of the warmup of one of your wrestling team members. Would you like to comment on this?

Mr. Spain:

Interviewer: Would you like to make any ending comments regarding this situation?

Mr. Spain:

Name ______________________ Date ____________

4–32

BRINGING IN THE NEW YEAR

Many cultural groups in the United States have different customs to celebrate the beginning of a new year. Read the facts below about the traditions practiced by many members of two cultural groups—Japanese Americans and African Americans. On the Venn diagram on the following page, compare and contrast these traditions. How are they similar? How are they different?

JAPANESE AMERICANS

1. The Japanese New Year is celebrated for three days.
2. The traditional food for New Year celebrations is mochi, a rice cake. Traditionally, men would pound the rice into a thick paste. Then women would put the paste on a board and mold it into flat balls.
3. A pair of bamboo reeds is placed over the front door on New Year's Eve; the Japanese believe that the reeds symbolize faithfulness in marriage and the family's ability to "bend and not break." A pine tree, a kadomatsu, is also placed at the front door; it symbolizes a long and healthy life.
4. The Japanese believe that joy or sadness on New Year's is an omen for the remainder of the year and, therefore, they allow no unhappiness during the New Year celebration. It is considered a time for forgiving, smiling, and cordiality to all.
5. Singers and carolers dressed in ancient Japanese costumes go from house to house beating a drum and singing happy songs.
6. The traditions for Japanese American New Year celebrations originated in Japan and were brought here by immigrants to America.

AFRICAN AMERICANS

1. Many African Americans celebrate Kwanzaa during the last seven days of the year.
2. The word "Kwanzaa" comes from the Swahili phrase "matunda ya kwanza." "Matunda" means "fruit" and "ya kwanza" means first.

3. Kwanzaa was begun in America in 1966 by African Americans who wanted to practice the traditions of the African "first fruit" festivals with their emphasis on gathering the people together to celebrate community.
4. On each day of Kwanzaa, a different communitarian African value is celebrated: Unity, Self-determination, Collective Work and Responsibility, Cooperative Economics, Purpose, Creativity, and Faith.
5. Many African Americans dress in African clothing (hats, scarves, dresses, shirts, pants) while celebrating Kwanzaa.
6. The seven basic symbols of Kwanzaa are: crops (symbolizing the rewards of collective productive labor), a mat (symbolizing the foundation of tradition), a candle holder (symbolizing African ancestors), seven candles, corn (symbolizing the hopes and challenges of children), the unity cup (symbolizing unity in the family and community) and gifts (symbolic of the fruits of a parent's labor).

SIMILARITIES AND DIFFERENCES OF KWANZAA AND JAPANESE NEW YEAR

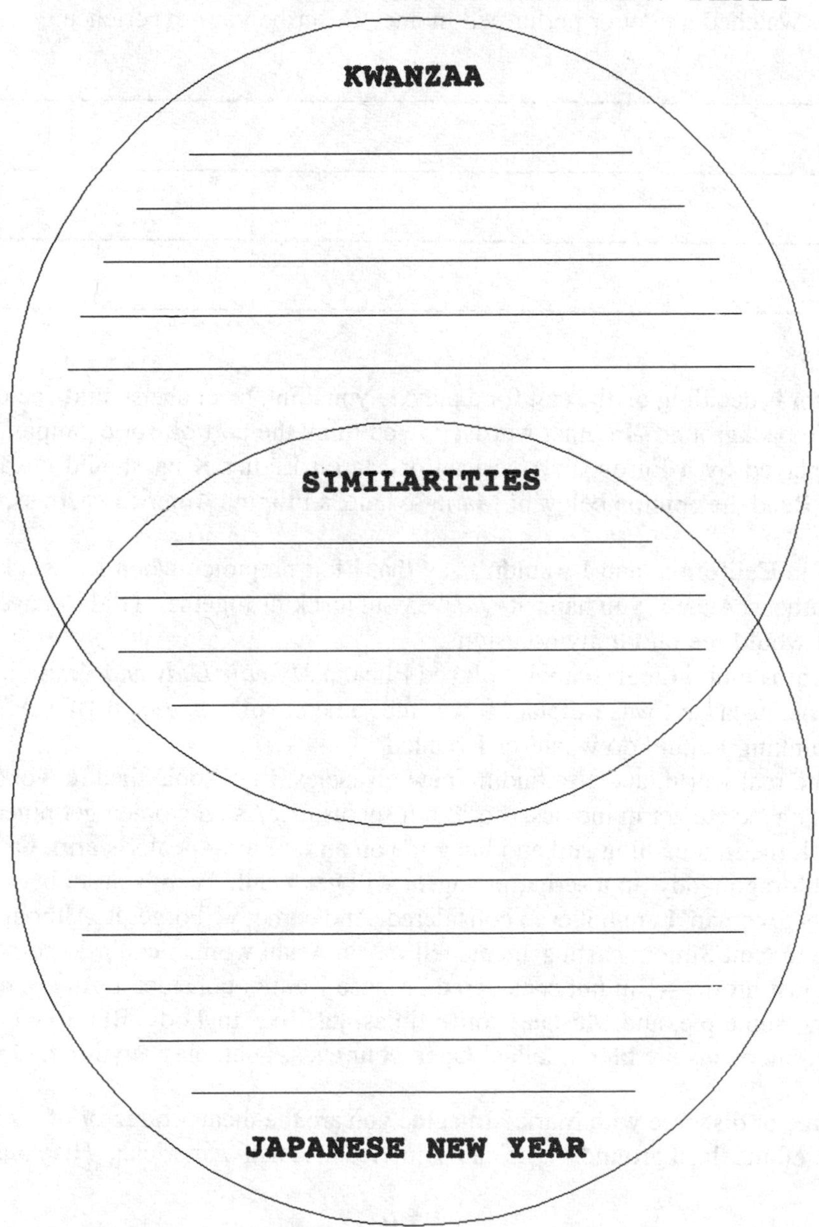

Name ________________________________ Date ______________

4–33
TYPECASTING

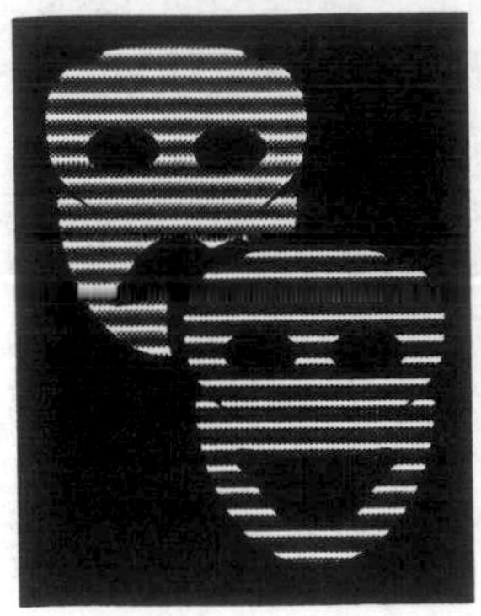

Have you ever watched a play or performed in one? Describe your experience.

____

____

____

____

When a director is deciding on the cast for a play do you think he or she should decide on the parts based on the actor's ethnic background? In other words, do you think the part of, for example, George Washington should always be played by a European American or Martin Luther King should always be played by an African American? Read the opinion below of Maria Aviado, a Filipino American actress, regarding this issue.

"I grew up in California, and I wouldn't say that I felt prejudice when I was a kid. I went to school with Mexicans, Southeast Asians, you name it. We were all just kids together. I didn't have one Filipino friend, just some cousins I would see on family occasions.

I was in the drama club in high school. I played Eliza in *My Fair Lady* and Emily in *Our Town*. No role was ever closed to me because I was Filipino. It was the same in college, too, at UCLA. I got plenty of leads and I got used to thinking I could do whatever I wanted.

Now I'm in the real world, and I'm finding new obstacles. I get some theatre work in the Los Angeles area, and I want the chance to act in movies, too. But it seems that Asian women get pigeonholed. I'm young, so they want to stick me in a bathing suit and hang me on an evil drug dealer's arm. Or if there's a manipulative, cold-hearted 'dragon lady' in a script, my agent will get a call. There's no in between. If there's a role for a gutsy, intelligent woman, I am not even considered. And comedy? Forget it. Although I've played everything from Moliere to Neil Simon, casting agents tell me an Asian woman can't do comedy.

So one day it just hit me—I'm not considered because I'm not considered *American*. I grew up in L.A. I like cheeseburgers, apple pie, and Mustang convertibles, just like anybody. But now I am considered exotic. . . . Hey, not all Americans are blond, fellas! Open your eyes. I can play anything. Open your minds."[(1)]

Do you agree or disagree with Maria? Imagine you are the theater director of a school where students of many different ethnic backgrounds (African American, Asian American, Hispanic American, Native

American, European American) audition for plays. What would be your casting policy? Would you let an Asian American play the part of Abraham Lincoln? Would you let a Hispanic American play the part of Malcolm X? What would you do if you were casting a play like *The Sound of Music* (a play about Europeans) or *For Colored Girls . . .* (a play about African American women) or *Dances with Wolves* (a film about Native Americans)? Write a conversation between yourself (the theater director) and the students who have auditioned for the play (one mentioned above or another with which you are familiar) you are going to produce this spring. The conversation takes place after an audition. You are letting them know which students received what parts for the upcoming play. Explain your reasoning for the casting.

Theater Director: Hello everyone! We are gathered here this afternoon so that I can tell you the casting for our upcoming production of ____________________________________.

Student 1:

Theater Director:

(Continue the dialogue in the space provided below.)

Name ______________________________ Date ______________

4–34
AMERICAN AS APPLE PIE?

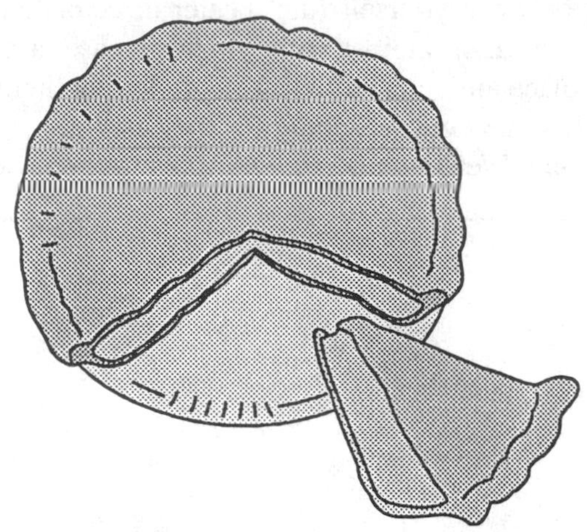

Because we are largely a country of immigrants, the United States has received many contributions from all over the world in the form of foods, arts, ideas, and people. In the list below you will find people and contributions from Italian Americans, East Indian Americans, Japanese Americans, French Americans, Dutch Americans, and Polish Americans. Read the list and decide which words belong with which ethnic group. Then place them in the appropriate piece of thc "Apple Pie" on the following page.

yogurt	Mario Cuomo	pizza
chess	Dalip Singh Saund	badminton
parcheesi	Santha Rama Rau	karaoke
Madonna	Seiji Ozawa	golf
cloves	Hideyo Noguchi	Kate Chopin
cumin	Amerigo Vespucci	sukiyaki
Mother Cabrini	Joe DiMaggio	Gobind Behari Lal
yoga	Theodore Roosevelt	Franklin D. Roosevelt
Geraldine Ferraro	Isamu Noguchi	mustard
tempura	Thomas Hopkins Gallaudet	omelette
Jack Kerouac	soup du jour	kimonos
Casimir Funk	city public playgrounds	Dr. Marie Elizabeth Zakrzewska
fondue	John James Audubon	ice skating
reservoir	vitamins	hors d'ouvres
Santa Claus	Martin Van Buren	French fries

PEOPLE AND CONTRIBUTIONS FROM MANY ETHNIC GROUPS

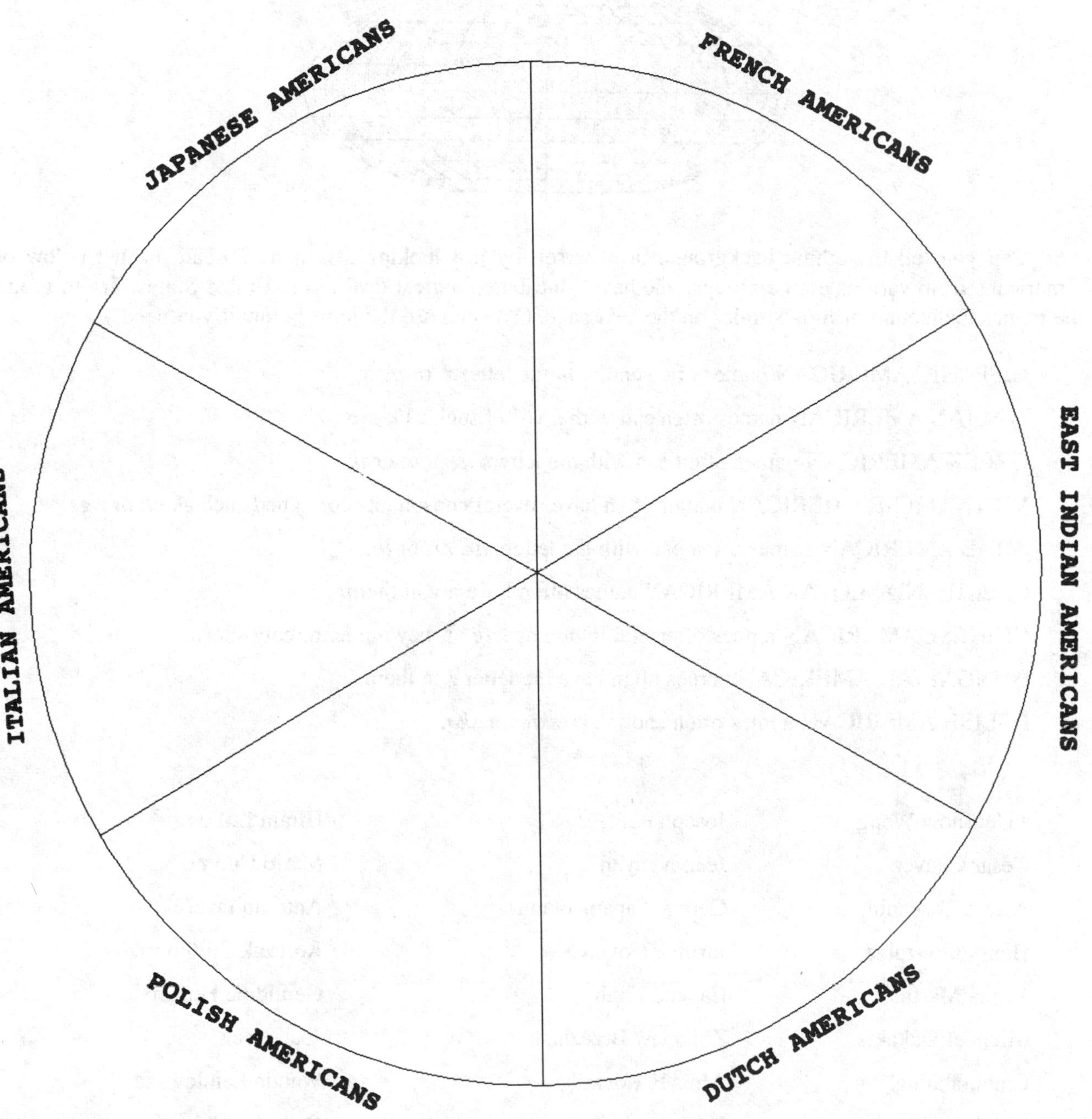

Name ______________________________ Date ____________

4–35
NAMES

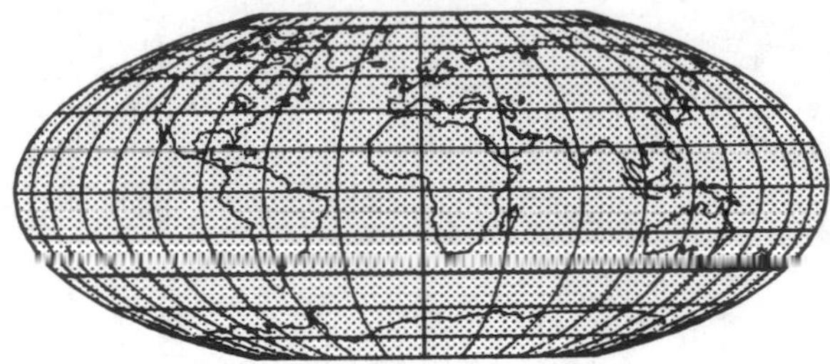

Can you tell the ethnic background of a person by just looking at a name? Read the list below of Americans from various ethnic groups who have contributed a great deal to the United States. Try to group the names that sound or look similar on the next page. (You can use the hints below if you need!)

HISPANIC AMERICAN names often end with the letter *z*, or *os*.

ITALIAN AMERICAN names often end with a vowel such as *i*, *a* or *o*.

GREEK AMERICAN names often end with the letters *is*, *aou*, or *ik*.

VIETNAMESE AMERICAN names often have several consonants combined such as *nh* or *ng*.

ARAB AMERICAN names often end with the letters *ar*, *er*, or *ib*.

CZECH AND SLOVAK AMERICAN names often have a *v* in them.

CHINESE AMERICAN names often end in *ong* or *ung* or they are extremely short.

HUNGARIAN AMERICAN names often have the letter *z* in them.

POLISH AMERICAN names often end in *ski*, *skie*, or *ska*.

Jade Snow Wong
Cesar Chavez
Arturo Toscanini
Henry Gonzalez
Vilma Martinez
Michael Dukakis
Chien-shuing Wu
Ralph Nader
Nghi Huynh
Frank Stella
Philip Habib
Adolph Zukor

Joseph Pulitzer
Jean Nguyen
George Papanicolaou
Jarmila Novotna
Eugene Trinh
Zbigniew Brzezinski
Alois F. Kovarik
Dr. Nguyen Anh Nga
Lawrence Ferlinghetti
Ieoh Ming Pei
Zsa Zsà Gabor
Connie Chung

Hiram L. Fong
Mario Cuomo
Antonin Dvořák
Korczak Ziolkowski
Geraldine Ferraro
Joan Baez
Wanda Landowska
Olympia Dukakis
Henry Cisneros
Mary Rose Oakar
Maya Lin
Edmund Muskie

4-35 (continued)

HUNGARIAN AMERICANS

VIETNAMESE AMERICANS

CHINESE AMERICANS

ITALIAN AMERICANS

GREEK AMERICANS

HISPANIC AMERICANS

CZECH AND SLOVAK AMERICANS

ARAB AMERICANS

POLISH AMERICANS

EXTRA CREDIT! Choose one person from each ethnic group and research them in your school or local library. Write a short description (one paragraph) of their lives and their contributions to U.S. society.

Name ______________________ Date ____________

4–36

MAJORITY-MINORITY

Every ten years, since 1790, the United States has taken a census of its population. Read the statistics below and then chart them on the graph provided at the bottom of the page.

Census Date	*Population*[1]
1790	3.9 million
1800	5.3 million
1810	7.2 million
1820	9.6 million
1830	12.9 million
1840	17.1 million
1850	23.2 million
1860	31.4 million
1870	38.5 million
1880	50.1 million
1890	63.0 million
1900	76.2 million
1910	92.2 million
1920	106.0 million
1930	123.2 million
1940	132.2 million
1950	151.3 million
1960	179.3 million
1970	203.3 million
1980	226.5 million
1990	248.7 million
2070 (estimated)	497.4 million

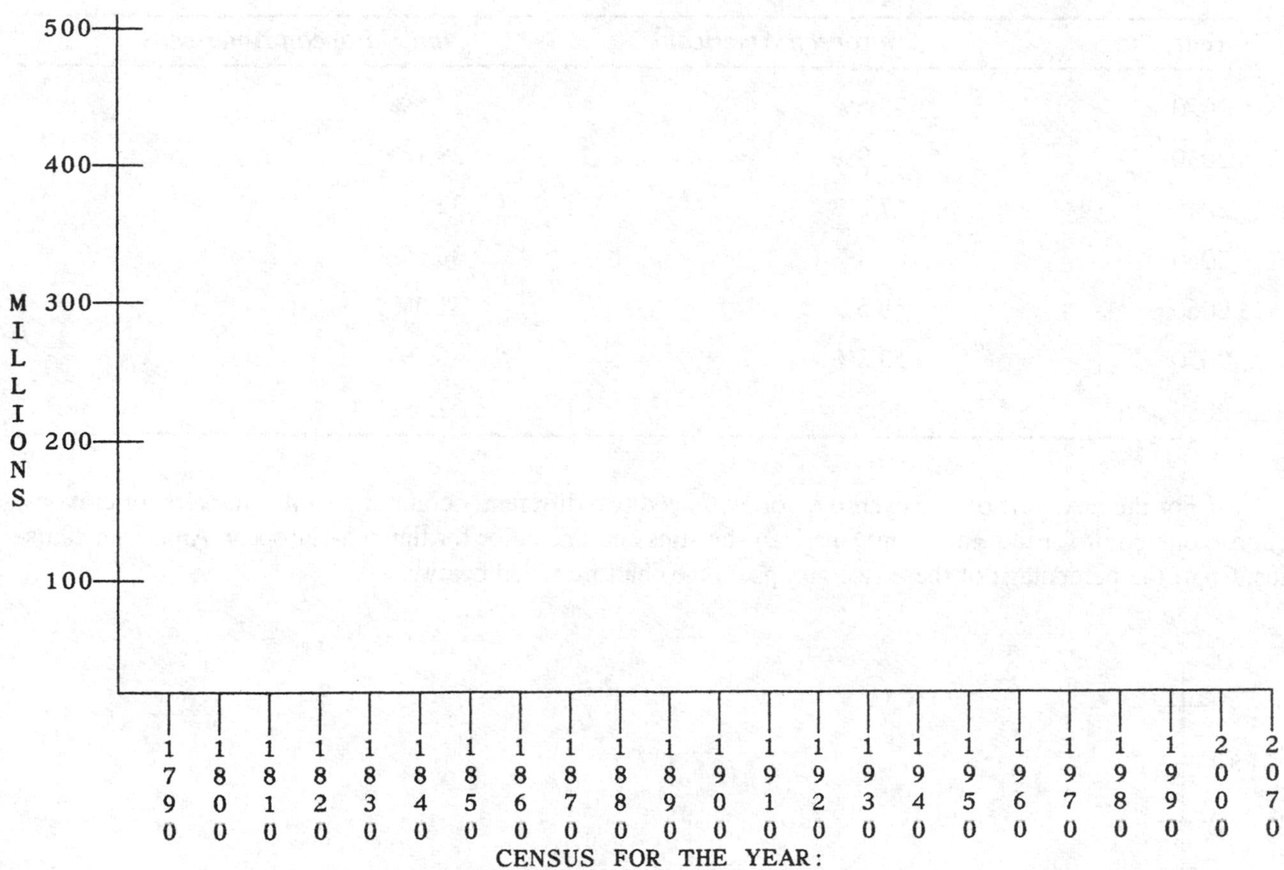

European Americans have been a majority of the U.S. population since the first census was taken in 1790; however, in the twenty-first century, it is predicted that the number of European Americans will drop below 50% of the U.S. population and therefore, become a minority. Look at the statistics below that show the European American and non–European American population since 1930 and projections into the twenty-first century.[(2)]

Year	*European Americans*	*Non-European Americans*
1940	89.8%	10.2%
1950	89.3%	10.7%
1960	88.6%	11.4%
1970	87.6%	12.4%
1980	85.9%	14.1%
1990	83.9%	16.1%
2000	81.5%	18.5%
2010	78.7%	21.3%

Year	*European Americans*	*Non-European Americans*
2020	75.5%	24.5%
2030	71.9%	28.1%
2040	67.8%	32.2%
2050	63.4%	36.6%
2060	58.5%	41.5%
2070	53.3%	46.7%
2080	47.5%	52.5%

For the next part of this exercise, you will need two differently colored pencils, markers, or crayons. Choose one color for the European American statistics and one color for the non-European American statistics. Chart the percentage of these two groups on the chart provided below.

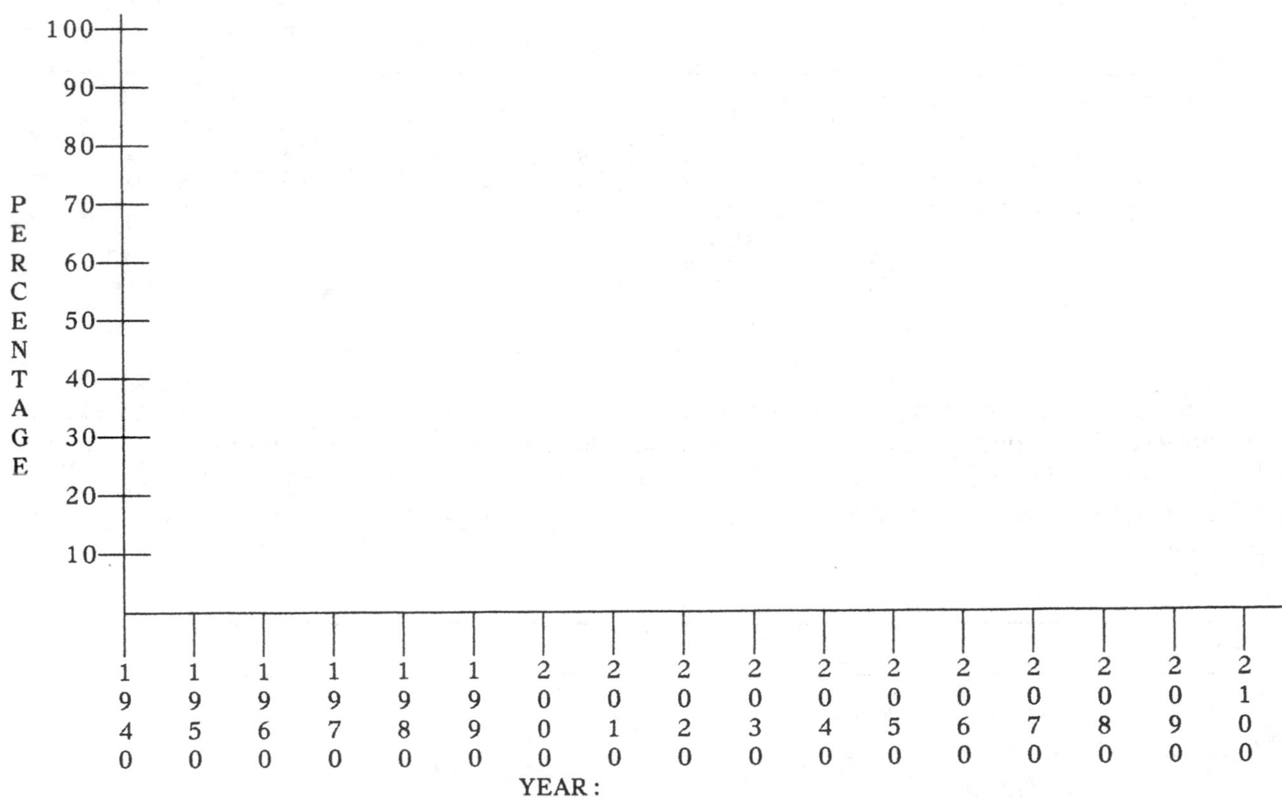

Based on the information you have charted above, in what year will European Americans become a *minority* in the U.S. population?

European Americans will become a minority in the year _____.

How do you think this will affect life in the United States? Write your answer to this question on a separate sheet of paper.

Name ______________________________ Date ______________

4–37

ANCESTRIES

Since 1790, the U.S. has taken a census every ten years. One of the questions asked in the census is the following: "Of what ancestry(ies) are you?" Some Americans can answer with just *one* category such as "Italian," or "Japanese." More and more Americans answer with two or three categories such as "German," "African," and "Mexican"; or "Filipino," "Chinese," and "Native American"! It is interesting to note which ancestries are most commonly mentioned when Americans are asked where they come from. The 1990 census revealed that, within the total U.S. population of 248,710,000, there were ten leading ancestries. Read the chart below of statistics taken from the 1990 census to find out what these ancestries are![(1)]

Americans who are **partially *or* fully:**	*Total*	*Percentage of American Population*	*Color Code*
German	57,947,000	23.3%	■
Irish	38,736,000		☐
English	32,652,000		☐
African	23,777,000		☐
Italian	14,665,000		☐
Mexican	11,587,000		☐
Scottish/Scotch-Irish	11,012,000		☐
French	10,321,000		☐
Polish	9,366,000		☐
Native American	8,708,000		☐

What percent of the *total* American population (248,710,000) is each of the ten leading ancestries? Look at the example below, then compute the rest and complete the chart above!

1. Americans who are partially or fully of German ancestry (57,947,000) are what percent of the total American population (248,710,000)?

STEP ONE: $57{,}947{,}000 = \frac{X}{100} \cdot 248{,}710{,}000$

STEP TWO: $X = \frac{57{,}947{,}000}{2{,}487{,}100}$

STEP THREE: X = 23.3% (rounded off to the nearest .1%)

For the next part of the exercise, you will need nine differently colored pencils, markers, or crayons. Choose one color for each American ancestry (except for German, which has already been color coded black) and color in the "color code" box on the chart. Then create a bar graph on the next page and show, visually the percentage each ancestry is of the total American population. (German has already been done in black as an example!)

4-37 (continued)

ANCESTRAL GROUPS IN THE U.S.

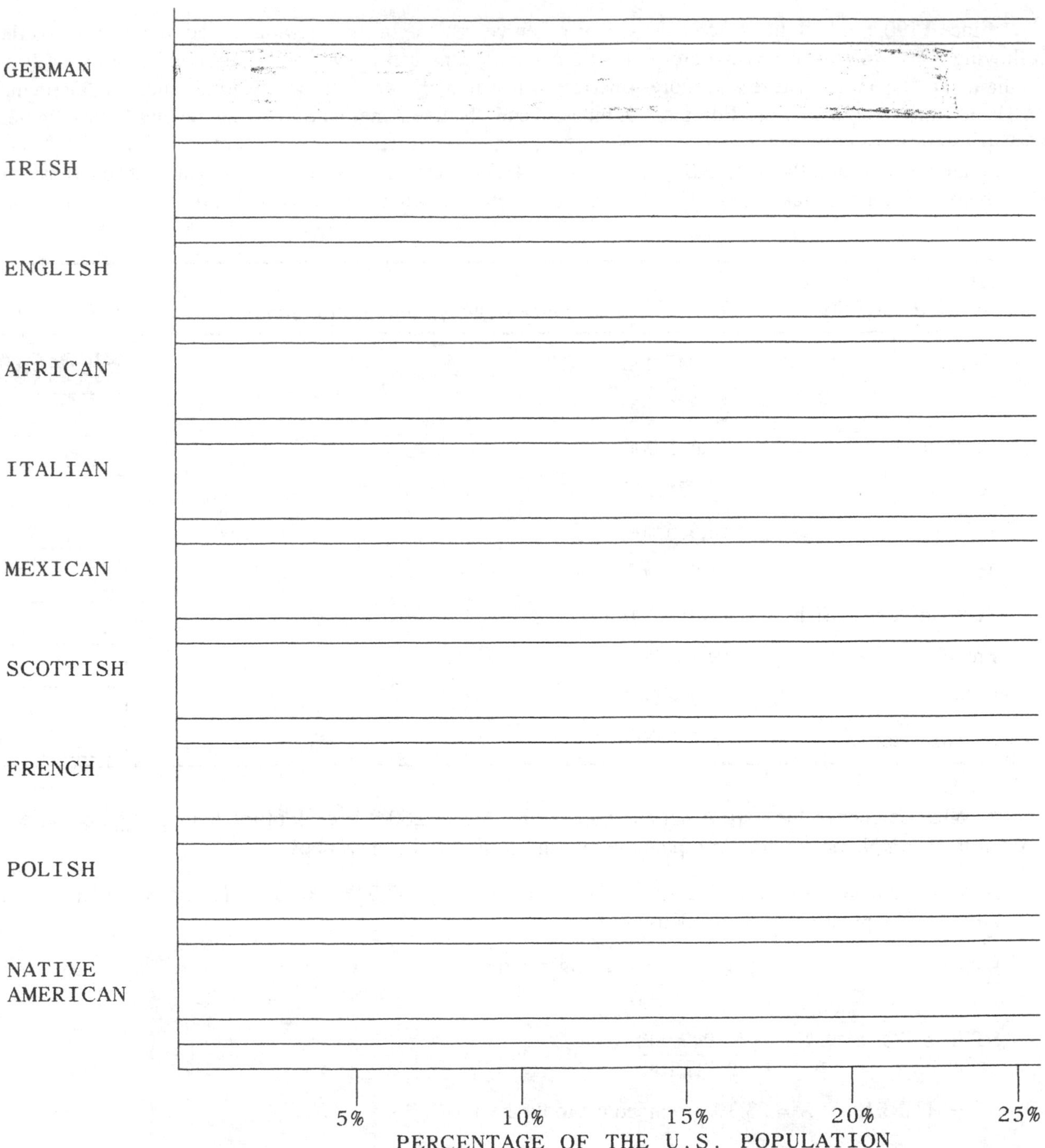

Name ______________________ *Date* ____________

4–38

ASIAN AND PACIFIC ISLANDER AMERICANS

The 1990 census revealed that a total of 7,274,000 Americans are of Asian and Pacific Islander descent. What are the origins of these Americans? Analyze the chart below of statistics taken from the 1990 census to find out![(1)]

Asian or Pacific Island Country	*Total*	*Percentage of Asian American Population*	*Color Code*
Chinese Americans	1,645,000	22.6%	
Filipino Americans	1,407,000		
Japanese Americans	848,000		
Asian Indian Americans	815,000		
Korean Americans	790,000		
Vietnamese Americans	615,000		
Laotian Americans	149,000		
Cambodian Americans	147,000		
Thai Americans	91,000		
Hmong Americans	90,000		
Pakistani Americans	81,000		
Hawaiian Americans	211,000		
Samoan Americans	63,000		
Guamanian Americans	49,000		
Others	263,000		

What percent of the *total* Asian and Pacific Islander American population (7,274,000) is each ethnic group? Look at the example below, then compute the rest and complete the chart above!

1. Chinese Americans (1,645,000) are what percent of the total Asian and Pacific Islander American population (7,274,000)?

STEP ONE: $1{,}645{,}000 = \frac{X}{100} \cdot 7{,}274{,}000$

STEP TWO: $X = \frac{1{,}645{,}000}{72{,}400}$

STEP THREE: X = 22.6% (rounded off to the nearest .1%)

For the next part of the exercise, you will need 14 differently colored pencils, markers, or crayons. Choose one color for each country from which Asian and Pacific Islander Americans come (except for China which has already been color coded black) and color in the "color code" box on the chart above. Then, create a bar graph on the next page and show, visually, the percentage each group is of the total Asian and Island Pacific American population. (Chinese has already been done in black as an example!)

4-38 (continued)

ASIAN AND PACIFIC ISLANDER AMERICANS

CHINESE

FILIPINO

JAPANESE

ASIAN INDIAN

KOREAN

VIETNAMESE

CAMBODIAN

THAI

HMONG

PAKASTANI

HAWAIIAN

SAMOAN

GUAMANIAN

OTHERS

5% 10% 15% 20%

PERCENTAGE OF TOTAL ASIAN AND PACIFIC ISLANDER POPULATION:

Name ______________________________ *Date* ______________

4–39

HISPANIC AMERICANS

The 1990 census revealed that a total of 22,354,000 Americans are of Hispanic descent. What are the origins of these Americans? Analyze the chart below of statistics taken from the 1990 census to find out![1]

Hispanic Country	*Total*	*Percentage of Hispanic Population*	*Color Code*
Mexico	13,496,000	60.4%	☐
Puerto Rico	2,728,000		☐
Cuba	1,044,000		☐
Other	5,086,000		☐

What percent of the *total* Hispanic American population (22,354,000) is each ethnic group? Look at the example below, then compute the rest and complete the chart above!

1. Mexican Americans (13,496,000) are what percent of the total Hispanic American population (22,354,000)?

STEP ONE: $13{,}496{,}000 = \frac{X}{100} \cdot 22{,}354{,}000$

STEP TWO: $X = \frac{13{,}496{,}000}{223{,}540}$

STEP THREE: X = 60.4% (rounded off to the nearest .1%)

For the next part of the exercise, you will need four differently color pencils, markers, or crayons. Choose one color for each country from which Hispanic Americans come (blue for Mexico, green for Puerto Rico, etc.) and color in the "color code" box on the chart above. Then, look at the pie graph, which visualizes the percentage each Hispanic ethnic group is of the total Hispanic population. Figure out which part of the pie represents the Mexican Americans, the Puerto Rican Americans, the Cuban Americans, and the "other" Hispanic Americans (e.g., Dominican Republic, Colombia, El Salvador).

4-39 (continued)

HISPANIC ETHNIC GROUPS IN THE U.S.

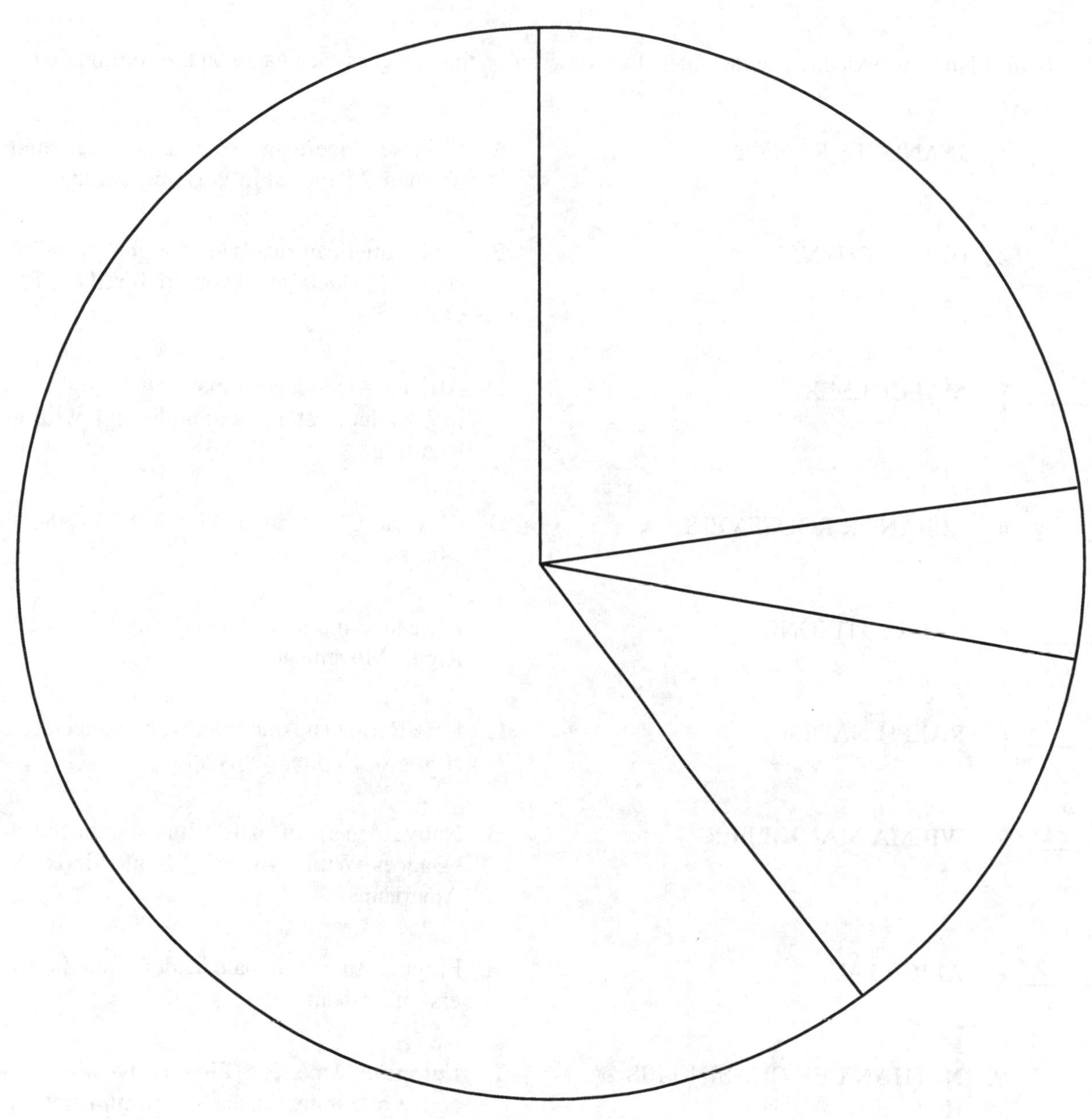

Name ______________________________ Date ______________

4–40

PEOPLE TO REMEMBER

In the blanks provided, write the letter of the description that matches each name on the column on the left.

____ 1. JEANETTE RANKIN	A. Chinese American woman who created the Vietnam Memorial in Washington, D.C.
____ 2. CESAR CHAVEZ	B. Arab American man who fought for safer consumer products and worked for the EPA and OSHA
____ 3. MALCOLM X	C. African American woman who fought against mob violence and lynching through writing and lecturing
____ 4. ELEANOR ROOSEVELT	D. Mexican American male leader of the farmworkers' movement
____ 5. LARRY ITLIONG	E. African American male leader of the Civil Rights Movement
____ 6. RALPH NADER	F. First European American woman elected to the House of Representatives
____ 7. WILMA MANKILLER	G. Native American male film star in the movie "Dances With Wolves" about Sioux Native Americans
____ 8. ALICE PAUL	H. Filipino American male leader of the farmworkers' movement
____ 9. NATHAN LEE CHASING HIS HORSE	I. European American First Lady who took an active role in her husband's administration
____ 10. MAYA LIN	J. One of the European American leaders of the women's suffrage movement in the early 1900s
____ 11. PEDRO ALBIZU CAMPOS	K. First Native American female chief of the Cherokee Nation
____ 12. IDA B. WELLS	L. Male leader of the Puerto Rican independence movement

References

INTRODUCTION

A–2 FROM ALL OVER THE WORLD

1. U.S, Bureau of the Census, *1990 Census of Population, General Population Characteristics, U.S.* (CP-1-1).

SECTION ONE—THE 1600s

1–5 GOING TO A DANCE?

1. Carolyn Niethammer, *Daughters of the Earth: The Lives and Legends of American Indian Women* (New York: Macmillan Publishing Co., 1977), p. 60.

1–8 POLISH AMERICANS LEAD THE FIRST LABOR WALKOUT

1. Joseph A. Wytrwal, *The Poles in America* (Minneapolis: Lerner Publications, 1969), p. 22.

1–9 ENSLAVED!

1. Charles Ball, *A Narrative of the Life and Adventures of Charles Ball, A Black Man*, 3d. ed. (Pittsburgh: John T. Shyrock, 1854), pp. 158–159.

2. Morris Hillyer, Library of Congress.
3. Josiah Henson, *Father Henson's Story of His Own Life* (New York: Corinth Books, 1962), pp. 17–18.
4. Russell Menard, "The Maryland Slave Population, 1658–1738: A Demographic Profile of Blacks in Four Counties," *Women's Monthly Quarterly*, 3d., 33 (1975), p. 36.

1–15 INDENTURED SERVANTS

1. Clifford Lindsey Alderman, *Colonists for Sale* (New York: McMillan Publishing Co., 1975), p. 33.
2. Ibid. p. 67.

1–16 GRILLED CHEESE SANDWICH

1. Laurel Thatcher Ulrich, *Good Wives: Image and Reality in the Lives of Women in Northern New England 1650–1750* (New York: Oxford University Press, 1983), pp. 20–22.

1–18 GUNS!

1. "Gun Swaps May Not Mean the Streets Are Any Safer," *The Record* (Jan. 8, 1994), p. A8.

SECTION TWO—THE 1700s

2–3 STEREOTYPES

1. D. Willian N. Fenton, ed. *Parker on the Iroquois,* Book III, pp. 30–31.

2–4 THE ENVIRONMENT

1. Ibid. pp. 38–39.

2–8 THREE CULTURES

1. Carolyn Niethammer, *Daughters of the Earth: The Lives and Legends of American Indian Women* (New York: McMillan Publishing Co., 1977), p. 119.
2. John P. McKay, Bennet D. Hill, and John Buckler *A History of Western Society* (Boston: Houghton Mifflin Co., 1991), p. 598.
3. Hallie Wannamaker, excerpt from diary written during 1989 trip to West Africa.

2–9 EUROPEAN AMERICAN MEDICAL CARE

1. John P. Mckay, Bennet D. Hill, and John Buckler, *A History of Western Society* (Boston: Houghton Mifflin Co., 1991), p. 644.

2–11 POINT OF VIEW

1. Joy Hakim, *From Colonies to Country* (New York: Oxford University Press, 1993), pp. 64–65.
2. Howard Zinn, *People's History of the U.S.* (New York: Harper and Row, 1980), p. 67.
3. John J. Rawls and Philip Weeks, *Land of Liberty* (New York: Holt, Reinhart and Winston Publishing Co., 1985), p. 118.
4. Leroy Bennet, *Before the Mayflower: A History of Black America* (New York: Penguin Books, 1984), pp. 59–60.

2–15 FOLLOW THE ARMY

1. Peter J. Albert and Ronald Hoffman, (eds.) *Women in the Age of the American Revolution* (Charlottesville: University of Virginia Press, 1989), p. 14.
2. Ibid. p. 15.
3. Ibid. p. 16.
4. Ibid. p. 15.
5. Ibid.

2–17 INSPIRATION

1. William N. Fenton, ed. *Parker on the Iroquois,* Book III, p. 49.

2–18 ABIGAIL ADAMS WRITES A LETTER

1. L. H. Butterfield (ed.), *Adams Family Correspondence*, Vol. 1 (Cambridge, MA: Harvard University Press, 1963), pp. 369–370.
2. Ibid. pp. 401–403.

2–20 THE IROQUOIS CONSTITUTION

1. *The United States in Literature*, p. 104.

2–22 THE CAJUNS

1. Polly Morrice, *The French Americans* (New York: Chelsea House Publishers, 1988), pp. 76–77.
2. Ibid.

2–24 *EVERYDAY LIFE*

1. Massachusetts Historical Society, *Collections*, 6th Ser., Vol. 4, pp. 228–229.

2–25 *WHAT IF?*

1. Malcolm X, *Malcolm X on Afro-American History* (New York: Pathfinder Press, 1970), p. 28.

2–27 *TRAGEDY*

1. James Axtell, *The European and the Indian: Essays in the Ethnohistory of Colonial North America* (New York: Oxford University Press, 1981), p. 259.
2. E. Wagner and Allen E. Stearn, *The Effect of Smallpox on the Destiny of the Amerindian* (Boston: Bruce Humphries Inc., 1945), pp. 44–45.
3. Russell Thornton, *American Indian Holocaust and Survival: A Population History since 1492* (London: University of Oklahoma Press, 1987), p. 89.
4. Ibid. pp. 84–85.

SECTION THREE—THE 1800s

3–3 *DECISIONS AND CHOICES*

1. Herbert Guttman, *The Black Family in Slavery and Freedom 1750–1925* (New York: Vintage Books, 1976), p. 353.

3–8 *TRAIL OF TEARS*

1. Ernest Thompson Seton, *Life Histories of Northern Animals* (New York: Charles Scribner and Sons, 1909), p. 300.
2. Russell Thornton, *American Indian Holocaust and Survival* (London: University of Oklahoma Press, 1987), p. 119.
3. Margot Liberty, "Population Trends Among Present-day Omaha Indians" *Plains Anthropologist*, Vol. 20, p. 228.
4. James Mooney, *Historical Sketch of the Cherokee* (Chicago: Aldine Publishing Co., 1900), p. 124.
5. Charles A. Eastman, (Ohiyesa) *From the Deep Woods to Civilization* (Boston: Little, Brown and Co., 1916), p. 111–112.

3–9 *WORKING CONDITIONS*

1. John R. Commons, *Documentary History of American Industrial Society* (Cleveland: A.H. Clark Co., 1911).

2. Carol Hymowitz and Miachele Weissman, *A History of Women in America* (New York: Bantam Books, 1978), p. 133.
3. Norman Ware, *The Industrial Worker, 1840–1860* (New York: Quadrangle, 1964).
4. "Report of the General Investigator," *Proceedings of the General Assembly of the Knights of Labor, 1887.*
5. "Case No. 45, Sadie G.," *Preliminary Report of the New York State Factory Investigating Commission.* Albany, NY 1912.
6. Elizabeth Gurley Flynn, *The Rebel Girl* (New York: International Publishers, 1973).

3–10 MEN, WOMEN, AND MONEY

1. Mary M. and W. Elliot Brownlee, *Women in the American Economy: A Documentary History, 1675–1929* (Clinton, Mass.: The Colonial Press Inc., 1976), p. 174–177. (permission of the publisher)

3–11 FIGHT, AND IF YOU CAN'T FIGHT, KICK

1. [Ophelia Settle Egypt, J. Masuoka, Charles S. Johnson] "Unwritten History of Slavery; Autobiographical Accounts of Negro Ex-Slaves," Social Science Documents No. 1 (Nashville, TN: Fisk Unversity, Social Science Institute, 1945, p. 284–291.

3–12 FREDERICK DOUGLASS

1. *Frederick Douglass,* Narrative of the Life of Frederick Douglass, an American Slave (New York: Literary Classics of the United States, Inc., 1994), pp. 180–182.

3–13 TELLING HER STORY

1. Harriet A. Jacobs, *Incidents in the Life of a Slave Girl* (Cambridge, Mass: Harvard University Press, 1987), pp. 114–116.

3–14 A WOMAN'S FATE

1. Thomas Weld, *American Slavery as It Is: Testimony of a Thousand Witnesses* (New York: American Anti-Slavery Society, 1839), p. 12 (narrative of Nehemiah Caulkins of Waterford, CT)
2. Josiah Henson, *Father Henson's Story of His Own Life* (New York: Corinth Books, 1962), pp. 12–13.
3. B.A. Botkin, *Lay My Burden Down: A Folk History of Slavery* (Chicago: University of Illinois Press, 1945), p. 155 (interview with Doc Daniel Dowdy).
4. Charles Ball, *Slavery in the U.S.: A Narrative of the Life and Adventures of Charles Ball, a Black Man* (Lewistown, Pennsylvania: J. W. Shugert, 1836), pp. 150–151.

5. Frances Ann Kemble, *Journal of a Residence on a Georgia Plantation in 1833–1839* John A. Scott (ed.) (New York: Alfred A. Knopf, 1961), pp. 224–241.
6. Solomon Northrup, *Narrative of Solomon Northrup, Twelve Years a Slave* (Auburn, NY: Derby and Miller, 1853), pp. 188–190, 198, 256–259.
7. Ida Hutchinson, Library of Congress.

3–17 DO YOU AGREE?

1. *American Medical Times*, (July 18, 1861), pp. 25–26, 30.

3–18 THE STORY OF TIN FOOK

1. Betty Lee Sung, *The Chinese in America* (New York: Macmillan Publishing Co., 1972), pp. 29–32.

3–19 I'VE BEEN WORKING ON THE RAILROAD

1. Oscar Lewis, *The Big Four* (New York: Alfred A. Knopf, 1938), p. 70.
2. Congressional Record (testimony by Oswald Garrison Villard).

3–25 AFRICAN AMERICAN SOLDIERS

1. *New York Evening Post*, July 19, 1863.
2. William Fox, *Regimental Losses in the American Civil War* (Albany, NY: Morningside Bookshop, 1889), p. 54.
3. *Official Records of the Union and Confederate Navies in the War of the Rebellion.* (Washington, DC: U.S. Governement Printing Office, 1894–1922, ser. 1, vol. 24, pt. 1m, p. 105.
4. Ibid. ser. 3, col. 3, pp. 733–734.

3–31 CHEYENNE NATIVE AMERICAN GAME

1. Carolyn Niethammer, *Daughters of the Earth: The Lives and Legends of American Indian Women* (New York: Macmillan Publishing Co., 1977), p. 201.

3–32 WHAT DO THEY HAVE IN COMMON?

1. Robert Ernst, *Immigrant Life in New York City* (New York: Columbia University Press, 1949).
2. Mary Antin, *The Promised Land* (Princeton: Princeton University Press, 1985), p. 5.
3. Richard Gambino, *Blood of My Blood* (Garden City, NY: Doubleday and Co., 1974), p. 71.

3–36 JEWISH AMERICANS

1. Mary Antin, The Promised Land (Princeton: Princeton University Press, 1985), p. 5.
2. Ibid. pp. 185–186.

3–38 THE GROWTH OF THE CITIES

1. Jacob Riis, *How the Other Half Lives* (Williamstown, MA: Corner House Publishers, 1972), pp. 43–44.

SECTION FOUR—THE 1900s

4–4 SHOVEL AND PICK

1. Gladys Nadler Rips, *Coming to America: Immigrants from Southern Europe* (New York: Delacorte Press, 1981), p. 8.
2. Constantine Pununzio, *The Soul of an Immigrant* (New York: Arno Press, 1969), pp. 75–77.
3. Willard A. Heaps, *The Story of Ellis Island* (New York: Seabury Press, 1967) pp. 36–37).

4–5 IDA B. WELLS FIGHTS MOB VIOLENCE

1. Calvin Lee, *Chinatown, U.S.A.* (New York: Doubleday and Co., 1965), pp 21–22.
2. Luciano J. Iorizzo and Salvatore Mondello, *The Italian Americans* (New York: Twayne Publishers, 1971), p. 69.
3. Linda Perrin, *Coming to America: Immigrants from the Far East* (New York: Delacorte Press, 1980), p. 122.
4. John Hope Franklin, *From Slavery to Freedom: A History of Negro Americans* (New York: Alfred A. Knopf, 1980), p. 314.
5. Jayne Clark Jones, *The Greeks in America* (Minneapolis: Lerner Publications, 1969), p. 33.

4–7 FIRST WOMAN IN CONGRESS

1. Hannah Josephson, *Jeanette Rankin: First Lady in Congress* (Indianapolis: Bobbs-Merrill Inc., 1974), p. 78.

4–9 THE SUFFRAGE MOVEMENT

1. G. Allen Foster, *Votes for Women* (New York: Criterion Books, 1966), p. 138.
2. Ibid.

4–12 WOMEN AND WORLD WAR II

1. Marynia Farnham and Ferdinand Lundberg, *The Modern Woman: The Lost Sex* (New York: Harper and Brothers, 1947), p. 370.
2. Ruth Young and Catherine Filene Strouse, "The Woman Worker Speaks," *Independent Woman*, 14, (October 1945), pp. 274–275.
3. Agnes Meyer, "Women Aren't Men," *Atlantic Monthly*, 86 (August, 1950), pp. 32–36.
4. Lucy Greenbaum, "The Women Who 'Need' To Work," *New York Times Magazine*, (April 29, 1945), p. 16.

4–13 INTERNMENT CAMPS FOR JAPANESE AMERICANS

1. Congressman John Rankin, *Congressional Record*, Dec. 15, 1941.
2. U.S. Government Poster, Executive Order 9066.
3. Linda Perrin, *Coming to America: Immigrants from the Far East* (New York: Delacorte Press, 1980), p. 88.
4. Dorothy Swain Thomas and Richard S. Nishimoto, *The Spoilage* (Berkeley: University of California Press, 1946), p. 367.
5. Letter, Father H. T. Laverty to President Harry S. Truman, *Pacific Citizen*, (September 24, 1949).
6. Heart Mountain Reports Division, May 1943, Heart Mountain Documents, Box 50, RG 210, National Archives.
7. Michi Weglyn, *Years of Infamy: The Untold Story of America's Concentration Camps* (New York: Morrow, Quill Paperbacks, 1976), p. 80.
8. Chief Judge William Denman, Ninth Circuit Court of Appeals, August 26, 1949.

4–15 WHERE WOULD YOU STAND?

1. Melba Patillo Beals, *Warriors Don't Cry—A Searing Memoir of the Battle to Integrate Little Rock High School* (New York: Pocket Books, 1994), pp. 108–111.
2. Juan William, *Eyes on the Prize: America's Civil Rights Years 1954–1965* (New York: Penguin Books, 1987), p. 112.
3. Ibid. p. 118.

4–19 THE VIETNAM WAR—PRO OR CON?

1. Seymour Hersh, *My Lai 4: A Report on the Massacre and Its Aftermath* (New York: Random House, 1970), p. 75.
2. Dorothy and Thomas Hoobler, *Vietnam: An Illustrated History* (New York: Alfred A. Knopf, 1990) p. 51.

4–21 WORKING OUTSIDE THE HOME

1. U.S. Bureau of Labor Statistics, Bulletin 2307.
2. William Greider, "Sinful Wages: Clinton Wavers on Raising Workers' Pay," *Rolling Stone* (Jan, 27, 1994), p. 30.

3. Fred Barnes, "Health Care Costs Are Going Down," *The American Spectator* (Feb., 1994), p. 36.
4. Anne Mitchell, "Day Care in the 90s," *Good Housekeeping* (Sept. 1992), p. 174.
5. Barbara Gilder, "Divorce Truths Everyone Needs to Know," *Glamour* (August, 1992), p. 138.

4–24 TRYING TO FIT IN

1. Piri Thomas, *Stories from el Barrio* (New York: Alfred A. Knopf, 1978), p. 43.
2. Piri Thomas, *Down These Mean Streets* (New York: Vintage Books, 1967), pp. 158–159.

4–25 IMMIGRATION BY SEA

1. Paul Rutledge, *The Vietnamese in America* (Minneapolis: Lerner Publications, 1987), pp. 28–29.
2. Gottlieb Mittelberger, *Gottlieb Mittelberger's Journey to Pennsylvania in the Year 1750 and Return to Germany* (Philadephia: John Joseph McVey, 1898).
3. Edward Barnes and Jacques Langevin, "Exodus from Haiti," (il) *Life*, 15 (April, 1992), pp. 52–60.

4–26 SWEATSHOPS

1. Milton Meltzer, *The Jews in America* (Washington, DC: Library of Congress, 1974), pp. 80–82.
2. *U.S. News and World Report*, 11/22/93, pp. 52–53.

4–27 THE FARMWORKERS AND NONVIOLENCE

1. " 'La Huelga' Becomes 'La Causa,'" *New York Times* (Nov. 17, 1968), p. 52.
2. Ibid.
3. Ibid.
4. Ronald B. Taylor, *Chavez* (Boston: Beacon Press, 1975), p. 135.
5. Ibid. p. 129.
6. Ibid. pp. 132, 135.
7. Mark Day, *Forty Acres: Cesar Chavez and the Farm Workers* (New York: Praeger Publishers, 1971), pp. 114–115.
8. Jan Young, *The Migrant Workers and Cesar Chavez* (New York: Simon and Schuster, 1972), p. 108.
9. Ibid. pp. 113, 139–140.

4–28 SEPARATION OR ASSIMILATION?

1. Milton Meltzer, *The Hispanic Americans* (New York: Thomas J. Crowell Junior Books, 1982), pp. 136–137.

2. Ibid.
3. Ibid.

4–29 A BASKETBALL STAR

1. Gary Smith, "A Woman of the People," (il.) *Sports Illustrated* 78 (March 1, 1993), pp. 51–64.

4–30 SMILES A LOT

1. Interview with Nathan Lee Chasing His Horse in *Seventeen* magazine (August, 1991), pp. 78–80.

4–31 ARAB AMERICANS

1. Merrel Noden, "They're Americans Too," v.74 *Sports Illustrated* (February 4, 1991), p. 9.

4–33 TYPECASTING

1. Alexandra Bandon, *Filipino Americans* (New York: Macmillan Publishing Co., 1993), pp. 82–83.

4–36 MAJORITY-MINORITY

1. U.S. Bureau of the Census, *U.S. Census of Population*
2. Ibid.

4–37 ANCESTRIES

1. U.S. Bureau of the Census, *1990 Census of Population and Housing Data Paper Listing* (CPH-L-133); and Summary Tape File 3C.

4–38 ASIAN AND PACIFIC ISLANDER AMERICANS

1. U.S. Bureau of the Census, *1990 Census of Population, General Population Characteristics, United States* (CP-1-1).

4–39 HISPANIC AMERICANS

1. U.S. Bureau of the Census, *1990 Census of Population, General Population Characteristics, United States* (CP-1-1).

Bibliography

Albert, Peter J., and Ronald Hoffman (eds.). *Women in the Age of the Amercian Revolution*. Charlottesville: University Press of Virginia, 1989.

Alderman, Clifford Lindsey. *Colonists for Sale: The Story of Indentured Servants in America*. New York: Macmillan Publishing Co., 1975.

Alternman, Hyman. *Counting People: The Census in History*. New York: Harcourt, Brace and World, Inc., 1969.

Antin, Mary. *The Promised Land*. Princeton: Princeton University Press, 1985.

Axtell, James. *The European and the Indian: Essays in the Ethnohistory of Colonial North America*. New York: Oxford University Press, 1981.

Bagia, Leona B. *The East Indians and Pakistanis in America*. Minneapolis: Lerner Publications, 1967.

Ball, Charles. *A Narrative of the Life and Adventures of Charles Ball, A Black Man*. 3d. ed. Pittsburgh: John T. Shyrock, 1854.

Bandon, Alexandra. *Filipino Americans*. New York: Macmillan Publishing Co., 1993.

Bannatyne, Lesley Pratt. *Halloween: An American Holiday, an American History*. New York: Facts on File, 1990.

Barker-Benfield, G. "Anne Hutchinson and the Puritan Attitude Toward Women," *Feminist Studies*, 1, (1972).

Barnes, Edward, and Jacques Langevin. "Exodus from Haiti" (il.) *Life*, Vol. 15 (April, 1992), pp. 52–60.

Barnes, Fred. "Health Care Costs are Going Down," *American Spectator*, (Feb. 1994), p. 36.

Baxandall, Rosalyn, Linda Gordon, and Susan Reverby. *America's Working Women: A Documentary History 1600–Present*. New York: Vintage Books, 1976.

Beals, Melba Patillo. *Warriors Don't Cry: A Searing Memoir of the Battle to Integrate Little Rock High School*. New York: Pocket Books, 1994.

Beard, Charles A., *An Economic Interpretation of the Constitution of the United States*. New York: Macmillan Publishing Co., 1913.

Bennett, Lerone Jr. *Before the Mayflower: A History of Black America*. New York: Penguin Books, 1984.

Botkin, B.A. *Lay my Burden Down: A Folk History of Slavery*. Chicago: University of Illinois Press, 1945, (interview with Doc Daniel Dowdy).

Brownlee, Mary M., and W. Elliot Brownlee. *Women in the American Economy: A Documentary History*, 1675 to 1929. Clinton, MA: The Colonial Press, Inc., 1976.

Brundin, Judith A. *The Native People of the Northeast Woodlands*. Spring Valley, NY: Intergraphic Technology, Inc., 1990.

Butterfield, L.H. (ed.), *Adams Family Correspondence*, Vol. 1 Cambridge, MA: Harvard University Press, 1963.

Cates, Edwin H. *The English in America*. Minneapolis: Lerner Publications, 1966.

Chester, Thomas Morris. *Black Civil War Correspondent*. Baton Rouge, LA: Louisiana State University Press, 1989.

Commons, John R. Documentary History of American Industrial Society. Cleveland: A.H. Clark Co., 1911.

Cornish, Dudley Taylor. *The Sable Arm: Black Troops in the Union Army, 1861–1865. Lawrence, KA: University Press of Kansas, 1987.*

Daley, William, *The Chinese Americans*. New York: Chelsea House Publishers, 1987.

Day, Mark. *Forty Acres: Cesar Chavez and the Farm Workers*. New York: Praeger Publishers, 1971.

Dennis, Henry C. *The American Indian 1942–1970*. Dobbs Ferry, NY: Oceana Publications, 1971.

Douglass, Frederick. *Narrative of the Life of Frederick Douglass, an American Slave*. New York: Literary Classics of the United States, Inc., 1994.

Eastman, Charles A. (Ohiyesa). *From the Deep Woods to Civilization*. Boston: Little, Brown and Co., 1916.

Ernst, Robert. *Immigrant Life in New York City*. New York: Columbia University Press, 1949.

Farnham, Marynia, and Ferdinand, Lundberg *The Modern Woman: The Lost Sex*. New York: Harper and Brothers, 1947.

Fenton, William N. ed. *Parker on the Iroquois*, Book III. Syracuse, NY: Syracuse University Press, 1968.

Flynn, Elizabeth Gurley. *The Rebel Girl*. New York: International Publishers Co., 1973.

Foner, Philip. *W.E.B. Du Bois Speaks*. New York: Pathfinder Press, 1970.

Foster, G. Allen. *Votes for Women*. New York: Criterion Books, 1966.

Fox, William. *Regimental Losses in the American Civil War*. Albany, NY: Morningside Bookshop, 1889.

Franklin, John Hope. *From Slavery to Freedom: A History of Negro Americans*. New York: Alfred A. Knopf, Inc., 1947

Gambino, Richard. *Blood of My Blood*. Garden City, NY: Doubleday and Co., 1974.

Gilder, Barbara. "Divorce Truths Everyone Needs to Know." *Glamour*, (August, 1992), p. 138.

Gordon, Irving L. *American History*. New York: Amsco School Publications, 1989.

Gracza, Rezsoe and Margaret Gracza. *The Hungarians in America*. Minneapolis: Lerner Publications, 1969.

Greenbaum, Lucy. "The Women Who 'Need' to Work." *New York Times Magazine*, (April 29, 1945), p. 16.

Greider, William. "Sinful Wages: Clinton Wavers on Raising Workers' Pay." *Rolling Stone*, (Jan, 27, 1994), p. 30.

Grossman, Ronald P. *The Italians in America*. Minneapolis: Lerner Publications, 1966.

Guttman, Herbert G. *The Black Family in Slavery and Freedom 1750–1925*. New York: Vintage Books, 1976.

Hakim, Joy. *A History of US: From Colonies to Country*. New York: Oxford University Press, 1993.

Hakim, Joy, *A History of US: Liberty for All?*. New York: Oxford University Press, 1993.

Hakim, Joy. *A History of US: Making Thirteen Colonies*. New York: Oxford University Press, 1993.

Hakim, Joy. *A History of US: Reconstruction and Reform*. New York: Oxford Unversity Press, 1993.

Hakim, Joy. *A History of US: The New Nation*. New York: Oxford University Press, 1993.

Hakim, Joy. *A History of US: War, Terrible War*. New York: Oxford University Press, 1993.

Hargrove, Hondon B. *Black Union Soldiers in the Civil War*. Jefferson, NC: McFarland and Company, 1988.

Heaps, Williard A. *The Story of Ellis Island.* New York: Seabury Press, 1967.

Henson, Josiah. *Father Henson's Story of His Own Life.* New York: Corinth Books, 1962.

Hersh, Seymour. *My Lai 4: A Report on the Massacre and Its Aftermath.* New York: Random House, 1970.

Hoobler, Dorothy, and Thomas Hoobler. *Vietnam: An Illustrated History.* New York: Alfred A. Knopf, 1990.

Hymowitz, Carol, and Michaele Weissman. *A History of Women in America.* New York: Bantam Books, 1978.

Iorizzo, Luciano J., and Salvatore Mondello. *The Italian Americans.* New York: Twayne Publishers, 1971.

Jacobs, Harriet A. *Incidents in the Life of a Slave Girl.* Cambridge, MA: Harvard University Press, 1987.

Johnson, James E. *The Irish In America.* Minneapolis: Lerner Publications, 1966.

Johnson, James E. *The Scots and Scotch-Irish in America.* Minneapolis: Lerner Publications, 1966.

Jones, Claire, *The Chinese in America.* Minneapolis: Lerner Publications, 1972.

Jones, Jayne Clark. *The Greeks in America.* Minneapolis: Lerner Publications, 1969.

Josephson, Hannah. *Jeanette Rankin: First Lady in Congress.* Indianapolis: Bobbs-Merrill Co., 1974.

Karenga, Maulana. *The African American Holiday of Kwanzaa: A Celebration of Family, Community and Culture.* Los Angeles: University of Sankore Press, 1988.

Katz, William Loren. *Black Indians: A Hidden Heritage.* New York: Macmillan Publishing Company, 1986.

Katz, William Loren, *The Black West.* Seattle, WA: Open Hand Publishing, Inc., 1987.

Kemble, Frances Ann. *Journal of a Residence on a Georgia Plantation in 1833–1839.* John A. Scott (ed.). New York: Alfred A. Knopf, 1961.

Kessler-Harris, Alice. *Out to Work: A History of Wage-earning Women in the U.S.* New York: Oxford University Press, 1982.

Kitano, Harry. *The Japanese Americans.* New York: Chelsea House Publishers, 1987.

Koehler, Lyle. "The Case of the American Jezebels: Anne Hutchinson and Female Agitation During the Antinomian Turmoil, 1636–1644." *Women's Monthly Quarterly*, 3d., Vol. 31 (1974), pp. 55–78.

Kunz, Virginia Brainard. *The French in America.* Minneapolis: Lerner Publications, 1966.

Lee, Calvin. *Chinatown, U.S.A.* New York: Doubleday and Co., 1965.

Lee Chasing His Horse, Nathan. "Interview with Nathan Lee Chasing His Horse," *Seventeen*, (August, 1991), pp. 78–80.

Lester, Julius. *To Be a Slave*. New York: Dell Publishing Co., 1968.

Lewis, Oscar. *The Big Four*. New York: Alfred A. Knopf, 1938.

Liberty, Margot. "Population Trends Among Present-day Omaha Indians," *Plains Anthropologist*, Vol. 20, p. 228.

Main, Jackson Turner. *The Social Structure of Revolutionary America*. Princeton, NJ: Princeton University Press, 1965.

Malcolm X. *Malcolm X on Afro-American History*. New York: Pathfinder Press, 1970.

Matthaei, Julie A. *An Economic History of Women in America*. Great Britain: Harvester Press Limited, 182.

McDonald, Forrest. *E Pluribus Unum: The Formation of the American Republic*. Boston: Houghton Mifflin Company, 1965.

McDonald, Forrest. *Novus Ordo Seclorum: The Intellectual Origins of the Constitution*. Lawrence, KA: University Press of Kansas, 1985.

McKay, John P., Bennet D. Hill, and John Buckley. *A History of Western Society*. Boston: Houghton Mifflin, 1991.

Meltzer, Milton. *The Hispanic Americans*. New York: Thomas J. Crowell Junior Books, 1982.

Meltzer, Milton. *The Jews in America*. Washington, DC: Library of Congress, 1974.

Menard, Russel. "The Maryland Slave Population, 1658–1738: A Demographic Profile of Blacks in Four Counties." *Women's Monthly Quarterly*, 3d., Vol. 33, (1975) pp. 29–54.

Meyer, Agnes. "Women Aren't Men." *Atlantic Monthly*, Vol. 86 (August, 1950), pp. 32–36.

Mitchell, Anne. "Day Care in the 90s." *Good Housekeeping*, (Sept. 1992), p. 174.

Mittelberger, Gottlieb. *Gottlieb Mittelberger's Journey to Pennsylvania in the Year 1750 and Return to Germany*. Philadelphia: John Joseph McVey, 1898.

Mooney, James. *Historical Sketch of the Cherokee*. Chicago: Aldine Publishing Co., 1900.

Morrice, Polly. *The French Americans*. New York: Chelsea House Publishers, 1988.

Mullins, Joseph G. *Hawaii: 1776–1976*. Honolulu: Mutual Publishing Company, 1976.

Murphy, Carole E. (ed.). *Understanding Our Country* (2d. ed.). River Forest, IL: Doubleday and Co., 1981.

Naff, Alixa. *The Arab Americans*. New York: Chelsea House Publishers, 1988.

Niethammer, Carolyn. *Daughters of the Earth: The Lives and Legends of American Indian Women*. New York: Macmillan Publishing Company, 1977.

Noden, Merrel. "They're Americans Too." *Sports Illustrated*, Vol. 74 (February 4, 1991), p. 9.

Northrup, Solomon. *Narrative of Solomon Northrup: Twelve Years a Slave*. Auburn, NY: Derby and Miller, 1853, pp. 188–190, 198, 256–259.

Norton, Mary Beth. "The Evolution of White Women's Experience in Early America." *American Historical Review*, Vol. 89, No. 3 (June 1984) pp. 593–619.

Painter, Nell Irvin. *The Exodusters: Black Migration to Kansas After Reconstruction*. New York: Alfred A. Knopf, Inc., 1976.

Perrin, Linda. *Coming to America: Immigrants from the Far East*. New York: Delacorte Press, 1980.

Panunzio, Constantine M. *The Soul of an Immigrant*. New York: Arno Press, 1969.

Rawls, James J., and Philip Weeks. *Land of Liberty*. New York: Holt, Rinehart and Winston, Inc., 1985.

Riis, Jacob. *How the Other Half Lives*. Williamstown, MA: Corner House Publishers, 1972.

Rips, Gladys Nadler. *Coming to America: Immigrants from Southern Europe*. New York: Delacorte Press, 1981.

Roucek, Joseph S. *The Czechs and Slovaks in America*. Minneapolis: Lerner Publications, 1967.

Rutledge, Paul. *The Vietnamese in America*. Minneapolis: Lerner Publications, 1987.

Ruttman, Anita, and Darrett Puttman. "Non-wives and Sons-in-Law: Parental Death in a 17th Century Virginia County." *The Chesapeake in the Seventeenth Century: Essays on Anglo-American Society*. Chapel Hill, NC: University of North Carolina Press, 1980.

Sacks, Karen. *Sisters and Wives: The Past and Future of Sexual Equality*. Westport, CT: Greenwood Press, 1982.

Seton, Ernest Thompson. *Life Histories of Northern Animals*. New York: Charles Scribner and Sons, 1909.

Smith, Gary. "A Woman of the People" (il.) *Sports Illustrated*, Vol. 78 (March 1, 1993), pp. 51–64.

Sowell, Thomas. *Ethnic America*. New York: Basic Books, 1981.

Stearn, E. Wagner, and Allen E. Stearn. *The Effect of Smallpox on the Destiny of the Amerindian*. Boston: Bruce Humphries, Inc., 1945.

Sung, Betty Lee. *The Chinese in America*. New York: MacMillan Co., 1972.

Taylor, Ronald B. *Chavez*. Boston: Beacon Press, 1975.

Thomas, Dorothy Swain, and Richard S. Nishimoto. *The Spoilage*. Berkeley: University of California Press, 1946.

Thomas, Piri. *Down These Mean Streets*. New York: Vintage Books, 1967.

Thomas, Piri. *Stories from el Barrio*. New York: Alfred A. Knopf, 1978.

Thornton, Russell. *American Indian Holocaust and Survival: A Population History Since 1492*. Norman and London: University of Oklahoma Press, 1987.

Ulrich, Laurel Thatcher. *Good Wives: Image and Reality in the Lives of Women in Northern New England 1650–1750*. New York: Oxford University Press, 1983.

Ware, Norman. *The Industrial Worker, 1840–1860*. New York: Quadrangle, 1964.

Weglyn, Michi. *Years of Infamy: The Untold Story of America's Concentration Camps*. New York: Morrow, Quill Paperbacks, 1976.

Weld, Thomas. *American Slavery as It Is: Testimony of a Thousand Witnesses*. New York: American Anti-Slavery Society, 1839, p. 12, (narrative of Nehemiah Caulkins of Waterford, CT).

Williams, Juan. *Eyes on the Prize: America's Civil Rights Years 1954—1965*. New York: Penguin Books, 1987.

Wytrwal, Joseph A. *The Poles in America*. Minneapolis: Lerner Publications, 1969.

Yee, Shirley J. *Black Women Abolitionists: A Study in Activism, 1828–1860*. Knoxville, TN: University of Tennessee Press, 1992.

Young, Jan. *The Migrant Workers and Cesar Chavez*. New York: Simon and Schuster, 1972.

Young, Ruth, and Catherine Filene Strouse. "The Woman Worker Speaks." *Independent Woman*, Vol. 14 (October 1945), pp. 274–275.

Zinn, Howard. *A People's History of the United States*. New York: Harper and Row, 1980.

Topical Index

AFRICAN AMERICANS

A–1 What Is Multicultural History?

A–2 From All Over the World

A–4 The "All American" Teenager

1–2 How Much Do We Know? (the 1600s)

1–6 Important Dates!

1–7 A Love Story

1–9 Enslaved!

1–11 Children or No Children?

1–12 Needs/Economic Interests

1–20 People to Remember (the 1600s)

2–2 How Much Do We Know? (the 1700s)

2–8 Three Cultures

2–11 Point of View

2–12 Whose Side Are You On?

2–13 What Did They Say to One Another?

2–19 Too Far or Not Far Enough?

2–23 Benjamin Banneker

2–25 What If?

2–28 The Du Sables

2–29 Benjamin Franklin's Parody

2–30 People to Remember (the 1700s)

3–2 How Much Do We Know? (the 1800s)

3–3 Decisions and Choices

3–5 York

3–11 Fight, and if You Can't Fight, Kick

3–12 Frederick Douglass

3–13 Telling Her Story

3–14 A Woman's Fate

3–15 Abolitionists Working Together

3–24 The Civil War—Who Would You Fight For?

3–25 African American Soldiers

3–26 Abraham Lincoln

3–27 Robert Elliot Brown

3–29 African American Pioneers
3–30 Cowboy Quiz
3–32 What Do They Have in Common?
3–40 People to Remember (the 1800s)
4–2 How Much Do We Know? (the 1900s)
4–5 Ida B. Wells Fights Mob Violence
4–6 Du Bois and Washington
4–6 World War I
4–14 The Civil Rights Movement
4–15 Where Would You Stand?
4–32 Bringing in the New Year
4–37 Ancestries
4–40 People to Remember (the 1900s)

ASIAN AMERICANS

A–1 What Is Multicultural History?
A–2 From All Over the World
A–4 The "All American" Teenager
3–2 How Much Do We Know? (the 1800s)
3–18 The Story of Tin Fook
3–19 I've Been Working on the Railroad
3–20 Lee Yick
3–32 What Do They Have in Common?
3–33 Immigration
3–34 Words We Use Every Day
3–40 People to Remember (the 1800s)
4–2 How Much Do We Know? (the 1900s)
4–5 Ida B. Wells Fights Mob Violence
4–8 World War I
4–13 Internment Camps for Japanese
4–18 Oral History Interview—The Vietnam War
4–19 The Vietnam War—Pro or Con?
4–25 Immigration by Sea
4–31 Arab Americans
4–32 Bringing in the New Year
4–34 American as Apple Pie?
4–35 Names
4–38 Asian and Pacific Islander Americans
4–40 People to Remember (the 1900s)

EUROPEAN AMERICANS

A–1 What Is Multicultural History?
A–2 From All Over the World
A–4 The "All American" Teenager
1–2 How Much Do We Know? (1600s)
1–6 Important Dates!
1–8 Polish Americans Lead The First Labor Walkout
1–10 Stepmothers and Stepfathers
1–12 Needs/Economic Interests
1–13 Economic Class Tension?
1–14 Tight Quarters
1–15 Indentured Servants
1–16 Grilled Cheese Sandwich
1–17 European American Women's Position in Society
1–18 Guns!
1–19 English American Names
1–20 People to Remember (the 1600s)
2–1 Draw!
2–2 How Much Do We Know? (the 1700s)
2–5 Spanish Colonization
2–6 French Colonization
2–7 Hats and Lingo
2–8 Three Cultures
2–9 European American Medical Care
2–12 Whose Side Are You On?
2–13 What Did They Say to One Another?
2–15 Follow the Army
2–18 Abigail Adams Writes a Letter
2–21 Which Side of the Road?
2–22 The Cajuns
2–23 Benjamin Banneker
2–24 Everyday Life

2–28 The Du Sables
2–30 People to Remember (the 1700s)
3–2 How Much Do We Know? (the 1800s)
3–6 Spelling
3–9 Working Conditions
3–10 Men, Women, and Money
3–15 Abolitionists Working Together
3–16 Susan B. Anthony Goes to Jail
3–17 Do You Agree?
3–24 The Civil War—For Whom Would You Fight?
3–26 Abraham Lincoln
3–30 Cowboy Quiz
3–32 What Do They Have in Common?
3–33 Immigration
3–34 Words We Use Every Day
3–35 German Americans
3–36 Jewish Americans
3–37 Little Bags of Irish Earth
3–38 The Growth of the Cities
3–40 People to Remember (the 1800s)
4–2 How Much Do We Know? (the 1900s)
4–4 Shovel and Pick
4–5 Ida B. Wells Fights Mob Violence
4–8 World War I
4–25 Immigration by Sea
4–26 Sweatshops
4–34 American as Apple Pie?
4–35 Names
4–36 Majority–Minority
4–37 Ancestries
4–40 People to Remember (the 1900s)

HISPANIC AMERICANS

A–1 What Is Multicultural History?
A–2 From All Over the World
A–4 The "All American" Teenager
3–2 How Much Do We Know? (the 1800s)
3–21 The Mexican War
3–22 Juan Nepomuceno Cortina
3–23 Mexican Americans
3–30 Cowboy Quiz
3–34 Words We Use Every Day
3–40 People to Remember (the 1800s)
4–2 How Much Do We Know? (the 1900s)
4–23 Puerto Rico—Commonwealth, State, or Independence?
4–24 Trying to Fit In
4–26 Sweatshops
4–27 The Farmworkers and Nonviolence
4–28 Separation or Assimilation?
4–35 Names
4–37 Ancestries
4–39 Hispanic Americans
4–40 People to Remember (the 1900s)

NATIVE AMERICANS

A–1 What Is Multicultural History?
A–2 From All Over the World
A–4 The "All American" Teenager
1–1 Draw! (the 1600s)
1–2 How Much Do We Know? (the 1600s)
1–4 Matrilineal Society
1–5 Going to a Dance?
1–6 Important Dates!
1–12 Needs/Economic Interests
1–20 People to Remember (from the 1600s)
2–2 How Much Do We Know? (the 1700s)
2–3 Stereotypes
2–4 The Environment
2–7 Hats and Lingo
2–8 Three Cultures
2–12 Whose Side Are You On?
2–17 Inspiration
2–19 Too Far or Not Far Enough?

2–20 The Iroquois Constitution
2–25 What If?
2–26 Sagoyewatha
2–27 Tragedy
2–28 The Du Sables
2–30 People to Remember (the 1700s)
3–2 How Much Do We Know? (the 1800s)
3–4 Sacagawea
3–7 Rewrite History
3–8 Trail of Tears
3–31 Cheyenne Native American Game
3–40 People to Remember (the 1800s)
4–2 How Much Do We Know? (the 1900s)
4–29 A Basketball Star
4–30 Smiles a Lot
4–37 Ancestries
4–40 People to Remember (the 1900s)

PACIFIC ISLANDER AMERICANS

A–1 What is Multicultural History?
A–2 From All Over the World
3–33 Immigration
3–39 Queen Liliuokalani
4–5 Ida B. Wells Fights Mob Violence
4–27 The Farmworkers and Nonviolence
4–33 Typecasting
4–38 Asian and Pacific Islander Americans
4–40 People to Remember (the 1900s)

WOMEN

1–2 How Much Do We Know? (the 1600s)
1–4 Matrilineal Society
1–6 Important Dates!
1–11 Children or No Children?
1–17 European American Women's Position in Society
1–20 People to Remember (1600s)
2–2 How Much Do We Know? (the 1700s)
2–8 Three Cultures
2–10 Childbirth and Midwifery
2–12 Whose Side Are You On?
2–13 What Did They Say to One Another?
2–14 Should Women Be Soldiers?
2–15 Follow the Army
2–16 Home Alone (with All the Work!)
2–18 Abigail Adams Writes A Letter
2–19 Too Far or Not Far Enough?
2–24 Everyday Life
2–30 People to Remember (the 1700s)
3–2 How Much Do We Know?
3–4 Sacagawea
3–10 Men, Women, and Money
3–11 Fight, and if You Can't Fight, Kick
3–13 Telling Her Story
3–14 A Woman's Fate
3–15 Abolitionists Working Together
3–16 Susan B. Anthony Goes to Jail
3–17 Do You Agree?
3–24 The Civil War—For Whom Would You Fight?
3–28 Close Quarters
3–39 Queen Liliuokalani
3–40 People to Remember (the 1800s)
4–2 How Much Do We Know? (1900s)
4–5 Ida B. Wells Fights Mob Violence
4–7 First Woman in Congress
4–9 The Suffrage Movement
4–12 Women and World War II
4–20 Gender Stereotypes
4–21 Working Outside the Home
4–22 Eleanor Roosevelt and Hillary Rodham Clinton
4–29 A Basketball Star
4–33 Typecasting
4–40 People to Remember (the 1900s)